Reverend Beecher
and Mrs. Tilton

Reverend Beecher
and Mrs. Tilton

Sex and Class in Victorian America

Altina L. Waller

The University of Massachusetts Press   Amherst

Copyright © 1982 by
The University of Massachusetts Press
All rights reserved
Printed in the United States of America

Library of Congress Cataloging in Publication Data
Waller, Altina Laura, 1940–
Reverend Beecher and Mrs. Tilton: sex and class
in Victorian America.
Bibliography: p.
Includes index.
1. Beecher, Henry Ward, 1813–1887. 2. Tilton,
Theodore, 1835–1907. 3. Tilton, Elizabeth M.
Richards, b. 1834. 4. Brooklyn (New York, N.Y.)—
Biography. 5. Marriage—United States—History—
19th century. I. Title.
BX7260.B31W34   285.8'32'0924 [B]   81–15982
ISBN 0–87023–356–4   AACR2

For Laura Louise and Andrew

Contents

ix   Preface

1   One. Introduction: The Brooklyn Scandal

Part I. The Personal Roots of Scandal: A Hunger for Love

18   Two. Henry Ward Beecher: The Emergence of the Gospel of Love

38   Three. Theodore Tilton: Making It in the Gilded Age

54   Four. Elizabeth Tilton: The Transformation of a Marriage

Part II. Social Origins of the Scandal

64   Five. "Plymouth: The Rock upon Which Mr. Beecher Stands"

82   Six. The Scandal and Local Politics: The "Radical Rumpus"

93   Seven. Two Churches: Money, Power, and Social Conflict in Brooklyn

Part III. The Scandal and Its Consequences

112   Eight. The Higher Sphere: Nesting on Brooklyn Heights

130   Nine. Theodore Tilton as Scapegoat: Retreat from the Gospel of Love

151   Notes

169   Bibliography

175   Index

Preface

SINCE 1873, when Mark Twain and Charles Dudley Warner published the novel whose title, *The Gilded Age,* gave a name to their generation, attempts to understand American life in the late nineteenth century have been hampered by the dominance of powerful and usually negative stereotyped images. In the popular mind—and among many historians as well—the post–Civil War period was perceived as flawed by crass materialism and greed, by political corruption and scandal, and—worst of all—by cloying sentimentality and hypocritical moral pretentiousness.

It is significant that the most extensive and probing studies of the political, social, and cultural history of the Gilded Age have focused on the minority who stood outside the mainstream or resisted its dominant currents: critics and skeptics like Mark Twain, Walt Whitman, and Henry Adams; quixotic political reformers like E. L. Godkin; isolated creative figures like Albert Pinkham Ryder and Kate Chopin; humanitarians like Jane Addams and Jacob Riis; or—at the other end of the spectrum—the anonymous masses who struggled for survival and a decent living against great odds. In short, historians have tried to salvage the Gilded Age for us by focusing on its redeeming qualities and its leavening minority.

Twentieth-century perceptions of what makes relevant history have dulled our sensitivity to the issues arresting the attention and concern of Americans living in the Gilded Age. Historians have chosen to study economic development and political reform because these things seemed most important to them. These issues did capture the attention of some segments of late nineteenth-century American society and they certainly deserve careful historical investigation, but our exclusive concentration on them has left us with a lopsided picture of the era. When it comes to the social and cultural contours of the era, we have studied the fringes, the atypical, the nay-sayers, but we have not yet penetrated the life of the majority to its core.

This book is an effort to correct the balance somewhat: to explore—on their own terms and through the medium of a single, traumatic event—some of the central concerns of a segment of the American middle class in the 1870s. Specifically, I propose to examine the sensational and highly publicized social scandal of the era: the 1875 adultery trial of the most popular American Protestant preacher of the day, Henry Ward Beecher.

Almost as soon as it was over, this event was relegated to the attic of American consciousness. Everyone knew about it, but few—certainly few historians—considered it worthy of serious attention. For a period of several years while awareness of the scandal dominated the national consciousness, no other event was more written or talked about. Reactions ranged from amusement to outrage: some were convinced it presaged the downfall of Christianity or heralded a social revolution, everyone knew about it, and everyone had something to say on the subject. I have proceeded on the assumption that no event, however melodramatic, that so engaged the national attention could be without historical interest or significance. A careful consideration of the circumstances, personalities, and ramifications of this famous scandal can help us understand some of the fundamental issues confronting middle-class Americans in the mid-Victorian era.

I have approached the Beecher-Tilton scandal not as narrative history, but as a study of institutional changes and their psychological ramifications. This means I will often touch only briefly on, and possibly neglect entirely some details of a complex story. My major purpose is not a dramatic re-telling but an exploration of what I perceive to be the underlying patterns. Further, I have not been overly preoccupied with the question of Beecher's guilt or innocence. It will soon be clear what my own conclusions are, but, nevertheless, I am willing to argue that whether or not Beecher was guilty, the same fundamental social dynamics are present. Actual adultery notwithstanding, many Americans perceived the Gospel of Love as a social philosophy conducive to such illicit liaisons. Thus, Beecher's most ardent supporters, while insisting that he was not actually guilty, were willing to censure the minister for impulsive, even irresponsible behavior in his involvement with Elizabeth Tilton. The real issues went far deeper than the guilt or innocence of one man—even when that man was Henry Ward Beecher. The intense social conflict the scandal engendered in Brooklyn and the national fascination with it attest to this point.

The scandal was first suggested to me by Professor Stephen Nissenbaum as a possible teaching unit in a course at the University of Massachusetts known as "New Approaches to History." After having successfully taught such units as Salem Witchcraft, Shays' Rebellion, and Lizzie Borden, the faculty was looking for a new topic amenable to the research-oriented methodology of the course. To facilitate the search, Professor Nissenbaum offered a graduate seminar designed to consider potential topics. Personally convinced that this particular unit would not be successful, I opposed its selection but was outvoted by the class. Ironically, I was the only graduate student enrolled in the seminar who was also on the staff of the New Approaches course and therefore was "volunteered" to develop the Beecher-Tilton scandal topic into a viable unit. In doing this, however, I had the good fortune of collaborating with Professor Gerald McFarland, who saw more teaching potential in it than I did.

Eventually, I was to teach the course on three different occasions from the fall of 1975 through the spring of 1977, discovering on each occasion that undergraduates could indeed become involved in the complex issues raised by the scandal. During the first semester that Professor McFarland and I taught the course, the students demonstrated their enthusiasm by organizing a trip to Brooklyn. We met one Sunday morning at five A.M., drove five hours to Brooklyn, and attended a service at Plymouth Church. Our efforts were rewarded, for Brooklyn Heights and Plymouth Church today still look much the same as they did in the 1870s. The present minister, Reverend Harry Kruener, and church secretary, Miss Beatrice Loennecke, proved gracious hosts who extended a warm welcome to our group. I am most grateful to them for hospitality and assistance in the weeks I spent at the church doing research, not only for the course, but for this book.

The teaching of this topic and its evolution into a book have proceeded hand in hand. My students shared my own excitement and commitment to unearthing increasing amounts of data. Each semester, more of the long list of church members was "fleshed out" as students uncovered long-buried data in local histories, newspapers, directories, and census records. But to the students in the final Beecher semester—fall 1977—I owe my greatest debt. It was this group who *systematically* searched the census for a random sample of Plymouth as well as Church of the Pilgrims members. The statistical tables which appear in chapter 7 are largely the result of their diligent perusal of the 1870 census schedules.

Indeed, at every stage, this research has been enhanced by the assistance and encouragement offered by many people. My students were only the first to contribute their enthusiasm as well as labor. Another committed research assistant was my daughter Laura Louise Wilson, who, at the ages of thirteen and fourteen, accompanied me to Plymouth Church to collect data on church members. Her careful work, dedication to the task, and extraordinary good humor imbued the weeks spent among the dusty church records with extremely pleasant memories. Recently, both my children, Laura Louise and Andrew, offered invaluable and patient service as proofreaders and sensitive editors of the manuscript. Laura also managed to serve as typist in the busy summer before she entered Yale. This book, as well as my entire graduate career, has been a family endeavor.

Success in locating, borrowing, or acquiring the sources for the Beecher-Tilton course and this book was due primarily to the American bibliographer at the University of Massachusetts Library, John Kendall. I can never thank him enough, not only for his actual help in ferreting out materials, but for his constant interest and encouragement.

To Leonard Lewis, who devoted significant amounts of time and energy to the collection of data at Plymouth Church and to discussing its interpretation, this study is also indebted.

Others, whose involvement has not been quite so direct, have endured my long periods of discouragement and inability to progress. For their patience, understanding, and faith, I am grateful to David Stamps, and my dear friends Liz Lewis and Pamella Weeks. During my two years at West Virginia University, vital support was always forthcoming from Peter and Laura Gottlieb, Barbara Rowe and Bob Withers, and one of my colleagues in the history department, John A. Maxwell.

I especially want to mention the intellectually rigorous yet emotionally supportive atmosphere of the history department at the University of Massachusetts. My work has benefited indirectly from many courses and informal conversations with Professors Leo Richards, Bruce Laurie, Robert Griffith, Miriam Chrisman, Robert Hart, Gerald McFarland, Ronald Story, Philip Swenson, and Stephen Oates. It is rare to find an academic environment so conducive to the scholarly sharing of information, ideas, and criticism.

Finally, I want to thank the two people who have had the longest and closest association with this project, Professors Stephen Nissenbaum and Paul S. Boyer. Professor Nissenbaum's ideas and fresh insights have repeatedly stimulated my thinking, while Professor Boyer's thoughtful suggestions and untiring patience with draft after draft of the manuscript provided the impetus for its completion.

To all these students, friends, and colleagues belongs the credit for whatever is worthwhile in the book. For its many failings, I alone am responsible.

Altina Waller
Memphis, Tennessee

1

Introduction:
The Brooklyn Scandal

THE BOMBSHELL

IT WAS DURING the last week of October 1872 that the Beecher-Tilton scandal first appeared in the press. Victoria Woodhull, a notorious advocate of women's rights, published an article in *Woodhull and Claflin's Weekly* accusing the most respected minister of the age, Henry Ward Beecher, of adultery. Her purpose, Woodhull wrote, was not to condemn Beecher's behavior, but to expose his hypocrisy to the world. Boldly declaring that the minister shared her own belief that marriage as an institution should be abolished, she claimed Beecher himself had said, "marriage is the grave of love." This sentiment came from the most unimpeachable spokesman for American Christianity, but, according to Woodhull, it reflected the view of her own group of social reformers as expressed in the phrase "Free Love." Far from advocating sexual promiscuity, asserted Woodhull, the Free Love movement sought to *free* both men and women from sexual slavery inherent in the institution of marriage. Sexual intercourse ought to result from pure romantic attraction rather than mere legal obligation. It ought to be as free and uninhibited as economic, political, or religious activity. Free Love, ought, in fact, to be the final culmination of the ideals of a free society. Moreover, any kind of coercion applied to the mysterious workings of love and its sexual expression would not only be ineffective but could easily damage or destroy its fragile purity. This, argued Woodhull, is what Beecher meant by identifying marriage as the grave of love.

Beecher's fault, Woodhull insisted, lay not in having practiced Free Love, but in his attempts at concealment. Why didn't the minister proclaim his beliefs publicly? Woodhull was sure it was simply expedience— he was afraid such an admission would ruin his career. But now Woodhull declared her intent of forcing a leadership role upon the reluctant Beecher. This, she hoped, would give courage to the many so-called respectable

Americans who, like Beecher, were actually practicing the precepts of Free Love while professing conformity to conventional moral codes. The revelation of Beecher's sexual commerce with his parishioner would, Woodhull prophesied, "burst upon the ranks of the moralistic camp like a bombshell."[1]

The flamboyant Woodhull had not underestimated public response. It was indeed a bombshell; "Free Lover" was perhaps the single most odious epithet one could attach to a respectable citizen in the post–Civil War era —something akin to an accusation of communism in the 1950s. One contemporary writer railed that Free Lovers were "anxious to bring their vile principles into favor . . . to degrade society to their own level . . . destroying all morality . . . their avowed programme—first to destroy the institution of marriage; second to abolish the Christian religion; and third, to inaugurate a reign of lust."[2] In short, more than sexual behavior was at stake— Free Lovers were out to subvert the very foundations of society.

Yet the intense fear of Free Love was relatively new to the post–Civil War period. Although ante-bellum America had produced such radical ideas as spiritual wifery, Perfectionism and Free Love, and such radical experiments as the Mormon Church, the Oneida Community, and Nashoba, most people had not taken these aberrations very seriously. Although these communities were ridiculed and sometimes—as in the case of the Mormons—persecuted, on the whole, middle-class Americans left them alone. In the aftermath of the Civil War, however, increasingly conservative attitudes characterized the country. Most uptopian communities had failed by then and the women's movement was struggling to survive. Radical social movements were, in fact, declining. Yet, paradoxically, at the moment of their decline, the frequency and emotional pitch of the rhetoric against them rose. The attackers, not content to ridicule the Mormons or Oneidians, shifted their focus to the ways in which ideas such as Free Love and Perfectionism had insidiously infiltrated a respectable society. Clearly the days of Free Love as a "harmless vagary" were over. In 1870 one fearful observer declared:

The evil principle of Free Love has spread with marvelous rapidity, until it has manifested itself in almost every class of society . . . it has . . . lowered the moral tone of society to an extent which is truly alarming. We see its workings in the looseness of public sentiment on questions of morality; in the infamous facilities for divorce which are increasing in our land; in the light esteem in which the marriage tie is held; and in the efforts to abolish the marriage relation. The evil has spread to such an alarming extent, that it is time some measures were taken to check it.[3]

No longer laughable, Free Love was not perceived as a challenge to fundamental social institutions. Such increased and widespread apprehension provided the background for Victoria Woodhull's accusation that Henry Ward Beecher had secretly adopted this subversive doctrine.

At the time she accused Beecher of adultery, Woodhull had reached the height of her meteoric career. Born in the frontier community of Homer, Ohio, of poor parents, her family soon discovered that Victoria—she had been named after Queen Victoria—had a talent for preaching and faith healing. Capitalizing upon the discovery, her parents began an itinerant existence—moving from town to town collecting fees for the "medical" services of Victoria and her sister Tennessee. During the course of her travels, Victoria married twice, first to a drunk named Woodhull and second to an impoverished genteel intellectual, Colonel James Blood. Blood was a philosophical anarchist as well as a spiritualist and a believer in Free Love; he provided Victoria with an intellectual framework for her talents in the popular healing art of "animal magnetism." Like Stephen Pearl Andrews, with whom Victoria was to become involved later, Blood was obsessed with early nineteenth-century notions of anti-institutionalism. Humanity, Blood and Andrews thought, had been dismally repressed by the negative attitudes toward human nature then inherent in organized religion and social institutions. Andrews posited that, given time and freedom from these repressive institutions, the innate goodness and purity in every human being would gradually emerge; he called his doctrine "individual sovereignty." Victoria was to combine the ideas of both these men with her own personal charisma and flamboyant style to create a brief, but stunningly successful career.[4]

With Colonel Blood's support, she and her family moved to New York where Victoria managed to become intimate with Commodore Vanderbilt, who, in January 1870, set her up in the brokerage business. She followed this success with an appearance before the Congressional House Judiciary Committee in December of the same year—the first woman ever to do so. This time her angel was General Ben Butler who arranged the appearance and wrote her speech on women's suffrage. However, although the speech was Ben Butler's, it was Victoria's demure yet personable manner that won the admiration of the congressmen. Because of this particular success, she was embraced by the leaders of the women's movement, Elizabeth Cady Stanton and Susan B. Anthony, as an influential spokeswoman for their cause. They introduced her to Henry Ward Beecher and Theodore Tilton. The dangers of an association with Woodhull soon became apparent, however, for Victoria was not content with limiting herself to suffrage reform. She openly advocated communism (she joined the International Workingmen's Association and printed Marx's *Communist Manifesto* in her paper) and spiritualism (she became president of the American Spiritualist Association). But most disturbing was her commitment to Free Love, which was evident in her scandalous personal behavior as well as in her public speeches. By now, Canning Woodhull, her first husband whom she had never divorced, had come to live with her and Colonel Blood in New York. And Victoria was quite willing to talk about the various men with whom she claimed to have had affairs—from office boys to Stephen Pearl Andrews. Ultimately, Victoria's charisma was not sufficient to overcome public censure of such behavior and ideas; in order to preserve the respectability of the suffrage movement, Stanton and Anthony denounced her. Undaunted, Victoria decided to form her own political party—the Equal Rights Party—in 1872. In May, about 500 followers nominated her for President of the United States on the Equal Rights Ticket. It was only after the election of 1872 that Victoria, irked by the lack of support from former friends and the public ridicule of her by Henry Ward Beecher's sisters, attempted to reveal the scandal. In the article she wrote exposing Beecher, she described her belief in Free Love as she had stated it to Theodore Tilton:

I told him that the fault and the wrong were neither in Beecher nor in Mrs. Tilton, nor in himself; but that it was in the false social institutions under which we still live, while the more advanced men and women of the world have outgrown them in spirit; and, that, practically, everybody is living a false life, by professing a conformity which they do not feel and do not live, and which they cannot feel and live any more than the grown boy can reenter the clothes of his early childhood.[5]

In her criticism of repressive social institutions, Woodhull was merely echoing the numerous social reformers of the ante-bellum period. She seemed more radical than they because she was willing to go beyond the criticism of government and religion; she extended her ideas to sex and marriage as well. Although most Americans reacted with simultaneous outrage and amusement, the possibility that Henry Ward Beecher might actually share these ideas—even to the point of practicing them—was extremely disturbing.

If Woodhull symbolized the disrepute into which American radicalism had fallen, Henry Ward Beecher seemed to represent the best in American culture. If one wants to observe a peculiarly American phenomenon, declared a contemporary journalist, attend Plymouth Church in Brooklyn

Thomas Nast's famous cartoon of Victoria Woodhull first appeared in Harper's Weekly *on February 17, 1872. Nast, a liberal reformer, feared the growing influence of the woman's movement.*

Heights where every Sunday Beecher preached to three thousand people.[6] These were the days before the Brooklyn Bridge, and each Sabbath morning the ferries from New York were so crowded with people bound for Plymouth Church that they became known as "Beecher boats." Beecher was, in fact, a well-known New York tourist attraction. In an era when public oratory seemed to be declining, Beecher could hold an audience spellbound. Thus it was only natural that Abraham Lincoln chose him to speak when the flag was raised victoriously over Fort Sumter. Beecher's sermons were recorded stenographically and published each week in newspapers throughout the country, and his articles in religious weeklies were read by thousands more. A book he wrote—not a very good book— became one of the top four best sellers in 1868. Beecher was an institution because he represented more than his own denomination of Congregationalism, or even Protestantism; he embodied the very essence of American purity and virtue. Indeed, many nonchurchgoers were personal followers of his. Therefore it is not surprising that Victoria Woodhull's revelation was a bombshell, or, as another journalist expressed it, a thunderbolt.[7]

And yet, precisely because Henry Ward Beecher had stepped beyond the traditional role of minister, many people were convinced there might be some truth to the accusations. They reasoned that his emphasis on the centrality of "love" in religion undercut the strength of traditional intellectual and moral standards. They accused Beecher of watering down and sentimentalizing Christianity. In attempting to popularize religion, they claimed, Beecher had irrevocably weakened religious institutions. The emphasis on love, or as Beecher liked to call it—"affinity"—could not help but spill over into secular areas—especially sex and marriage. Beecher's confounding of the distinction between love of God and love between men and women could only lead to immorality. This prospect was frightening enough, said Beecher's opponents, but the scandal provided tangible evidence that Beecher's "Gospel of Love" constituted a set of ideals dangerously imitative of Free Love.

The scandal, then, posed the question, not of the validity of Victoria Woodhull's radical notions, but of the extent to which, wittingly or unwittingly, Henry Ward Beecher and his thousands of respectable admirers had come to accept those ideas. It caused many Americans—both admirers and enemies—to examine more closely the origin and implications of Beecher's famous social philosophy known encompassingly as the Gospel of Love.

In the "bombshell" article, Woodhull, after asserting that Beecher was a believer in the "most advanced doctrines of free-love and the abolition of Christian marriage," went on to supply the "sordid" details of the scandal.

She had learned them, she said, from the husband of the woman involved, Theodore Tilton. The exposé article claimed that Tilton first learned the "tale of iniquitous horror" from his twelve-year-old daughter. When confronted by her husband with this evidence, Mrs. Tilton, who was pregnant, did not attempt any "palliation." Tilton concluded that her unborn child was not his, and "stripped the wedding-ring from her finger." Crazed with jealousy, he "tore the picture of Mr. Beecher from the wall and stamped it in pieces." Within a few months, Elizabeth miscarried and a frantic Tilton could be found "walking to and from that grave, in a state bordering on distraction."[8]

Woodhull's tale was worthy of a Victorian novel. It surpassed the almost pathological sensationalism characterizing the popular fiction of the day. Truth, it seemed, was not so different from fiction after all. However, as Beecher's defenders quickly pointed out, Woodhull was an unreliable troublemaker—she had a reputation for attempting to blackmail prominent men by threatening to expose their relations with prostitutes. Beecher himself responded to Woodhull's story with a condescending "policy of silence." After a brief flurry in the press, this strategy proved effective—the scandal faded from public attention. But it was not dead, only dormant, as its sporadic reappearance in the press demonstrated. Finally, during the "scandal summer" of 1874, the whole affair came to light and dominated the national press.[9] Although the facts were somewhat less lurid than Woodhull's portrayal, they still gripped the imagination of a fascinated public.

THE STORY

Theodore Tilton and Henry Ward Beecher had first become friends when they worked together on the popular religious journal, the *Independent*. The minister, along with others in Plymouth Church, had been instrumental in obtaining a position for Tilton on the paper, later promoting him to editor. Tilton, twenty-two years younger than Beecher, regarded the minister as a father figure. Anxious that Beecher's friendship include his wife and children, he repeatedly urged the preacher to visit his home. These invitations were ignored until 1866 when Tilton began a series of lecture tours that kept him away from Brooklyn three or four months every year.

During these absences, Beecher began calling upon Mrs. Tilton every week—indeed, he became almost a part of the household, reading the children stories and putting them to bed. Elizabeth Tilton, flattered by attention from this "great man," described these visits in letters to her husband. Despite her openness, however, Tilton's suspicions were aroused. He vacillated, however, between feeling flattered and, increasingly, jealous. Significantly, Tilton was not alone in his suspicions, for many Plymouth Church parishioners, who were neighbors of the Tiltons, had noticed the frequent visits. Beecher had a reputation as a nonvisiting minister; he made no secret of his aversion to this particular pastoral duty. Mrs. Tilton was a notable exception.

Whatever rumors may have circulated, nothing was said openly for four years after the visits began. From 1866 on, however, it was clear that the Tiltons experienced marital difficulties, while the discord between Henry Ward Beecher and his wife Eunice was common knowledge. Rumors surfaced that Beecher had sought sympathy and sexual solace from other female members of his congregation. Despite the gossip, however, the Tiltons continued their friendship with the minister. Elizabeth Tilton even suggested to her husband that the two of them—with "pure" friendship—might cure Beecher of some of the "delusions" he had about himself.[10]

Apparently, the Tiltons were more deluded than Beecher, for on October 10, 1868, the pastor probably succeeded in seducing Elizabeth. She told her husband later that she had "surrendered" only after "long moral resistance . . . and . . . repeated assaults . . . upon her mind with overmastering arguments." She had weakened only because of her "tender state of mind" and her need of consolation following the death of her infant child. Beecher's arguments that "pure affection and a high religious love" justified their sexual union were indeed "overmastering." They convinced Elizabeth that, despite the affair, she remained "spotless and chaste." But her contention that "pure" love should be honest and open, and that she should therefore inform her husband of their relationship, was vehemently resisted by Beecher. He insisted, she said, that the vulgar world would not understand such purity; they must practice "nest-hiding."[11] Keeping their love a secret was necessary to preserve its integrity.

On July 3, 1870, Elizabeth finally did confess to her husband. Clearly, however, she intended the revelation only for Theodore—it was not a public statement. At the time of her confession, Theodore offered to keep her secret and help heal her "wounded spirit." Despite intentions of secrecy, however, the scandal almost became public the following December when Tilton quarreled with his employer and fellow Plymouth Church member, Henry C. Bowen. Bowen as publisher and Tilton as editor of the *Brooklyn Union* had come to disagree on the paper's editorial policy toward Plymouth Church. In the heat of the dispute, Tilton revealed to Bowen his wife's adultery with Beecher. The impact of this information on Bowen was startling. He already harbored numerous grievances against the minister, one —possibly—for the seduction of his own wife Lucy eight years before. Bowen himself had been the source of the earlier rumors about Beecher. This evidence of another Beecher adultery offered Bowen the opportunity for revenge. He urged Tilton to demand the minister's resignation. Caught off guard by this turn of events, Tilton wrote such a letter but then confided to his long-time friend Frank Moulton what had occurred. Moulton, suspicious of Bowen's motives, urged Tilton to destroy the letter, but it was too late; it had been delivered by Bowen himself. Beecher as well as Tilton, badly shaken by the possibility of public exposure, now welcomed Moulton's offer to "manage" the affair. Thus began a four-year attempt to cover up the scandal. The "mutual friend," as Moulton later became known, planned the cover-up strategy—suddenly becoming an important figure in the lives of both men.

Moulton, in fact, accompanied the preacher as he confronted Elizabeth Tilton. It was the first time they had seen each other since Beecher's discovery of her confession. During that encounter, the minister persuaded Elizabeth—who was recovering from a miscarriage—to write a retraction of the confession; he even dictated its contents. Tilton, upon discovering this maneuver on Beecher's part, insisted that his wife write yet another letter, this time denying her retraction and indicating that Beecher had dictated it. She abjectly agreed.

The next day, in one of the more dramatic episodes of the case, Moulton called on Beecher, took a pistol from his coat, and chided the minister for obtaining from Mrs. Tilton a letter which he "knew to be a lie." Some accounts claim that it was common for those who had business along Brooklyn's waterfront to carry pistols, although others insisted that Moulton was deliberately threatening Beecher. Significantly, the preacher surrendered the retraction to Moulton amidst "great sorrow and weeping" and protestations that the "sexual expression" of his love for Elizabeth Tilton was as natural as its "verbal expression."[12]

For a time, Moulton was extremely effective in concealing the scandal and persuading Tilton and Beecher to resume their friendship. Because Henry Bowen had fired Tilton, Moulton and his business partners, with financial help from Beecher, backed a new weekly paper, the *Golden Age*, with Tilton as editor. Moulton also sent off to boarding school a young girl who had been living with the Tiltons and who knew of Beecher's affair with Mrs. Tilton. He even persuaded Beecher to pay the girl's expenses.

Moulton might have congratulated himself on his astute handling of the

scandal if Woodhull, through her connections with Susan Anthony and
Elizabeth Cady Stanton, had not heard rumors of the affair. In the spring
of 1871 came the first hints that she knew of the scandal—causing Moulton, Beecher, and Tilton to begin frantically, and somewhat comically,
conspiring to keep her quiet. The three conceived a plan whereby Tilton
would placate Woodhull by putting her under "social obligation" to them.
He accomplished this by flattering her and offering to compose an admiring biography.[13] (Woodhull later claimed that he had also become her
lover for more than six months.) The appeasement policy succeeded for a
year, until 1872, when Woodhull, angered by the attacks upon her by Beecher's sisters, Catherine and Harriet, published her story.

This time, despite Moulton's frantic schemes to avoid it, the scandal
erupted. One after another of the incriminating letters and documents was
published in the papers—but it was still a full year and a half before any
formal action was taken. Curiously, it was *Tilton* who was first attacked
for his part in the scandal. In 1873, Plymouth Church dismissed him from
membership, citing his "slander" of the minister and association with
Woodhull! Even then, however, Tilton's commitment to silence was unshaken. Had it not been for a Brooklyn Congregational Council's demands for an investigation, the affair might once again have faded from
public notice. The council had no real power, but it inspired a series of articles in the *Independent* by a Yale divinity professor—a friend of Beecher's
—who referred to Tilton as a "knave" and a "dog."[14] Tilton could not
stand this public degradation; in June 1874, he responded with a long re-
ply, which he sent to the major New York and Brooklyn newspapers, stating his version of the case and voicing his refusal "to sacrifice my good
name for the sake of *his*."[15]

By July 1874, public outcry was so great that Beecher abandoned the
policy of silence. Taking the offensive, he appointed a Church Investigating Committee (which consisted of six of his closest friends) to hear the
charges. During August the committee took testimony which the newspapers published verbatim. A fascinated public hung on every word. Elizabeth Tilton, determined to defend Beecher, appeared the day after leaving
her husband, revealing with touching pathos a sad tale of "domestic unhappiness," but denying the adultery.[16] Tilton, now joined by Moulton in
an effort to expose Beecher, presented a mass of documentation—including Beecher's own letters—which constituted almost irrefutable evidence.
But, not surprisingly, the committee issued a report completely exonerating Beecher. "The evidence," stated the Investigating Committee, established "to the perfect satisfaction of his church" Beecher's "entire inno-

cence and absolute personal integrity." Because of their pastor's "unmerited sufferings," the committee members reiterated that they now felt a "sympathy more tender and a trust more unbounded" than ever before. When Moulton protested the report at a full church meeting, he was threatened with violence and the police were called to "escort" him from the hall.[17]

Tilton, angered by Beecher's private system of justice and smarting under the sharp insulting rebuke of the committee, filed criminal charges against the minister. The ensuing trial was the greatest national spectacle of the 1870s. For six months—from January to June 1875—the most renowned lawyers in the country dedicated their talents to the case. Opening and closing statements alone took two months; opera glasses were sold in the courtroom and bouquets of flowers were showered on Beecher and Tilton. The trial became known as the "flower war." In the end, the jury could not agree and Beecher was acquitted. His congregation staged a huge celebration, voting to raise his salary by $100,000 in order to pay the lawyers. It was all a magnificent vote of confidence which demonstrated the overwhelming devotion of Beecher's congregation.

Because the result of the trial was equivocal, Plymouth Church sought to make the verdict conclusive by calling a second church council in 1876. In that council, Henry C. Bowen, for the first time, came forward, testifying that he knew Beecher to be a "libertine and a seducer."[18] Nevertheless, the council—which consisted of churches carefully chosen because of their sympathy with Beecher—followed the lead of Plymouth in completely exonerating Beecher. Bowen, Emma Moulton, and others who had testified against the minister were promptly excommunicated. The purge was completed in the spring of 1878 when Elizabeth Tilton, in a startling reversal of the stand she had taken all through the trial, made a public confession of the adultery and was also excommunicated.

The members of Plymouth Church were both numerous and powerful in Brooklyn and New York and their revenge against the Tiltons was complete. Ostracized by Plymouth Church, Elizabeth Tilton died in 1897, lonely and blind, at the home of her daughter in Brooklyn. The influence of Beecher's wealthy parishioners in journalistic circles prevented Theodore Tilton from earning a livelihood and he fled to Paris where he lived in poverty, writing poetry, and playing chess.

Beecher, despite his continued popularity in Plymouth Church and as a lecturer, did suffer from the scandal. The religious newspaper he edited, the *Christian Union,* lost a significant number of subscribers and the publishing firm that depended for most of its profit on the sale of Beecher's books went bankrupt. Though respected and popular until his death in 1887, Beecher never again enjoyed the same universal reverence of the pre-scandal days.[19]

HISTORIANS AND THE SCANDAL

After his death and until very recently, Beecher's reputation (among those who have chosen to remember him at all) continued to decline. Most historians have treated Henry Ward Beecher as one of the worst examples of hypocritical moralism in the Gilded Age. Though lauded for his promotion of antislavery and women's suffrage, his involvement in the scandal and his later reactionary political and social views precluded serious study of his career. One exception, Paxton Hibben's *Henry Ward Beecher: An American Portrait* (1927), used Beecher's story as a vehicle to debunk the motives of prominent leaders—attempting to prove that the pursuit of wealth, power, and selfish pleasure were common failings among "great men." Hibben's bias led him to portray Beecher as the sole culprit in the whole affair: he seduced a simple-minded and devoted female parishioner, the wife of a hard-working and long-suffering friend, and then proceeded to make false and shameless accusations against them in a brazen attempt to cover up his own guilt. Beecher's selfishness and hypocrisy were, to Hibben, a perfectly satisfactory explanation for the whole imbroglio.[20]

Victoria Woodhull's biographers, as well, accepted this version of the scandal. Emanie Sachs, writing in 1928, although not endorsing her subject's views on free love, defended Woodhull's courageous exposure of Beecher's hypocritical philandering.[21] Thus, by the 1930s Beecher had become a stereotyped whipping boy for American historians and an embarrassment to American religion. His niche in nineteenth-century social history as the purveyor of a watered-down Protestantism to a self-satisfied middle class and the symbol of Victorian moral hypocrisy seemed permanently fixed; few historians were moved to subject his career to further scrutiny. Those who did venture to study the periods of his life devoted to antislavery dismissed as "trivia" his involvement in the scandal. Beecher appeared in textbooks as the abolitionist who sent Sharps rifles, or "Beecher Bibles," to aid in the bloody struggle for Kansas, and as the brother of Harriet Beecher Stowe of *Uncle Tom's Cabin* fame. There his case rested until 1954.

In the early 1950s, Robert Shaplen, a writer for the *New Yorker* who lived in Brooklyn, became interested in the scandal as a piece of local color.

After publishing a two-part article in the *New Yorker* in June 1954, he expanded the piece into a book, *Free Love and Heavenly Sinners*. The book itself is as astute as its title, for Shaplen delved more thoroughly into the scandal than any previous writer. Not intended to be a work of historical scholarship, it is a popular, dramatic, accurate portrayal of the people and events of the scandal. It is the best single work on the subject.[22]

More recently, several scholars have begun to renew interest in Beecher as an illuminating figure in the development of Victorian culture. In *The Meaning of Henry Ward Beecher,* William G. McLoughlin resurrects Beecher as one of the most important representative figures of the entire century. With McLoughlin's opening statement, Beecher was restored to a place of serious consideration in American history:

Henry Ward Beecher is treated as something of a joke by most Americans and many history books. He is the pompous ass who got caught off base. . . . This book is not an attempt to make Beecher appear a neglected hero of American history. But it does attempt to explain how and why such a man achieved such fame, popularity, and fortune in the half-century after 1840. . . . What is significant is what he said, why he said it, why so many people believed it, what it meant to them, and therefore why Beecher seemed to most middle-class church-going Americans of his day a very important man.[23]

This book probes Beecher's articulation of "the shifting values of mid-Victorian America," primarily through an analysis of his only novel, *Norwood* (1868). McLoughlin argues that there Beecher laid out his ideas in "orderly fashion" and the novel constitutes "whatever claim Beecher has to historical importance."[24] Thus, McLoughlin sees Beecher's significance in his genius for articulating the values and thoughts of middle-class Americans in the mid-nineteenth century. He does not deal with the scandal, but his work is extremely helpful in illuminating Beecher's theology and social philosophy.

Paul Carter is the first historian to investigate seriously the fascination of millions of Americans with the Brooklyn scandal. In his single chapter in *The Spiritual Crisis of the Gilded Age,* Carter suggests the ways in which freedom threatened most morality-conscious Americans; their major concern, he says, was not with Beecher's pompous hypocrisy, but with the obvious characteristics of his personality—the warm heartiness and vigor with which he enjoyed life. He was a man of enthusiasm and passion. This freedom was far too frightening to Americans concerned about social and personal discipline in an emerging industrial society. They found Beecher's indulgence in such socially destructive antics titillating yet frightening.[25]

Clifford Clark's recent book, *Henry Ward Beecher: Spokesman for Middle-Class America,* in the same vein as McLoughlin and Carter, attempts to trace the evolution of Beecher's life and thought as a paradigm for the newly urbanized middle class. According to Clark, Beecher's followers simply could not accept Beecher's guilt because "to admit that Beecher might have been guilty . . . was to admit that their own moral perspective on life might be wrong and they were simply unwilling to entertain this thought."[26]

There has been so much focus on Beecher's character and role as a "spokesman" for an amorphous middle class that writers have given too little attention to the other principals—Theodore and Elizabeth Tilton, Henry Bowen, and Richard Salter Storrs. The one exception is Ann Douglas; in *The Feminization of American Culture* (1977), she uses Elizabeth Tilton (whom she gratuitously refers to as "Libby") as a representative woman, demonstrating the shallow personality of the middle-class woman who turned to sentimentalized fiction for a definition of her own role. Douglas argues that "Libby" was a confused nonentity until fiction offered her a role to play—in short, she could not function as a genuine person, but only as an imitation of some external idealized model. This assessment of the middle-class woman has been common for some time—and with it the tendency to dismiss her as a weak, simpering, indeed, almost worthless human being. Thus, a concentration on female heroes such as Margaret Fuller, Susan B. Anthony, and Victoria Woodhull has become common. However, in this book, I will focus on the intense pressures that had to be exerted before Elizabeth Tilton, Eunice Beecher, and others like them were "domesticated." Simply because they failed in resisting dominant social currents does not mean they lacked character or courage.

HISTORICAL CHANGE IN PERSONAL PERSPECTIVE: THE TILTON MARRIAGE

Much has been written in recent years about the historical changes in the role and structure of the family. The old idea that actual family structure was transformed from extended to nuclear in the nineteenth century has been discredited by research showing the pervasiveness of the nuclear family before as well as during the colonial period. Beyond this structural similarity, however, it is undeniable that the internal dynamics of family relationships and expectations of family life changed radically during the nineteenth century. Earlier concepts of duty and responsibility were replaced by a spiritualized romantic love that acted as a defense against the debilitating intrusions of the outside world.[27]

The radical shift from the function of the family as a "Little Commonwealth" which should extend and enforce the values of the larger community to a "haven" protecting its members from the temptations of a competitive world has been well documented in sermons, novels, and private letters. Historians have successfully shown that this change in the role of the family did occur. What has been less often demonstrated is the process, on an individual level, of how and why it occurred. These are startling changes, after all, even on an aggregate social level; how much more startling and confusing they must have seemed to individuals caught up in what we can now see as a sweeping historical trend. How did these changes manifest themselves in the lives of people growing to maturity and marrying at mid-nineteenth century? What specific events and problems did they have to face and solve in new and unfamiliar ways? These are areas which need exploring before the larger, more abstract patterns can be fully understood.

The Tilton marriage offers a compelling case study not simply because ordinary marital difficulties brought about a national scandal, but because these rapidly changing family ideals led explicitly and directly, if unwittingly, to the scandal. Elizabeth and Theodore Tilton were intelligent, articulate, and often perceptive individuals. They formulated and expressed to each other their evolving ideas and anxieties about the tension between "old" assumptions about marriage, contrasting them with "new" values. In great detail, they explored what this meant for them, their parents, children, and friends. In discussing love, sex, and fidelity, they focused on the problem of involuntary return to old patterns they had explicitly rejected. Indeed, they might be compared to modern couples who reject the traditional sex roles in marriage but continue, unwittingly, to act them out. Thus, to understand the Tiltons is to understand changing cultural values through a set of unique personal problems. The dissolution of this marriage as a result of adultery and the resultant notoriety do not negate the lessons to be learned. The scandal, in fact, enhances the value of the study, for it brings into bolder relief the confusion in attitudes undoubtedly felt by many couples who were never called upon to articulate their feelings. The Tiltons' testimony at the trial and the testimony of friends, neighbors, and servants add a depth and color to the usually sketchy outline available to the historian when dealing with family and personal history. On the shadowed stage of Victorian family history, the Beecher trial shines a bright spotlight on one family—thereby illuminating the contours of nine-teenth-century family dynamics.

RELIGIOUS AND POLITICAL CONFLICT IN THE SCANDAL

Another aspect of the scandal that has been universally ignored in the literature is the religious and political conflict in which it was rooted and which it exacerbated. Paxton Hibben's biography of Henry Ward Beecher intriguingly suggested that political divisions existed in the trial of 1875—but then dropped any further discussion of the nature of these divisions.[28] Robert Shaplen assumes that Beecher was the spokesman for the wealthy, complacent, respectable residents of fashionable Brooklyn Heights.[29] Spurred on by these hints that the scandal represented more than conflicting values in the minds of *all* middle-class Americans, I wanted to determine if the patterns that emerged in the conflict over Beecher's guilt or innocence reflected more than personal whim or circumstance. The results suggest that the scandal and its response reveal more than a lurid exposé of Victorian sexual hypocrisy.

The most obvious division between Beecher's supporters and opponents was based on religious ideology. Though Beecher was minister of a large Congregational church in Brooklyn Heights, his parishioners had long been proud of the nonsectarian nature of his preaching. The minister scorned such fine dogmatic arguments as the method of baptism—he would baptize anybody any way he or she desired. "All denominations can claim him," enthused one contemporary, "for he is broad enough in his sympathies, and comprehensive enough in his sweep of the truth to afford a support for all."[30] Beecher was the most prominent spokesman in nine-teenth-century America for liberal Christianity; any indictment of him threatened the validity of the liberal approach to Protestantism.

But on another level, Beecher's parishioners perceived the charges against their pastor as charges specifically aimed at Plymouth Church, for they responded as though attacked. Any dissension in the congregation over Beecher's possible doctrinal looseness disappeared as the members closed ranks in almost unanimous support. This support could hardly have been due to personal friendship with the minister because there were about 3,000 members of the church. Beecher himself admitted he barely knew or could recognize most of the members.

By contrast, Beecher's opponents displayed an implacable hostility. Two orthodox Congregational churches in Brooklyn persisted in demanding an investigation and were unrelenting in their attempts to discredit

Beecher. One of the ministers, Richard Salter Storrs, even threatened to change the denomination of his church to Presbyterian if Beecher and Plymouth Church were not expelled from the Congregational Association. Thus, Beecher's enemies perceived the scandal as more than a single instance of immorality; they considered it a threat to the religious institutional life of their community as well.

The second striking ideological division was in the arena of politics. Hibben's guess that political conflict shaped the trial was a shrewd one. Since the late 1860s there had been a reshuffling of political alignments in Brooklyn politics; older, simpler divisions between Republicans and Democrats had broken down into a scramble for power among factions. Reform wings of both parties had recently rebelled against the "bossism" rampant in the structures of the regular party "machines." The struggle for power between these factions caused confusion, election fraud, and bitter confrontations in Brooklyn.

These patterns were reflected in the adultery trial. Theodore Tilton as well as his lawyers was actively involved in the movement for political reform; Beecher's lawyers, on the contrary, were committed "regular" party politicians. Moreover, both local and national newspapers tended to reflect these political divisions in their editorial comments on the affair. The scandal, then, far from being an event removed from the web of social and religious life in Brooklyn, was an essential element of the political rivalry already raging.

How can these striking religious and political divisions that emerged in the controversy over the scandal be explained? What were Beecher's ideas about sex, love, and marriage, and how did they become entangled with ecclesiastical organization and political party alignments? Why did reform politicians and orthodox Christians strive to have Beecher exposed and convicted of adultery, while regular politicians and liberal Christians insisted, just as tenaciously, on his acquittal? Why did it matter so much? In this study I will address these questions by documenting hitherto untold aspects of the scandal and exploring the links between it and social conflict in the city of Brooklyn.

2

Henry Ward Beecher:
The Emergence of the Gospel of Love

O N JANUARY 3, 1866, soon after he began visiting Elizabeth Tilton, Henry Ward Beecher wrote to his editor describing the novel later published as *Norwood; or Village Life in New England*. "I propose to make a story which shall turn, not so much on outward action (though I hope to have enough to carry the story handsomely) as on *certain mental* or inward questions. I propose to delineate a high and noble man, trained to New England theology, but brought to excessive distress by speculations and new views. . . . The heroine is to be large of soul, a child of nature, and, although a Christian, yet in childlike sympathy with the truths of God in the autumn world, instead of books. These two, the man of philosophy and theology and the woman of nature and simple truth, are to act upon each other, and she is to triumph."[1] Significantly, it was *Norwood*—with its focus on the conflict between a male intellectual world and the intuitive, childlike nature of what Beecher perceived as a feminine world—which fostered the bond between him and Elizabeth. As he wrote each chapter, Beecher would read it aloud to Elizabeth. In these discussions of the novel and its themes of pure love and affinity was born the sexual affair that was eventually transformed into the greatest scandal of the nineteenth century.

The point is that when Henry Ward Beecher importuned Elizabeth Tilton with phrases such as "high religious love," "pure" friendship, and "nest-hiding," he was not speaking hypocritically. He was expressing a desperately felt need—one, in fact, not significantly different from ideas and yearnings apparent in the rhetoric of his public utterances—not only in the novel *Norwood*, but in his sermons. Indeed, with such titles as "The Primacy of Love" and "Moral Affinity the Ground of True Unity," it is not surprising that Beecher's philosophy came to be known as the Gospel of Love. These sermons, no less than the novel, condemned the world of Beecher's youth as oppressive, rigid, and emotionally barren, while his ideal world promised freedom, simplicity, and love. Such rhetoric may seem timeworn, but only because we are observing from the perspective of the twentieth century. In Beecher's day, for thousands of Americans, this was a new way of thinking about the world. Before *Norwood,* writes William McLoughlin, "It is difficult to find . . . in American evangelical writing such an explicit statement of the romantic basis of love as distinct from the older contractual or sacramental basis." Love, based on the new idea of romantic attraction—Beecher's favorite term was "affinity"—was the cornerstone of his gospel in public as well as private life. Beecher's success, as McLoughlin has pointed out, was not in developing an original doctrine —similar ideas had long been preached by the Transcendentalists and Methodists—but was in bringing such ideas to a middle-class public: "Beecher reached a much wider audience than any of those theologians who struggled so hard to say on a high plane of system and consistency what could only strike home at a much lower and nonrational plane."[2]

Given the attractiveness of Beecher's gospel to thousands of Americans, it is hardly surprising that Elizabeth Tilton found both the minister and his ideas difficult to resist. However, the nature of their early interaction reveals another side to Beecher that, no less than his explicit philosophy, characterized the Gospel of Love. When Beecher was questioned in court as to why he turned to Elizabeth for criticism of the novel, he replied that having so little confidence in his ability to write he needed someone to provide "uncritical praise."[3] His honesty here was somewhat disarming because, of course, Elizabeth thought he appreciated her critical abilities—he "respected me," she said in her testimony.[4] The truth was that Beecher generally cultivated people who admired and worshiped him. In fact, much of his famous magnetism seemed to emanate from his almost desperate need to win the praise and approval of everyone—from family and friends to his congregation. Paxton Hibben has suggested that the only consistent goal in Beecher's life was satisfying his hunger for love and power. Though his theology was vague, his moral standards flexible, and his reform efforts sporadic, the pursuit of love and power was always evident.[5] In admitting that he sought "uncritical praise" from Mrs. Tilton, Beecher revealed a need that had shaped his entire life.

Born on June 24, 1813, in Litchfield, Connecticut, Beecher was the eighth child of famed evangelical preacher Lyman Beecher. Barely three years after Henry Ward was born, his mother Roxanna died and his care was left to his older sisters and stepmother. Much has been written on the entire Beecher family, several of whom became influential ministers or

writers. Historians who have studied the various children of Lyman Beecher agree that this controversial minister was also a domineering father
who irrevocably shaped, for better or worse, the lives of his children.[6]
Henry Ward was no exception; references to his parents and his childhood
occur in Henry's sermons and writings until the end of his life. Although in
these reminiscences it is clear that Beecher respected his father—"I never
saw my father do a thing that had duplicity in it in my life," he once wrote
—for the most part he recalled a childhood fraught with pain and anger.
Often he felt neglected and cheated of the love he thought every child deserved: "My father was so busy, and my mother had so many other children to look after, that except here and there, I hardly came under the parental hand at all."[7] Beecher's older sister, Harriet, confirmed this assessment of his childhood but attributed it to prevalent practices in raising
children. "The community did not recognize them," she said, "there was
no child's literature; there were no children's books . . . the childhood of
Henry Ward was unmarked by the possession of a single child's toy as a
gift from any older person or a single fête."[8]

Whether this treatment was standard for the period or not, Henry Ward
resented it, feeling that when he did receive attention from his father, it was
negative. Love, in the Beecher household, he remembered, had been conditional and judgmental; he was frightened and bewildered by the expectations of his father. Lyman Beecher's habit was to relate to his children by
challenging them to intellectual debates over points of religious doctrine,
rewarding those who exhibited the most agility of mind. "I was brought
up," Beecher recalled, "in the school of dispute."[9] Henry Ward consistently rated lower in these contests than any of his siblings, including sisters
Catherine and Harriet. Beecher referred to these episodes of humiliation as
going through the "colic and anguish" of "hyper-calvinism." Although
Lyman Beecher was associated with the New Haven theology that did
much to challenge the rigid doctrine of predestination and introduce flexi-
bility and free agency into Calvinism, these liberalizing tendencies did not
seem to temper his stern style, either in preaching or in dealing with his
children.[10] Not surprisingly, young Henry was "mortified" and developed
a stutter that impaired his speech until late in his college career. Beecher
never forgave his father, brothers, and sisters for treating his efforts to be
heard with contempt and embarrassment; in a lecture-room talk forty
years later, he referred emotionally to his own "shame" and their "ungra-
cious" behavior.[11]

Not only did young Henry Ward fail to measure up intellectually, but he
seemed also to lack the moral character to resist "wrong-doing." In refer-

ring to his childhood, Beecher once said that it was most often characterized by "shame and terror."

I had not the courage to confess, and tell the truth . . . shame hindered me; second,
fear. . . . And when I got to going wrong I went on going wrong. . . . I was afraid of
being found out . . . when my father came home, I would watch his face to see if he
looked as though he knew it . . . and out of that depression and low state it was easier to be tempted again . . . and I became more and more uneasy.[12]

Henry apparently spent the better part of his youth ashamed, fearful, and
convinced of his inadequacy. His stepmother referred to him as "deceit-
ful" and he himself wrote to his sister Harriet that "I find no place with so
little sympathy as home."[13]

For Beecher, then, home was a place of fear, judgment, and stern retri-
bution. He conceded that his father had been "kind" to him, but had never
demonstrated the love Beecher craved so intensely—a love not dependent
on intellectual prowess or righteous conduct. Beecher reacted by rejecting
not only what he saw as an incomprehensible theology but the father and
siblings responsible for his suffering. In a remarkable sermon in 1868 he
denounced the ties of family as merely "mechanical." "We cannot choose
who shall be our companions in the cradle. . . . And whether they be suit-
able or not, they are our brothers, they are our sisters, they are our
parents."[14]

Beecher's rejection, however, applied only to his father—because as a
young man he did come to regard one member of his family as his "salvation." That person was the mother who died when Beecher was three years
old. When he was eighteen, Beecher discovered some letters his mother
had written and confided to his diary: "I found out more of her *mind* than I
ever knew before—more of her *feelings,* her *piety*. And I could not help observing that her letters were superior—more refined and conclusive than
the corresponding ones of father."[15] As this image of his mother evolved,
Beecher came more and more to believe that he could actually remember
her. By the end of his life, he spoke as though she had been a constant presence throughout his childhood. The year before his death, Beecher "recalled" that she had a "wonderful depth of affection" and while his father
was "tormenting himself," she "threw the oil of faith and trust on the
waters and they were quieted." Beecher insisted that all his good qualities,
all his accomplishments originated in his mother's undemanding and unconditional love—the only counterpoint to his father's inflexibility.
"From her," he said, "I received my love of the beautiful, my poetic temperament . . . simplicity . . . and childlike faith in God."[16] The image of

woman as more refined and superior was eventually to be a key force in the development of the Gospel of Love.

At the same time that Beecher was developing a mythical profile of his mother and rejecting the demands of his father, he was still very much under the authority of the powerful Lyman. The elder Beecher insisted that all his sons become ministers, but he encountered obstacles with Henry Ward. From the beginning it had been obvious that this son was neither theologian nor scholar. In addition, he stuttered. And finally, when the family lived in Boston, the young man threatened to run away to sea. Lyman promptly sent his recalcitrant son to Mt. Pleasant Academy in Amherst.[17] Besides removing Henry from Boston ships, it was hoped that he would improve enough academically to be sent to Yale, where several of his brothers had gone. When the time came, however, it was clear that Henry could not measure up to Yale. The father's dissatisfaction was evident in the letter he wrote to the president of Amherst College, informing him that after "much deliberation and some hesitation" he had decided to send Henry to Amherst. At Mt. Pleasant, said the elder Beecher, Henry had been taught "carelessly" and learned his lessons "superficially."[18] Lyman hoped that Amherst College could somehow "retrieve" the losses.

In this hope, Lyman Beecher was disappointed. During his college years at Amherst (1830–1834) the young man gained a reputation for his lack of interest in scholarship. He liked the social activities and eventually overcame the stutter that had bothered him for so long—but this may have had more to do with his physical distance from the father of whom he was so frightened. Most of the time, however, Henry Ward spent cultivating what his sister Harriet was later to call his "genius for friendship."[19] Apparently, Henry had finally found some friends who appreciated him, people who made him feel loved and important. The first of these was a Greek student, Constantine Fondolaik, with whom Beecher made a pact of friendship which he called "a marriage of man to man."[20] An antidote to his "mechanical" family, Fondolaik represented Beecher's first friendship based on affinity.

Besides cultivating friends who made him feel positive about himself, the young man began to develop his oratorical ability. It was in a somewhat different direction than his father might have hoped, however. Beecher formed a working partnership with another Amherst student, Orson Fowler, later to become famous for his books on phrenology, love, and sex. Fowler introduced Beecher to the new "science" of phrenology then just becoming popular in America. Later in the century, phrenology was treated as a joke, sarcastically referred to as the science of bumps; but in the pre–Civil War period, many intelligent people were taking the new theories seriously. Phrenology taught that different areas of the brain controlled each human attribute or faculty, and that the skull, because it conformed closely to the shape of the brain, would indicate which of the faculties were well developed and which underdeveloped.[21] For example, the area of the skull at the base of the neck was believed to represent "amativeness" or interest in love and sex; several areas at the front of the head, reason. Thus, by closely examining an individual's head, a phrenologist could produce a character analysis. Orson Fowler was eventually to become the most successful phrenologist in America—and Beecher was one of his earliest disciples. The two traveled around western Massachusetts, Beecher delivering speeches explaining phrenology while Fowler examined heads and wrote out mental profiles.[22]

Beecher was fascinated by this new approach to the study of human nature. It seemed to liberate one from the constraints of a family background by offering the opportunity of discovering and working with one's own natural propensities. Phrenology was later interpreted as being essentially conservative and elitist because it assigned the best head shapes to the Anglo-Saxon race, but Beecher's generation saw it as a way to escape the confining institutions and expectations of the past. "It gives a new power," he declared, "over the intellect and the will."[23] For a young man like Beecher, oppressed and guilt-ridden by his father's intellectual demands, this new "science" offered a more benevolent and hopeful way to explain and justify his own temperament.

The influence of phrenology on Beecher's religious ideas was immediately apparent in a "conversion" he experienced at about this time. Because he related this event much later, when he was almost eighty, it is probable that the recollection may have been distorted. Indeed, every time he recounted the experience in later life, he altered the details as to where and when it took place, so there is some question as to whether it happened in any such dramatic way at all. Perhaps Beecher simply realized there were some psychological changes taking place in him at about that time, but there is no doubt that during these college years, Beecher's fear of his father, his adoration of his mother, his unconscious rejection of the theological complexity of his youth, and his introduction to phrenology combined to produce a conversion experience, not *to* his father's religion, but *from* it.

One morning the "light" broke upon his mind, Beecher said, revealing to him God's "infinite, universal" love. This was a dramatic revelation because it came to him in spite of his consistent inability to "do the things that were right." Surprisingly, God wanted to *help* him, not condemn him to eternal damnation. When this insight occurred, Beecher said, "One might have thought that I was a lunatic escaped from confinement." This assurance that he might be accepted for himself along with all his imperfections was exactly what Beecher always had longed for. Before this, he had painfully concluded that with the death of his mother he had lost the possibility of compassion and understanding. The conversion revealed most clearly, however, that God was like his mother, rather than like his father —in short, a sympathetic figure instead of a judgmental one. His conversion symbolized freedom from the emotional grip of a domineering father. "I ran up and down," Beecher recalled, "through the primeval forest . . . shouting, Glory! . . . All the old troubles gone, and light breaking upon my mind, I cried, 'I have found my God, I have found my God!' "[24]

If this conversion really happened, it constituted the beginnings of what gradually evolved into the Gospel of Love. This emphasis on freedom, love, and forgiveness eventually led Beecher to publicly reject the doctrines of predestination, hell, and atonement upon which his father's theology was based. Instead, he moved toward toleration and universal salvation. Beecher's gospel, however, was not original, but a popularization of ideas developed at about this time by a group of New England intellectuals known as the Transcendentalists. The group, led by Ralph Waldo Emerson, argued that God, as a kind of benevolent mystical force, was immanent in nature; He manifested Himself in moral and ethical principles that transcended the doctrinal differences between organized churches. Universal love formed the bonds between people, not membership in a particular denomination, family, or community. The Transcendentalists scorned the ideas of predestination, hell, and election, arguing that essential goodness, if allowed to develop freely, would come to the surface. At the time Beecher was in college, however, the Transcendentalists were still considered heretics. If the young man was influenced by them—as he certainly must have been—he would not have dared to begin voicing their sentiments openly.

In his years at divinity school and in his first two small parishes in Indiana, the conversion experience was a well-kept secret. In order to be licensed for preaching, Beecher had to appear traditional in his views on hell, original sin, and predestination. And his style if not the substance of his preaching remained much like his father's. He attempted to invoke fear in his congregation—not so much for lack of doctrinal sophistication as for moral lapses. In one of his first widely successful endeavors, Beecher delivered a set of lectures designed to guide young men into righteous paths as they ventured out into the world. This *Seven Lectures to Young Men,* first published in 1843, was so successful that it was published in book form and reprinted many times.[25] Many other preachers, at this time, produced similar manuals, but Beecher's was one of the most popular. As the stable communities of early America were breaking down and forcing young men to migrate either West or to the cities, many found this a dangerous journey—both physically and emotionally—and moral guidebooks became standard reading.

In his *Seven Lectures,* however, Beecher did not stress the understanding and forgiveness that were later to become the heart of his preaching. Apparently, he was still convinced that *fear* best preserved morality. For example, in one lecture concerning "sensual habit"—presumably masturbation—Beecher compared the results of this habit with the tortures endured by blacks on the slave ships: "The agony of midnight massacre, the frenzy of the ship's dungeon, the living death of the middle-passage, the wails of separation, and the dismal torpor of hopeless servitude—are these found only in the piracy of the slave-trade? They are all among us! Worse assassinations! Worse dragging to a prison-ship! Worse groans ringing from the fetid hold! Worse separations of families! Worse bondage of intemperate men, enslaved by that most inexorable of all taskmasters sensual habit."[26] It was noticeable that Beecher did not devote much time to theological doctrine and when he did, his comments were often inconsistent. Yet his emphasis—as in the above passage—on colorful rhetoric, projection of emotion, and dramatic style began to win followers. Aware that his success did not depend on consistency, Beecher later said of his early preaching: "I had time to sow all my ministerial wild oats without damage to my people, for they knew little whether I was orthodox or not. . . . I said a great many extravagant things in my pulpit and preached with a great deal of crudeness."[27] This was a period of trial and error for Beecher and he used it well, admitting later that he "tried everything."[28] It soon became clear to the struggling young minister that what he needed to do was determine what most of his congregation wanted to hear. "I got this idea," he remembered later, "that the Apostles were accustomed first to feel for a ground on which the people and they stood together; a common ground where they could meet." Then the minister should concentrate on that "knowledge" which "everybody would admit" and reiterate it with "excited heart and feeling."[29]

This attitude was a striking reversal of traditional ideas about a minister's role. The older idea was that the minister had certain knowledge to impart to his flock, whether they liked it or not. What was right was im-

Henry Ward Beecher at age 46. (Beecher Family Papers, Yale)

mutable and people had to be molded to fit the truth. This attitude was apparent in Beecher's father. Although Lyman Beecher was responsible for
much of the softening of earlier Puritanism, he never seemed to doubt his
own ability to arrive at the truth through some internal logic. Once he was
convinced of the efficacy of any given doctrine, his mission was to convince others, both those more conservative and those more liberal. From
his father Henry Ward received the strong impression that the truth proceeded from the minister to the people, but the younger Beecher was beginning to adopt the reverse notion that truth emanated from a general consensus of the people. If he could only define and articulate that consensus,
success would follow. His father's primary concern had been to be right,
while Beecher's was to be popular. Thus, Beecher was able to find more
than personal reasons for rejecting his father; professional success required it as well.

Beecher had adjusted, unconsciously perhaps, to the fact that ministers
were not exempt from the competitive market economy of nineteenth-century America. As Ann Douglas and Daniel Calhoun have documented, by

the time Beecher launched his career, the ministerial profession had lost the authority and social status it held in colonial society. Economic problems, the proliferation of denominations, and the secularization of society had combined to deprive the minister of his respected status. No longer could a young minister emerging from college or seminary count on a secure lifetime position. Forced to appeal to masses of people, Henry Ward Beecher became the most successful minister of his century in packaging his ideas and style in response to the market.[30]

In rejecting the traditions and authority of his father, Beecher was not alone. In dealing with the emotional struggle an individual encountered as he left home and turned from parental values, Henry Ward Beecher was touching a chord common to his generation. In fact, one of the reasons for his remarkable empathy with thousands of listeners was the similarity between his plight and theirs. In traditional society, fathers had been able to provide their sons, not only with moral and religious values, but with a concrete economic foundation and a social identity. Patriarchal authoritarianism was solidly based in real economic power over the lives of children. With the increase in population and the diminishing land supply of the late eighteenth century, this power was considerably weakened, leaving only the shell of religious and moral authority. Sons, in particular, had to leave their childhood homes and learn to make their livelihoods in very different occupations than the agricultural pursuits of their fathers. Eventually, of course, the moral authority of a father was diminished along with his economic power. [31]

An 1873 sermon "Through Fear to Love" is a good example of Beecher's explanation and justification for the radical changes he made in his father's theology and social philosophy.[32] Beecher postulates a theory of moral evolution, beginning with the primitive imperative of fear and ending in love. Describing the world in terms of "universal destructiveness," Beecher evoked the image of big fish eating smaller ones. "The whole world," said Beecher, "is an open mouth, and destroying goes on everywhere." Fear, therefore, means "preservation," said Beecher, because it stimulates man to "look out for danger, and to reduce the evasion of danger to habit . . . to an intuition." Fear, for example, motivates parents to protect children and children to obey parents. In fact, fear is a positive good: "The beginnings of morality and virtue are in fear; for although men may finally be organized so highly that they shall work for the love of working, as men do that are in health and are well cerebrated, yet in the beginnings, among low and rude people, men do not work because they like it." The implications for his own background are instructive. He was not necessarily pronouncing his father's stern moralistic religion "bad" or "wrong"—it was simply that in those earlier days people had not "ripened" to the "nobler plane." And even now, Beecher believed, there were still many men who "as yet . . . are so low in the scale that they must needs have the ruder treatment. They are not yet carried up to that sphere in which they can do the works of true manhood by the attraction of goodness."

But gradually, Beecher maintained, the motive of fear gives way to "other feelings" and finally "ripens" into love—which is the "highest element." Love, for Beecher, was the result of an internalization of the values that had previously been enforced by fear of an *external* force—God, family, or community. In a prefiguring of Freudian thought, Beecher told his listeners that they could, indeed, survive on their own in a world without the accustomed external moral guidelines. Astutely he argued for internal discipline while using the theory of evolution to justify the past. Beecher sympathized with those still in the lower spheres and granted them time to advance beyond coercion, but he glorified those individuals who "have by culture and training, passed out of the lower states into the higher ones," the higher state being characterized by "love." Although Beecher denied being a Perfectionist, he seemed to carry the ideal of moral evolution to its logical conclusion: eventually, any social institution or authority would be superfluous to those most highly evolved. Because "love" in "higher-sphere" individuals could only result in exemplary behavior, doing the right thing is, for them, Beecher claimed, almost as normal as breathing. These individuals have risen to a "likeness of God," they live in a higher sphere and on a "nobler plane."

For Beecher, this conception of fear as the lowest stage of moral development justified the continuance of coercive social institutions. Still necessary were authoritarian tactics in the social control of unevolved segments of the population such as children and immigrants. The authoritarian dogma of Roman Catholicism, thus, was appropriate to the stage of moral development of the immigrants. Beecher asserted that "low and rude" people —readily identified as the Irish and German immigrants inhabiting the slum sections of Brooklyn—basked in the sun, gorged themselves with food when they had it, and starved when they had none. Only fear, reiterated Beecher, could stimulate them to build houses, cultivate land, and plan ahead. "Fear is the strongest impulse," he said, "toward improvement on the lower range in the scale of human life."

Oddly enough, Beecher's hierarchy resembles the seventeenth-century Puritan concept of the "elect"; his higher and lower spheres constitute a nineteenth-century version of predestination in a heterogeneous urban setting. In traditional New England, however, the saints or elect were presumed to be visible; they were those born to high social status. Beecher, however, rejected the idea of inherited status and adopted instead a merit system. He and his parishioners may not have inherited the highest social standing, but they had moral sensitivity, and were therefore surely on a higher plane of existence. Such individuals, however, were in the minority —especially in an urban environment such as Brooklyn. Therefore, for society as a whole, fear in the form of law was necessary. But for individuals who have reached the "higher and nobler plane . . . fear no longer has any function."

Beecher never seemed to doubt that such highly evolved moral individuals should be released from the arbitrary constraints of social institutions and tradition, but he was not entirely clear about what should take their place. Instead of reason, he recommended emotion; instead of organized religion, love; instead of duty, spiritual affinity. How these vague concepts would preserve social order, he never specifically articulated. But this ambiguity did not seem to bother his followers. Beecher's brand of Protestantism, after all, did not depend on logic or intellect; his role as minister was based on an emotional and spiritual inspiration.

Like the nineteenth-century woman—perhaps like the mother he so idolized—Beecher expected to inspire rather than inform. If religion in nineteenth-century middle-class culture had become feminized, so too had the image of the minister.[33] Because of Beecher's own background, it was an image he readily embraced—acting out successfully the same kind of inspirational role for his church that he perceived his mother having done for her husband and family. Beecher's success is evident in descriptions of the 1872 "Silver Wedding" Anniversary of Plymouth Church. This not only illustrates his image of himself as a model of feminine goodness but also the phenomenal popularity he achieved. Celebration of Beecher's twenty-five years with Plymouth Church occupied an entire week in October 1872. On the first day, a procession of children and adults from the various Sunday schools marched past Beecher's house with drum rolls and band music. The minister himself stood on his front porch, his face "wreathed" in smiles of expectation. As the column approached "expressing by the delight depicted upon their faces their happiness at seeing him and love for him in their hearts," pandemonium broke loose: "Handkerchiefs were waved, banners held aloft, smiles everywhere, cheers triumphant rent the air, and to complete one of the most joyous demonstrations that any one clergyman was ever made the recipient of, a perfect shower of the choicest bouquets were cast at Mr. Beecher's feet . . . one of the urchins succeeding with admirable precision in planting a rosebud on Mr. Beecher's eye." Gratified by this touching display, Beecher followed the "Wedding Procession" to the church for another round of cheering. One of the banners posted over the platform read, "One family in heaven and earth."[34]

As part of this commemoration, Beecher reminisced about his first connection with Plymouth Church. In characteristic emotional style, he made his business negotiations with the church's representative sound like a seduction! He was living in Indiana in 1846, Beecher recalled, when an "innocent-looking" gentleman appeared and introduced himself; he "proved to be a conspirer against my person. He induced me to go with him on fishing excursions, for drives and other amusements, and when he had got out of me what he wanted, he told of his deep-laid scheme of getting me away from the land of the West."[35]

In 1871, Beecher had made explicit his tendency to identify religion, God, and Christ with feminine gentleness rather than male authority: "The opening phrase [of the Lord's Prayer], *Our Father,* is the key to Christianity. God is father; government is personal. All the tenderness which now is stored up in the word 'mother' was of old included in the name 'father.' "[36] Simply translate "father" to read "mother" and all the mysteries of religion are explained. If any doubt remains as to his vision of himself, or his congregation's acceptance of that image, the following quote from the "Plymouth Silver Wedding Anthem" composed by the church organist especially for the occasion should dispel it:

> Who speak of aught but joy?
> Five and twenty years together
> We have trod the Way of life
> Shared its fair and stormy weather
> Church and Pastor—Man and wife![37]

This obvious equation—church equals man, pastor equals wife—is, of course, completely contrary to the usual representation of the church as bride with Christ as bridegroom. Once again, Beecher had successfully reversed traditional symbolism.

Henry Ward Beecher was certainly not the initiator of this concept of the divine nature of womanhood. He was merely an extraordinarily popular spokesman for a general cultural shift. The ubiquity of this view obviates any need to explain Beecher's idealization of woman in Freudian terms by relating it to the loss of his own mother at an early age. More significant is the fact that the majority of the young men who were attracted to Plymouth Church had, like Beecher, witnessed the erosion of their fathers' ability to exert authority—and, as Beecher did, had turned to the feminine model for guidance.

Beecher's genius was that he articulated for the uprooted individuals of his congregation a set of values that might replace contractual bonds with affinity—a mysterious, psychological attraction that most closely resembled the intuitive emotions of women. Intuitive love was far superior to older values of duty; indeed, Beecher argued, it was in a "higher religious sphere," and should be a model for all types of human relationships; husband-wife, parent-child, male as well as female friendships. Further, not only would the intuitive love of the higher sphere improve relations between people, it would provide an individual with an affinity for purity, truth, and morality. No longer would such a person need the external coercion of government, doctrine, or family in order to lead an honest, moral, successful life.

In his sermons, Beecher never dealt directly with the problems of a higher individual whose inner moral direction instructed him to disobey the law—he always assumed that all laws were good and benevolent in nature and those people on the higher stage of moral development would obey them automatically. However, his own marital problems and his need for love eventually created just such a dilemma in his own life.

Beecher had met his future wife Eunice Bullard when he was a student at Amherst College. The daughter of a prosperous farmer in Sutton, Massachusetts, she was at the time of their meeting teaching school. In 1837, after a seven-year engagement, they were married. Very little is known of their early relationship—in addition to some exceptionally nonrevealing correspondence, there is only the novel Eunice Beecher wrote in 1859 entitled *From Dawn to Daylight: The Simple Story of a Western Home,* a thinly veiled account of their early years together. These sources, however, do contain some hints as to the nature of their marriage.

Apparently, during the early years Eunice was the recipient of all the love and attention that Henry Ward, with his "genius for friendship," was capable of lavishing on anyone. At least one letter Eunice wrote to Beecher before their marriage referred to long, intimate dialogues concerned with the possibility of perfecting their friendship as well as their love.[38] It was just the kind of uncritical adoration that Henry Ward craved. In fact, if one is to judge from the letters the couple exchanged when apart, the first ten to fifteen years of their marriage were characterized by a deep affection and regard for each other. Many of those surviving letters have been carefully censored, however, presumably by the family. For example, in 1847 (ten years after their marriage) Beecher wrote to Eunice, "I shall not write again —I do despise writing—especially when I *feel*, Oh how much better would one look at . . . [two lines inked out], be than ten thousand letters." The letter was signed, "Your more than ever loving and affectionate husband."[39]

The first ten years in small parishes in Indiana seemed to be the most difficult for Eunice. Disappointment at being separated from her parents and community, as well as disillusionment with the role of wife and mother, combined to produce chronic unhappiness. Paxton Hibben reports that it was common knowledge among the Indiana parishioners that Eunice was miserable and complained incessantly. Hibben claims Eunice's hair turned gray when she discovered, about 1841, that Henry Ward was having affairs with other women.[40] However, there is no direct evidence of any such affairs. Of course, later, when the same rumors surfaced in Brooklyn, many of his contemporaries as well as historians jumped to the conclusion that they had begun in Indiana.

Even if these early rumors were false, Eunice had ample reason for being discontent with the kind of life that marriage brought. In *From Dawn to Daylight*, Eunice discusses the frustrations she encountered. First was the trauma of leaving the home of her childhood—parents, brothers, and sisters—to join her husband in Indiana: "The joys and sorrows, hopes and fears, belonging to those last days, when a young, warm-hearted girl prepares to leave father and mother, brother and sister, to go forth, with the chosen one, need no description." Eunice, significantly, stressed the anguish more than the joys: "Will he deal gently with her always—remembering that he is now her all—that for his dear sake, she leaves every tie, and each familiar scene, to follow him into a land of strangers."[41] As we shall see, it was a sentiment Elizabeth Tilton and many other middle-class women would echo.

More than just separation from home, however, troubled Eunice after the move. She found life in Indiana extreme in its physical demands, and the people crude and unfriendly. Her husband was too busy to spend much time with her; in addition, she did not possess his "healthful elasticity of spirit" and "natural mirthfulness" to help cope with "life's burdens." Often, when she felt her strength and "capacity for exertion diminishing," she wrote, her "youthful aspirations were brought vividly back to her mind. . . . To spend a lifetime in this wearisome, unchanging routine—caring only for bodily wants—to cook—to wash and mend—was that all woman was born for?" Eunice's uneasiness sprang from her conclusion that a woman who devoted her entire efforts to housekeeping and child

Eunice Bullard Beecher as a young mother. (Beecher Family Papers, Yale University Library)

care could not possibly be a fit companion for a husband of "high intellectual" abilities. As she perceived their early intellectual communication slipping away, it caused her "periods of despondency," which she tried to keep "carefully hidden" from Henry Ward.[42] *She* may have thought her feelings were hidden but obviously her unhappiness was interpreted by parishioners, and by her husband himself, as whimpering complaints and unreasonable demands for *his* precious time.[43]

Eunice, however, did make an effort to solve her domestic frustration. She learned, as she said in her novel, "to place a higher estimate on purely domestic qualifications—to feel that a woman's proper ambition should be the endeavor to relieve her husband . . . from those homecares which are incompatible with high mental effort—that he may turn, when wearied and perplexed with parochial or public duties, to his own hearth as a *resting place*—the sweetest earthly refuge from care and trouble."[44] Eunice made a self-conscious and intense effort to convince herself that domesticity and devotion to her husband offered the greatest possible rewards. Although Eunice adopted what was to become a widespread solution to this problem, she belonged to a generation of women for whom this represented a radical departure.

This solution, however, did not remedy the problem; Henry Ward Beecher and Eunice continued to grow apart. Beecher's letters to his wife became more impersonal and perfunctory. More and more he vented his emotional frustration in his sermons. In 1859, he analyzed in thinly veiled generalizations the reasons for the deterioration of his marriage: "Domestic unhappiness comes from the fact that people do not know or do not recognize the peculiarities of each other's natures. They expect impossible things of each other. If a flaming demonstrative nature and a cool, undemonstrative nature come together, neither of whom understands or makes allowance for the peculiarities of the other, there can hardly fail of being unhappiness."[45] It is clear that Beecher had come to think of Eunice, not as his worshipful admirer, but as "cool," "undemonstrative," and *critical*. In fact, Beecher may have compared Eunice's recent judgmental tendencies to those of his father. Neither father nor wife understood Beecher's own "flaming demonstrative" nature.

As a result, Beecher apparently turned to someone who did understand and sympathize—the wife of his closest friend in Plymouth Church, Lucy Maria Bowen. She was the daughter of abolitionist Lewis Tappan, a powerful member of Plymouth Church, and her husband, Henry Bowen, was the church's principal founder. Little is known of the liaison between Beecher and Lucy Maria. The affair cannot actually be proven, but a variety of evidence strongly suggests it did take place. For example, Lucy's husband seems to have discovered the affair around 1858, for in a letter to Beecher in 1863, Bowen claimed to have been a "silent sufferer from about 1857–1858 on.[46] Later, in his testimony before the Church Council, Bowen stated he learned Beecher was a "libertine" and an "adulterer" around 1860 from a "lady" whose veracity he could "hardly doubt."[47] Plymouth Church records also indicate that this was the approximate time Bowen, although still retaining his pew, ceased to attend church meetings.[48] Most damaging, however, was Bowen's letter to Theodore Tilton in 1863 which darkly hinted that "one word" from him (Bowen) would cause a "*revolution* in Plymouth Church."[49]

Further evidence is Beecher's own agitated state of mind during the same period. Bowen's discovery of the affair with Lucy seems to have brought on an attack of anxiety of the kind Beecher had not experienced since childhood. In his trial testimony, as Beecher described the course of his ministerial career, he noted that between 1856 and 1858 he experienced "violent" but "elusive" symptoms which he at first attributed to apoplexy but soon concluded were due to "excessive cerebral activity and fatigue-over-action of the mind."[50] In a letter written to a friend in 1858 Beecher begged off from a social engagement because he was so "nervous" and "sleepless" that he "could not bear social excitement during the day."[51] The pattern that emerged recalled his childhood—one he could not alter, the wrongdoing, followed by shame, fear, dread, and anguish. But fortunately, Beecher was learning how to translate his anguish into more general terms that would enhance rather than diminish his effectiveness as a minister.

In 1856—possibly as a result of his affair with Lucy—Beecher delivered a sermon entitled "The Seducer." It was often his habit to give sermons on topics that were of immediate concern to him, and this was the case in this instance. In "The Seducer" he accomplished two purposes, both of which were important to his psychological well-being. The more obvious one was indirectly to confess his guilt to his public and heap upon himself all the condemnation he perhaps thought he deserved. "The polished scoundrel betrays her to abandon her," Beecher cried, "and walks the street to boast his hellish deed." Worst of all, lamented the minister, the seducer is "courted, passed from honor to honor. . . . On her mangled corpse they stand to put the laurels on her murderer's brow!" Why do you honor me, when I am such a guilty sinner? he seemed to be asking. And much as Beecher believed in the Gospel of Love and forgiveness, in *this* sermon, he reverted to his father's stern style. "When I see such things as these," thundered Beecher, "I thank God that there is a judgment and that there is a hell!"

The second objective Beecher manages to achieve in this sermon is more indirect. Strangely enough, although the sermon is entitled "The Seducer," its focus is primarily on the suffering of the victim. This is presented at such great length and in such graphic detail that it almost seems as if Beecher himself identified not with the seducer, but with the innocent victim! We have seen that as a child, Beecher often did things that got him, or threatened to get him, into trouble with his father, when, in fact, what he felt he needed was attention, love, and understanding. Now, however, his behavior threatened to bring about public censure when he thought of himself as the innocent victim of a sinful world. This interpretation is suggested by the beginning of the sermon when Beecher hastens, gratuitously, to inform his listeners that the seducer's victim cannot be considered an "accomplice," and therefore, share the guilt. She is a "sufferer" who has been "betrayed" by the seducer who played upon her "noblest affections."

Surely, Beecher is grappling with the notion that he, himself, has given in to temptation only because of an honest, deeply felt need for affection. In a long section, Beecher pours out his own terrible fears of the consequences: "The accursed sorcerer opens the door of the world to push her forth. She looks out all shuddering; for there is shame, and sharp-toothed hatred, and chattering slander, and malignant envy, and triumphing jealousy, and murderous revenge—these are seen rising before her; clouds full of fire, that burn but will not kill."[52] Beecher's growing identification with women only increases the plausibility of such an interpretation. He, after all, had been seduced by both sex and power. His intellectual and psychological surrender of the values and doctrines of his youth may well have made him feel guilty as well as victimized: as guilty as he felt over his own seduction of Lucy, his most intense response was anxiety over the consequences. He was probably describing what he thought was in store for him if Bowen chose to reveal the affair. For reasons we shall examine in chapter 5, Bowen concealed the adultery from the church and the public; Beecher had escaped disgrace.

At the same time Henry Ward Beecher was exorcising guilt by delivering his emotional sermon, he simultaneously became acquainted with a set of beliefs that would help alleviate his guilt as well as shape the Gospel of Love. During the time that the minister was experiencing both guilt and victimization by sexual temptation, he became acquainted with a leading social radical. Appearing one evening in 1856 at a meeting at Beecher's home was Stephen Pearl Andrews.[53] Andrews was a radical political and social philosopher, who, like Beecher, carried the concept of freedom to its ultimate conclusion. Unlike Beecher, however, he argued publicly that man could be perfected and therefore become capable of making all his own decisions without governmental or religious institutions. Marriage, Andrews proclaimed, was just another oppressive institution and ought to be abolished. Perfect love, not human law, ought to determine sexual relationships.[54]

Beecher was fascinated by Andrews's theories, because they coincided with his own obsession with freedom and the satisfaction of emotional needs. But what attracted him most was the idea that spiritual, holy love, rather than the legalistic bonds of marriage, justified sexual relations. If true, this would explain his own unhappiness with Eunice—their love had vanished long ago—and his affinity for Lucy Maria.

Another influence that may have helped buttress these ideas was a book on love and sex written by his college friend Orson Fowler. In *Love and Parentage,* published in 1843, Fowler explicitly stated that "spiritual love" was equal to matrimony and "entitled to its prerogatives [sex] . . . without the least regard to the presence or absence of the legal cere-mony."[55] Thus, the real marriage takes place when the couple recognizes their attraction for each other, not when the ceremony occurs. Though Fowler remained conservative on the surface, continuing to argue that the only place for this spiritualized romantic love was within marriage, he made it very clear that a marriage should be dissolved if love were not pres-ent. In short, people should adjust their legal obligations to their *feelings,* not their feelings to their obligations. This philosophy expressed Beecher's temperament almost perfectly.

Still, the minister was a perceptive enough judge of the public temper to realize that most middle-class Americans, although generally welcoming the new notions of romantic love, were not ready to contemplate the aboli-tion of marriage. In fact, ironically, just the opposite was true; most people became more rigid regarding marriage, demanding not only legal commit-ment, but exalted love. We will explore later how this changing ideal of marriage brought emotional turmoil as well as structural change to the Til-ton marriage. So, although Beecher in his sermons focused more and more on the importance of emotion and love as guiding principles of society, he always stopped short of condemning marriage. In fact, when asked about the "new theories of marriage"—meaning the absence of legal marriage—Beecher responded that the aspirations of reformers like Stephen Pearl Andrews were "unrealistic" because they assumed *all* men were "perfect," when in reality *most* men still required "external law" to keep them from a "plunge into utter ruin."[56] Undoubtedly, in his mind, Beecher reserved the right of those like him who had reached the higher spheres to act upon their intuition without regard for external forms.

By the late 1860s, then, Henry Ward Beecher's personal charisma and distinctive formulation of the Gospel of Love had achieved for him the popularity and public approval he had always sought. One aspect of this success was his appeal to the women of his congregation.[57] Given his nature, Beecher found it very difficult, even impossible, to resist the praise and adulation of these women, even though it might threaten his career. The minister was so hungry for love, both personal and public, that he was willing to risk the one for the other. Thus, he was irresistibly drawn to the "uncritical praise" of Elizabeth Tilton. However, even before Henry Ward Beecher became personally entangled in the lives of the Tiltons, his concept of the "higher sphere" was to alter both Theodore's and Eliza-beth's fundamental assumptions about their lives, their marriage, and their very identities.

3

Theodore Tilton: Making It in the Gilded Age

ON OCTOBER 2, 1855, Theodore Tilton and Elizabeth Richards were married by Henry Ward Beecher in Plymouth Church. At that time, the minister was acquainted with the young couple in only the most cursory way. Theodore had joined the church two years before and had been active in the Sunday school, and Elizabeth had been a schoolmate of Beecher's daughter. There was no reason for Beecher to take any particular note of the two young people; they were typical of the over 700 members of this rapidly growing church on Brooklyn Heights.

In eight years as minister of Plymouth Church, Beecher had established a reputation for attracting young people of unsophisticated backgrounds—and the Tiltons were no exception. Although both Theodore and Elizabeth had been born in New York City, their parents had migrated there from rural New Jersey. Both of their fathers were artisans, Theodore's a shoemaker and Elizabeth's a jeweler. Both, however, had more education than their parents—Theodore had attended the Free Academy of New York and Elizabeth, the Brooklyn Female Seminary. In 1855 Tilton was only an obscure reporter on the *New York Observer*, but he hoped to "make a name for himself and rise before the world."[1] Theodore Tilton is a fascinating case study of the psychological shifts which many of Beecher's parishioners felt as they struggled to succeed in a market economy. Like Tilton, they found comfort and encouragement in the interpretation Henry Ward Beecher articulated for their struggles. Ironically, however, for Tilton, Beecher's social philosophy was also to plant the seeds of marital unhappiness and eventual scandal. A step by step examination of his career is therefore essential.

At first glance, Theodore Tilton's life, like many others in Plymouth Church, bears a striking resemblance to the Horatio Alger stories that became so popular in the late nineteenth century. Like Ragged Dick in one of the first Alger novels, Tilton seems to appear from nowhere, find a benefactor, join a Bible class, and begin a steady climb to success. However, as we shall see, Tilton's success was only the beginning, rather than the end, of his story.

On October 2, 1835, two years after his father Silas Tilton first appears in a New York City directory,[2] Theodore Tilton was born. The family had New England origins but had come from Monmouth County in New Jersey and "was considered an old one." Apparently, Silas Tilton's shoemaking business proved profitable; many years later he retired to comfortable respectability in his native Monmouth County. His five brothers (Theodore's uncles) were not so fortunate; they remained itinerant artisans—blacksmiths, carpenters, and shoemakers—who did odd jobs. According to a hostile account in the *Brooklyn Eagle,* they all had a reputation for drunkenness as well.[3]

During Tilton's boyhood, his father converted from the Methodist Episcopal to the Baptist church. With this background, it is unclear why Tilton as a boy attended an orthodox Presbyterian church. "I was brought up from childhood," he later testified, "in the Old School Presbyterian Church . . . my earliest religious bent was toward extreme Calvinism." Whatever the reason for the difference in churches, however, it is obvious that Tilton was as serious as his father in his religious attitudes, later referring to his youthful beliefs as "extreme and rigid."

I was accustomed to take, those dread and majestic views of life and of the future, the magnificence of God's greatness, the perfection of His purity, in comparison with which any human character was dwarfed and shriveled. All the early years of my life I spent very much—I was going to say—like a monk in a monastery. I was a religious ascetic. . . . I was brought up to the conviction that all men were miserable sinners.[4]

This condemnation of the harsh doctrine of his childhood sounds remarkably similar to Henry Ward Beecher's rejection of *his* father's religion. But this was not unusual. Many parishioners at Plymouth Church described their religious upbringing as "gloomy," "rigid," or "harsh." Henry Ward Beecher's appeal was his assurance that religion could be joyous, forgiving, and flexible. His Gospel of Love translated the nature of God's love from the judgmental love of a stern father to the unconditional love of a self-sacrificing mother.[5] "Christ only can save you," Beecher cried, "because you *are a sinner,* not because you aren't one!"[6] Tilton once said of the religious changes he experienced under Beecher's preaching, "I gave up a doctrine [Calvinism] that I could not understand."[7]

Two centuries in New England had shaped Calvinism into a set of doc-

This drawing of Theodore Tilton first appeared in the middle of the "scandal summer" in Frank Leslie's Illustrated Newspaper, *August 8, 1874.*

trines that reflected the relatively static, agricultural society that flourished there. Predestination, original sin, election, all emphasized and reinforced the social precepts of stability, harmony, and deference to authority. But by the time Tilton's generation was growing up, the static social order was being rapidly transformed into a fragmented, competitive society. The unprecedented religious ferment of the early nineteenth century was in part a reflection of the search for a set of religious beliefs that would explain and mitigate social and economic insecurity. Calvinism could no longer suffice. Tilton, like others in Plymouth Church, was experiencing confusion over the discrepancy between the static values of the past and the fluidity of the present. The strength of the Gospel of Love was its emphasis on observable realities rather than enshrined tradition.[8]

Tilton's introduction to Plymouth Church, which did so much to "soften" his early religious views, apparently came about initially because of Elizabeth Richards, his future wife. At the age of ten, he was introduced to her by a schoolmate. Elizabeth was a small, dark-eyed brunette, whose seriousness and piety matched Theodore's. They quickly became inseparable. When in 1850, Elizabeth's widowed mother moved the family across the river to New York's newest suburb, Brooklyn, Tilton became a frequent visitor. The same year that Elizabeth and Theodore became engaged —1851—the Richards family officially joined Plymouth Church. Undoubtedly, Tilton's visits across the river had included Sunday services at Elizabeth's church, for by 1853, he himself became a member. Church records indicate that both young people were active and enthusiastic members of the church; they taught Sunday school and served on several committees.[9]

Sometime during his youth, Tilton committed himself to the antislavery crusade and made it the major focus of his early life. In fact, Tilton was more than an antislavery man; he was among the small minority of abolitionists. Association with Plymouth Church intensified this commitment to abolitionism and at the same time encouraged a rejection of traditional orthodox Christianity: "These views [antislavery] were taught us in Plymouth Church. . . . We all despised the slaveholding Christianity of that day; we were all of one mind concerning it. Mr. Beecher preached against it."[10]

Tilton's association with Plymouth Church, however, did far more for him than simply provide philosophical and social support for his liberalizing religious ideas and antislavery principles. It was of direct economic benefit as well. Shortly after Tilton joined the church in November 1853, he was forced, probably by economic necessity, to leave the Free Academy of New York. He then took a job working for a religious newspaper, the *New York Observer,* where his major assignment was to report stenographically the sermons of Henry Ward Beecher.[11]

It appears that soon after Tilton was married, several members of the church were instrumental in locating him a position that led directly to his later success as editor of the leading religious journal in the country, the *Independent.*[12] This initial influence, however, did not come from Beecher. Though Tilton admired Beecher, the two men did not become friends until 1861.[13] This earlier influence on Tilton's behalf probably came from Joseph Richards, Elizabeth's brother, who was the publisher of the *Independent,* or from Daniel Burgess, another church member. Perhaps both men persuaded Henry Bowen, the owner of the paper, to give Tilton a chance. Thus, Tilton owed his opportunity to work as a clerk on the *Independent* to his wife's family and to Plymouth Church.

Tilton's experience was similar to that of other church members. In many cases Plymouth Church functioned as a medium for business and social contacts. Beecher recognized the need for his members, most of whom were newcomers to the city, to establish relationships which would help them secure jobs as well as find friends.[14] He emphasized social gatherings to a greater degree than most other ministers in Brooklyn. These parishioners found in Plymouth Church a social environment, as well as a religious orientation, which enabled them to deal with the practical difficulties of getting ahead in the city.

It was not long, however, before Theodore Tilton proved his capabilities to Henry Bowen. As a colleague on the paper later observed, he soon became a favorite of Bowen, who liked his "epigrammatic and yet somewhat poetical style."[15] Moreover, it was obvious to Bowen that Elizabeth's assessment of her husband as a "pretty hard worker" was true; Tilton worked day and night at the office.[16] At this point in his life, Tilton's ambition and intense devotion to antislavery were highly compatible. The fervor and sincerity that he displayed in religious and antislavery articles enhanced his vivid literary style and brought recognition from Bowen.

As yet, however, he received no public attention because he was not important enough to write signed articles or editorials. When his articles were signed, it was with the name of someone else—the name, in fact, of Henry Ward Beecher. Beecher was notorious for the slowness and inefficiency with which he worked. Writing was especially difficult for him and articles that he had promised to contribute were often never delivered. Because many people bought the paper to read Beecher pieces, these lapses were a constant source of friction between Beecher and Bowen, but the owner did find a way to remedy the situation. Discovering Tilton's knack for imitating Beecher's style, he contracted with Tilton to ghost-write the popular Beecher articles. Between 1856 and 1860, Tilton wrote at least thirty Beecher columns.[17]

Tilton's first real break came in 1861. In that year, the *Independent* went through a crisis that threatened its very survival. Because the owner's other business—a dry-goods firm—went bankrupt, the paper was also placed in grave financial danger. The crisis engendered disputes between the three editors and Bowen, resulting in the resignations of all three.[18] Bowen hoped to save the paper by making Henry Ward Beecher the editor; the minister's name alone could be counted on to increase circulation. But Bowen also knew that Beecher, notwithstanding his promises, would not devote enough time and attention to the paper. His solution was a shrewd one. He invited Beecher to be the editor, but assured him that Theodore Tilton would do all the work.[19] This arrangement pleased everyone. Bowen's paper not only survived but prospered, Beecher had the rewards but not the work, and Tilton was promoted to assistant editor.

Although this promotion did not raise Tilton's salary significantly, there were other benefits. As assistant editor he had to work closely with Beecher, a man he had admired for a great many years, and with whom he now developed something like a father-son relationship. Tilton later was to say that he had been "dazzled" by Beecher whom he came to love "as he had no other man."[20] Besides their work together, the two spent hours in intimate conversation, on long walks and in visits to shops and galleries.[21] Tilton had every reason to be proud; at the age of twenty-six he was the assistant editor of a nationally circulated religious newspaper and the closest friend of the most famous minister in the country. Further, he had the opportunity to meet and correspond with established reformers and intellectuals. William Lloyd Garrison, Charles Sumner, Lydia Maria Child, Salmon P. Chase, and Anna Dickinson were suddenly part of his circle, visiting his home whenever they were in Brooklyn. Trips to Washington and Philadelphia, where he delivered political addresses, were frequent. His influence grew rapidly.

In 1864 Beecher resigned as editor of the *Independent* with the stipulation that his friend would become the chief editor. Finally, the younger man would have the recognition of the public as well as the inner circle. Bowen was only too happy to comply with Beecher's parting request, because Tilton's colorful, sometimes vitriolic prose had steadily increased circulation. Suddenly, new opportunities opened up for Tilton. Although his salary as editor was to increase only moderately, his fame and visibility would allow him to make additional income by embarking on the flourishing lecture circuit. Beginning in 1864, Tilton spent three or four months a year on tour.[22]

Tilton made the *Independent* into one of the leading organs of the radical Reconstructionists and according to his biographer, was the first "important" abolitionist to call for the impeachment of Andrew Johnson.[23] His effective journalistic style so impressed Henry Bowen that he asked Tilton to become editor of another of his papers, the *Brooklyn Union*. At the same time, Tilton, who had been involved in the women's rights movement since 1866, became president of a suffrage group. As a colleague at the *Independent* put it, Tilton "was in the heyday of his fame," and possessed "a large knowledge of men and things, and absolute confidence in himself."[24] There seemed no limit to what this man could accomplish.

In the Alger novels, the attainment of success and respectability is always accompanied by a steadiness and peace of mind, a kind of ordering and integration of the young man's life which had been absent previously. For Theodore Tilton, however (and, one suspects, for many of the rising young men of Brooklyn and New York), this dramatic rise to fame did not have such a result. For during the same years that Tilton attained popularity, his anxiety and depression undermined that part of his life hidden from the public—his marriage. It is Tilton's treatment of Elizabeth that reveals most vividly the cost exacted by the urban competitive world.

For Tilton, as well as other young men, upward mobility required association with a new social set or circle; conversely, this often resulted in the severing of past friendships and family ties. In a dilemma common to many of Beecher's parishioners, one lonely young man from Vermont repeatedly urged his father to visit Brooklyn, only to experience acute embarrassment at his father's unsophisticated country manners.[25] The pain felt by this young man stemmed from the conflict between his continuing love for his parent and his need to belong to an urbane, sophisticated world. The social class he aspired to join in the city was not that of his father. In fact, his father was a hindrance rather than a help. To such men, Beecher's own family experiences and his genius at articulating them provided a solution for this dilemma. The ties of blood, said Beecher, do not always represent the "highest" human relationships. "Jesus," he claimed, "felt instantly that there were affinities and relationships far higher and wider than those constituted by the earthly necessities of family life." Family ties, in fact, were "mechanical" and therefore of a "lower" order.[26]

What Beecher was suggesting was not a complete repudiation of one's family, but rather a search for an entirely new set of associates—a circle based upon the natural affinity of "like natures."[27] Thus, affinity was not limited to sexual or romantic attraction between a man and a woman; in Henry Ward Beecher's scheme, it was much more broadly construed. Indeed, the doctrine of affinity served to rationalize the social mobility aspired to by the young men of Plymouth Church. Rather than perceive abandonment of parents and friends as self-serving social climbing, they could believe they were following natural affinities. Moving up in the world became not only economically advantageous but internally honest —more honest, in fact, than continuing traditional ties out of mere mechanical habit. Thus, affinity, as the cornerstone of the Gospel of Love, functioned as a justification for the intense concern with social status common to Beecher's parishioners.

Theodore Tilton's experience is a remarkable example of the process that Henry Ward Beecher was describing; it is also illustrative of the internal tensions created by this attempt to replace traditional contractual bonds with affinity. For Tilton, in fact, the seeds of marital discord were planted when he began to perceive that his affinities lay with a different intellectual and social class from that of his wife and her family. His own parents remained in New York and he did not see them often. As a youth he had been more often in the Richards household than his own, and after he and Elizabeth were married they boarded with Elizabeth's mother. The boardinghouse was located on Harrison Avenue in the sixth ward of Brooklyn—not in the more fashionable Brooklyn Heights (see map on page 108). The boarders and neighbors were similar to the parents of Theodore and Elizabeth—small merchants, clerks, carpenters, stonecutters.[28] Many other members of Plymouth Church lived close by and the couple's social life centered around this group. Elizabeth later recalled that for the first five years of their marriage, she and her husband belonged to the same social circle.[29]

Elizabeth's family had done much for her husband; they had accepted him into their household, encouraged his ambition, and helped him get a better job. However, when Tilton began to fulfill his ambition to "make a name for himself" and in the process acquired friends and colleagues of higher social and intellectual standing—Elizabeth called them "public" men and women—he was caught in a dilemma. He was embarrassed to bring his new friends to the boardinghouse to meet his unsophisticated family—country folk in appearance and language. They had not acquired the urbanity of city life, nor were they interested in the great issues of the day such as antislavery and women's suffrage. They concentrated on making a living and, as Theodore put it, "chattering" endlessly. Contrasted with Charles Sumner and Elizabeth Cady Stanton, Tilton perceived his family as "boring" and "distressing."[30] In Beecher's terms, Theodore's true affinity lay not with his family but with his new intellectual circle.

As a result, Theodore withdrew from Elizabeth's family and social activities at Plymouth Church: he built a new social and intellectual framework centered on the issues of abolition and Reconstruction.[31] When speaking in Boston, Washington, or Philadelphia, Tilton associated with these public people and constructed his identity around them. The principle of antislavery that united them created a supportive community that sustained Tilton's dissatisfaction with his home life.

In the spring of 1860, attempting to lower his level of frustration at home, Tilton rented a house on Oxford Street in a better section of Brooklyn. Here the couple lived for three years, but this solution ultimately failed: Tilton was not yet making enough money to afford a house, and Elizabeth was obviously distressed about being separated from her family. By 1863, they moved back to the boardinghouse.[32]

From Theodore's perspective, the next three years were the worst yet. During this period, as we have seen, he became editor-in-chief of the *Inde-*

pendent and the closest friend of Henry Ward Beecher; his reputation as editor, lecturer, and reformer grew; and he was accepted as an important influence in national affairs. Still, he was not living like the important figure he had become! Tilton's distress waxed more and more acute as time went on. The young editor blamed Elizabeth's family. "My life has been marred," he chided his wife, "by social influences coming from your mother."[33]

Finally, however, in 1866, with earnings from his lecture tours, Tilton was able to afford a house on the Heights which reflected his higher social status. Here the young editor satisfied two of his basic desires: he escaped from the "mildew"—as he called it—of the boardinghouse, and he could entertain his friends in style. Proud of his fashionable three-story "establishment" with its complement of servants, Tilton anxiously began to urge his fellow intellectuals to visit as frequently as possible. Horace Greeley was to have a room of his own with a desk and the particular kind of ink he liked. Henry Ward Beecher was repeatedly invited to make the Tilton house a second home. Tilton also demanded lavish expenditures on food and furnishings. He ordered a series of paintings by the well-known artist William Page. (Among the figures he commissioned Page to paint were Beecher, Greeley, and Sumner!) Instructing Elizabeth to cultivate friendships with such people and to spare no expense to make them comfortable, he hoped that she and the children would reflect his success as well. "Spend all the money you need to make yourself comfortable," Theodore instructed Elizabeth in 1865, "don't fail to ride out plentifully—never mind the cost."[34]

This final symbol—the house—of Tilton's success ironically laid the groundwork for the scandal, the dissolution of his marriage, and the ruin of his career. The problems created by his success eventually overwhelmed him. He had effectively separated himself from his extended family, but his wife remained a continuing embarrassment. True, Theodore recognized that Elizabeth was a devoted mother, a loving wife, and a sympathetic, generous, and intelligent woman. A maid in the Tilton household testified that on numerous occasions Theodore asked his wife to criticize articles he had written before they went to press. And Tilton once told a friend of the family that "Elizabeth was undervalued in her intellectual character, she was so domestic and so quiet; but that she was the finest critic he ever had."[35]

Yet, as his own social status rose, Theodore became increasingly embarrassed by Elizabeth's public demeanor and conduct. His problem seems to

The Tilton Residence, 174 Livingston Street. (Frank Leslie's Illustrated Newspaper, *August 8, 1874*)

have had more to do with what Elizabeth was *not* than with what she was. Affection, honesty, and sympathy could not make up for her inability to measure up to Theodore's new circle. Tilton summed up his complaints this way to a friend: Elizabeth was a "small woman, without presence, without port [deportment], not a woman of society, not a woman of culture." This same friend also reported Tilton's regrets that "he had married her young, and that he had grown and developed, and that she had not, and that there was a disparity between them."[36] In this same vein, another friend criticized Theodore for "disparaging" Elizabeth many times for "using the English language incorrectly."[37] Elizabeth herself later described two upsetting incidents:

I will tell you a little incident to explain this feeling in regard to my personal appearance (my presence was always mean, I know): I had often been invited to go with him to meet his friends, and very much against my will, I have gone; I never could appear as a lady; of course, I never could dress as other ladies did; that was not my taste; and when I have been there with them, going at his own desire, he has turned around to me and said, "I would give $500 if you were not by my side," meaning that I was so insignificant that he was ashamed of me . . . he seemed unwilling that I should be as the Lord made me . . . one occasion I remember very well; there was a large company of friends at our house; they were all his friends—a gathering of woman's rights people—and he particularly requested me not to come near him that night; it was very evident to me that he did not want comparisons made between us . . . it hurt me very much to know it.[38]

It may have hurt Elizabeth to know that Theodore was ashamed of her, but only because it made *him* discontent. She continued to find the unsophisticated life style in which she had been raised satisfactory; dressing as other ladies did, she poignantly notes, was not to her "taste." Upon reflection, Elizabeth concluded that the root of her difficulties with Theodore was her continued association with "persons that he would find it a perfect bore to talk with. . . . That was a great annoyance to Mr. Tilton, and he said I gathered about me the most distressing sort of people, and he frequently had to go away; many persons that were pleasant to me were repulsive to him."[39] Most of these "distressing" people were former friends of Theodore's from Plymouth Church with whom Elizabeth continued to associate after the move to the new house; this enraged Theodore and he angrily ordered Elizabeth not to encourage their visits. They embarrassed him. Elizabeth, to the detriment of their marriage, did not share Theodore's sensitivity to issues of social class.

If, however, Theodore's only source of dissatisfaction had been his wife's social ineptitude, he might have been able to deal with it in a less dramatic and violent fashion. But, after the move to the new house in 1866, other circumstances compounded his anxiety. After the move, Elizabeth lamented, Theodore "spent a great deal of his time at home in moods of dissatisfaction with the surroundings, yearning and wanting other ministrations; there was nothing in our home that satisfied him."[40] This change in behavior was also observed by a maid who had been with the family since 1864. "He was at times kindly, and at times very unkindly," she said, "he would be very restless, and walk about the house with his hands in his pockets, and look very sullen; and he would seem to make everybody around him feel unhappy."[41] Theodore himself admitted to a family friend that he regretted his moods, recognizing that they made life difficult for everyone, but that they were "beyond his control." Groping for the roots of his anxiety, Tilton speculated that his depressive moods were the "moods of genius . . . it was the penalty that genius had to pay."[42]

What Theodore did not realize was that he was not unique in his uneasiness and anxiety. Henry Ward Beecher, however, was aware that doubt, confusion, and anxiety were a natural state for the young men of Plymouth Church. Especially those with higher "sensitive" natures, he told his congregation in 1868, could not help but be tormented by the "passions whirling within";[43] these passions arose from the loosening of community and family control and the glittering, if elusive, possibilities for success. Indeed, a careful analysis of Theodore's letters suggests that the source of his problems was in the way his ambition was continually undermined by a web of economic, professional, and personal insecurity.

First, economic pressures increased significantly with the purchase of the new house. All the lecture tour earnings were required to pay the mortgage and keep it functioning. In 1868, three years after obtaining the mortgage, he wrote to Elizabeth, "At the beginning I did not understand the magnitude of the task which I had undertaken. To start out on a pilgrimage for the raising of $20,000 looked like an easier thing than it proved to be. . . . Every cent of the money with which I am paying for my house has cost me a throb of my pulse, and heart and brain."[44] This situation created a conflict for Tilton between his desire for the rewards of his climb up the social ladder and his distaste for money-grubbing. "I don't believe in squandering one's life in fortune seeking," he complained, "I have not dedicated my life to . . . buy, sell, and get gain."[45]

The tension led to an ambivalence toward money that baffled Elizabeth. While insisting that everything in the house be of the finest quality, Tilton continually upbraided his wife for spending above her budget. A servant confirmed that his ambivalence was most apparent after the move to the new house. He was, she said, "very fastidious, very difficult to please," and that he would lock himself in a room with Elizabeth where, in a loud voice, he berated her management of the household.[46]

Tilton's fear of losing his economic gains proved a continuing theme of his letters home. His travels gave him the opportunity to observe the fluctuations in fortunes of those who speculated in the expansive economy of post–Civil War America. Recounting stories of men who had diligently built comfortable fortunes only to have them wiped out by depressions in the economic cycle, Tilton expressed his apprehension. "Mr. G—— once told me," he wrote in 1868, "that he was worth a million dollars! Now his wife is a beggar! What a world this is for doing and undoing—for crown-

Theodore and Elizabeth Tilton (Frank Leslie's Illustrated Newspaper, September 5, 1874. Courtesy American Antiquarian Society, Worcester, Mass.)

ing and discrowning!"[47] It was an era of American history when such fears had basis in reality, particularly for people like Tilton whose marginal status made them vulnerable to ups and downs in the economic cycle. They had no savings to provide a cushion: "Ever since last October I have been lecturing every week—sometimes every night, and the proceeds have all been swallowed up in my extravagant debts. . . . Not one penny of all my lecture earnings for years has ever yet gone into a bank."[48]

For the upwardly mobile, the realistic fear that money and status could be lost as quickly and mysteriously as acquired, caused constant anxiety. Henry Ward Beecher himself was quick to recognize Tilton's fears; one of the recurrent themes of his sermons was this fear of loss, not simply of money, but of the social position and reputation that accompanied it. In a sermon in 1868, Beecher sympathized with those like Tilton who experienced "the awful fear—no, not of being engulfed in poverty, but of exposure; the dread of shame; the horror of disgrace."[49] It was not the fear of poverty per se then, but rather the fear of disgrace brought by decreased income that was crucial. It seemed to be a recognition that the days of genteel impoverishment were gone, that money had become the sole measure of one's social status and personal worth!

Second, insecurity in Tilton's professional life seemed rooted in a loss of purpose. He described it this way: "I became editor of the *Independent* when I was quite young, and my hands were immediately filled with public questions—the anti-slavery movement, the prosecution of the war, the reconstruction of the Union. . . . But, when slavery was abolished and the war was over, . . . my occupation, in a certain sense, was gone. . . ."[50] Tilton had spent all his adult life as a crusader; the passage of the Fifteenth Amendment seemed to resolve all the issues for which he had fought so hard, and thus to create a void in his professional life. True, there were other reform issues that attracted his attention—political corruption and women's rights, for example, but these simply could not command the zeal and dedication that he had poured into the antislavery movement. When Tilton could no longer define himself as an abolitionist or a radical, the crucial elements of his identity were disrupted. His yearly lecture tours, primarily dedicated to raising money for himself, seemed tawdry compared to his previous goals.

More important, the lecture tours created enforced leisure time in isolation not only from his family, but worse, from the circle of journalists and reformers who had given his existence meaning. He wrote to Elizabeth that in contrast to his days of crusading in Washington, the lecture circuit was interminably boring. "I do nothing all day," he wrote, "but sit either in a car or a hotel, and wait for the evening." As a result, he complained, "I am driven nowadays to live much in the imagination." This enforced introspection led the editor to some dismal conclusions about his accomplishments and career. "I have always been earnest and straightforward," he acknowledged, "but always too much in the interest of myself."[51]

These two areas of anxiety—economic instability and loss of "occupation"—along with the young man's sense of social isolation, created a void in his life that was both new and frightening. And during the winter of 1866–67, Tilton used his solitude for what he referred to as his "winter of meditation."[52] "Of late," Theodore wrote to Elizabeth, "I have been thinking much of my own life . . . endeavoring to ascertain what are my earthly ambitions, to struggle with them and to conquer them." Though it seemed to Tilton's friends and colleagues that his hard work and dedication to principle proved him a model of honesty and selflessness, the young man himself now denigrated his previous activities. "I am a weak man, supposed to be strong; a selfish man, supposed to be the world's lover and helper; an earthly minded man, supposed to be more Christian than my fellows. I cannot endure the mockery—it breeds agony in me."[53]

Economic and professional insecurity combined with isolation from family and community to produce an excruciating loneliness new to Tilton. In a letter to Elizabeth he touched on the key to the problem. "I am passing daily through multitudes of strangers," he complained, "who glide among one another without mutual recognition or mutual interest in each other's welfare."[54] The anonymity and sense of isolation that plagued Theodore led him to experiment with some new patterns of behavior.

Indeed, sexual affairs with one or more women were the apparent result of this gloomy "winter of meditation." Immediately overwhelmed by guilt, Tilton's moral lapse came to be the symbol of an accumulating disillusionment with his own character. "In most of us," he lamented, "innocence or guilt depends more on the measure of our temptation than on the measure of our virtue. Many a strong man is conquered and falls, while many a weak man escapes because unattacked."[55] Clearly, Tilton was convinced that *he,* up until that point, had been the "weak" man who escaped simply because he had not been tempted.

Again, Tilton's dilemma was not unique. Beecher preached often about the dangers and temptations that beset young men when they left home. The watchful eyes of parents and neighbors served as the external restraint curbing individual behavior. The young man, suddenly "set at liberty," Beecher said, was bound to surrender to temptation. As the minister put it, "men . . . that begin to feel their freedom, are like birds that have long been in a cage . . . they fly out, and fly to their peril." It was, Beecher insisted, a natural phase for a young man to go through—a temporary but natural result of an "intoxication with liberty."[56] Through this trial and error process, in fact, would develop the *internal* discipline necessary for survival in a world of freedom. This transitional state of confusion and doubt common to all "sensitive" natures, Beecher said, was an inevitable stage in "moral evolution." Man was in the lowest possible moral state when he defined his conduct simply by mindlessly obeying unexamined rules—the rigid doctrines of Calvinism in which most New Englanders had been raised, for example. The next higher state was rooted in moral and ethical beliefs that were personally chosen; Tilton's abolitionist and reform principles were an example. But, the "highest" of all was the state in which each man possessed such a strong *internal* sense of identity and worth that no external moral or institutional coercion was necessary. Young men, Beecher thought, would soon get over the confusion and enter a higher sphere, where freedom and confidence went hand in hand.[57]

Tilton, however, was not as sanguine as Beecher. Terrified that his obsession with money, status, and sex was not just a temporary stage, but instead revealed his essential character, he groped for some central point around which to reconstruct his self-respect—his very identity. Ironically, Theodore was to put the burden of responsibility for his own psychic rehabilitation on his marriage—a marriage that until now he had considered a hindrance to his intellectual development and his social advancement.

This struggle for self-respect, juxtaposed with his continued efforts to maintain his new social standing, were to coalesce in a manner that would alter his marriage, produce a scandal, and sharpen the lines of social conflict in Brooklyn. Ironically, Henry Ward Beecher—ever fond of theatrics —had set the stage and written the script, and it was he who was also to play the leading role in Theodore Tilton's passion play.

4

Elizabeth Tilton: The Transformation of a Marriage

I
F THEODORE TILTON is illustrative of the hundreds of young
men in Beecher's congregation who were struggling to adjust
their values to the necessities of market competitiveness, Elizabeth Richards Tilton is equally representative of the women of
Beecher's congregation. Beecher was best known for his ability to attract
large numbers of young men, but women made up fifty-eight percent of the
membership.[1] Middle-class women of the mid-nineteenth century, like
their male counterparts, had some very dramatic adjustments to make and
Henry Ward Beecher had something to say to them as well. Beecher was
one of the many spokespeople for a developing view of the spiritual sphere
of home and woman's priestesslike role within it.

The difference between the oppressive "mechanical" family Beecher so
disparaged in his remarkable sermon on "Moral Affinity" and the spiritual haven he advocated so often was, of course, the quality of the bonds
holding it together. Simply being born into a particular family meant little
—that could be characterized as "mere contiguity." "It is," Beecher insisted, "the mother's and father's *heart* that makes the family dear."[2] It
was not enough, he said, for parents to provide the basics of existence to
their children; they had the responsibility to develop an affinity with each
child that would ensure its purity and virtue as an adult. Obviously arguing from his own experience, Beecher advocated an unconditional affection, which would inspire the child.

Yet the bonds of this ideal affinity that would transform the family from
the coercive institution of the past into a romantic utopia would not depend on both parents equally. Given the necessity for men to be involved in
what Beecher termed the "swinish herd" of the outside world, women
must preserve the nobler virtues for their husbands and children. Thus, although on the surface a wife's lot might appear "dreary," "lonesome,"
and "restrained," Beecher urged women to "hold on" for "death will be a

revelation" in which it would become clear that women are "most like God" and in heaven will be "highest."[3]

What this rhetoric reflects, of course, is the reality of women's increasing confinement to domesticity. Indeed, it was this expectation that women embody Christ-like perfection, coupled with the social reality of isolation and loneliness that helped create what we have come to think of as the classic syndrome of nineteenth-century female disorders: nervousness, anxiety, and often physical illness.[4]

The consequences of such tensions are dramatically illustrated in the Tilton marriage. Theodore's struggles and his loss of purpose and identity provoked him into a search for a more secure foundation in an unpredictable world. In desperation, he turned to marriage as the stabilizing influence in his life. In doing so, he profoundly altered the nature of his marriage. Formerly, marriage had been only one of a set of integrated social institutions that defined identity. Theodore's attempt to isolate marriage was a radical departure.

For Elizabeth Tilton, the transition was sudden and devastating. During her childhood and the early part of her marriage, extended kin group and church had interacted to provide a variety of stabilizing forces in her life. Indeed, as Theodore's disapproval mounted, Elizabeth was sustained by social and family contacts outside her marriage. Attributing his irritable and sometimes insulting behavior to his genius and ambition, Elizabeth was not afraid to hold her own in family squabbles by hurling insults back at her husband. One gets the impression from references in correspondence as well as later testimony that there were regular free-for-alls in the boardinghouse which, as we have seen, included Elizabeth's mother, brother, friends of the family, and the boarders—as well as the young couple.[5] For the most part, the others took Elizabeth's side; she, apparently, had been "idolized" since childhood for "earnestness," "piety," and devotion to duty. They felt no hesitation in stepping in to reprimand the young husband for his "neglect" and "ill-treatment" of his wife.[6] So, in spite of the fact that Elizabeth was becoming more and more "self-conscious" in Theodore's presence, unable any longer to converse with him naturally or freely, the continued interaction with her family helped preserve her sense of self-respect.[7] In their company, she continued to be her own unpretentious self, "chattering" happily away in defiance of Theodore's criticism.

A portent of things to come later can be observed in the brief time the couple lived in their own house on Oxford Street. With no money for servants, Elizabeth was isolated with two young children, aged one and two. She became ill for long periods of time, later testifying that the doctor's diagnosis was "trouble in her mind." Concurring in this assessment, she insisted that part of the cause was Theodore's objection to visits from her mother.[8] Although Elizabeth attempted to become friends with the public men and women who now came to see her husband, she felt ill at ease, knowing that Theodore was ashamed of her. For her, the move back to the boardinghouse came as a welcome relief.

It was the permanent move to the Brooklyn Heights brownstone in 1866 that constituted the real turning point in Elizabeth's life. Even though the house was only a few blocks from her family, Theodore's disdain for her relatives effectively cut off daily contact with them. Now that they could afford servants, he insisted there was no longer any reason for her relatives to embarrass them by visiting. In reality, her new position as "lady" of the house was extremely intimidating. Always shy with strangers, she became more nervous, timid, and frightened of exercising authority over the Irish servants. Like her husband, Elizabeth also sensed a loss of function and identity.

As insecurity and loneliness mounted, these two troubled people began to consider a new possibility: that of deriving their identity *solely* from each other. To replace Theodore's causes and Elizabeth's family—the very things that had provided support and protection against their dissatisfaction with each other, they now turned inward, focusing attention on one another with an almost exclusive intensity. "We must both," Elizabeth proposed, "cultivate each other's self-respect."[9] As early as 1865, Theodore had discovered the "wonderful simplicity of God's plan for binding together human society . . . by creating in each breast some strong and dominating love for *one* human being." Implicitly acknowledging the weakening of external buttressing elements in both their lives, Theodore expressed their mutual need when he wrote to Elizabeth, "I find . . . I need your presence and influence not only for the comfort of my life, but for the stability of my mind."[10]

To understand the causes of the shift in marital expectations, we must first return again to Theodore, for it was in his mind that the outlines of what he called the "new marriage" first took form. As we have seen, anxiety arising from a sense of professional fraudulence had been channeled into guilt specifically related to his own sexual infidelity. During the winter of 1866–67, lonely, despondent, and without significant fear of discovery, Theodore succumbed to sexual temptation. This event had shocked him into realizing that without a social deterrent, he lacked the "innate vir-

This drawing of Elizabeth Tilton was included in the published volumes of the adultery trial transcript.

tue of discipline" to prevent sin. His previous assumptions of "moral strength" and "unbending rectitude" were swept away in a confused orgy of self-denunciation.[11] "I once thought myself a good, true, and upright man," he confided to Elizabeth in 1866, but now, "I find myself a constant sinner. I feel myself scarred, spotted, miserable, and unworthy . . . an inward revelation of a man's self to himself is an awful thing."[12]

Far from alleviating his loneliness and despondency, Theodore's sexual encounters destroyed his faith not only in himself but in human nature. "Perhaps because I do not entertain so good an opinion of my own character," he wrote despondently, "human characters do not seem so lovely to me as they once did." Theodore's guilt haunted his thoughts and letters to Elizabeth; but because she as yet knew nothing of his infidelity, speculations on the dangers of physical passion were an attempt to persuade *himself* that "the noblest part of love is honor, fidelity, constance, self-abnegation—not the clasp of the hand nor the kiss of the lips, nor the ecstasy of fondness."[13] This sudden, real, and frightening prospect that his impulses were uncontrollable convinced Theodore that "what most delights the heart [body] cheats the soul." Concluding that spiritual or platonic love must transcend unpredictable passion, he wrote Elizabeth of his desire that theirs should become a "soul-mated" marriage—one based on "a love that swells in the soul rather than in the heart [body]."[14]

Whether Tilton absorbed these changes in attitudes toward love and sexuality from Henry Ward Beecher or came to them himself, they do bear a remarkable similarity to the minister's ideas: "The end to be sought in this life, then, is the suppression of the passional man, of the animal disposition, and the development of the germs of heart-life which are planted in the soul." In fact, Beecher assured his listeners, "Love . . . is that which *subjugates* the passions."[15] Thus, in a remarkable reversal of traditional assumptions about the inevitability of emotional and physical excitement connected with love and sex, Beecher severed sex from love and held up the latter as a calming force. No longer should love represent disruptive sexuality, but passionless love should replace duty as the basis for marriage. Romantic love had found its first popularizer in mainstream American society.[16]

To Elizabeth the mysterious and powerful nature of romantic love was a new idea. Intrigued and attracted by the possibilities inherent in "soul-loving," early in 1867 she expressed to Theodore her fascination as well as her doubts: "You write today of the love of two interlocked souls remaining wedded for immortality, and ask whether such love is not more tenderly beautiful than those same souls can possibly feel toward God. Darling, I live in profound wonder and hushed solemnity at this great mystery of soul-loving to which I have been awakened the past year. Am I your soul's mate?"[17] This is not a star-struck teenager speaking, but a mature married woman! After twelve years of marriage, Elizabeth had awakened to the potential of romantic love!

But in spite of her "profound wonder" and "hushed solemnity," Elizabeth was still painfully aware of Theodore's complaints that she was the one person with whom he could *not* communicate because of her inability to relate to "intellectual" prople. In recognition of this, Elizabeth attempted to bring her husband's "imagination" more in line with reality: "When my sweet, will you *talk* to me as you write? Pretending always that you think I am the best and loveliest of little wives."[18] Though their letters to each other were tender and loving, their actual encounters were usually hostile. This was painfully evident when Theodore returned from his first winter on tour and their marriage resumed its old patterns: Theodore's complaints and insults, followed by Elizabeth's scoldings. Much as they tried, neither could function in the romantic, loving way in which they had begun to write to each other. Indeed, Elizabeth actually began to fear Theodore's homecoming: "In the early part of your absence it was well enough to suffer you to believe in my perfection, but as you near home," she warned, "it is wise to dispel the infatuation little by little and convince you of the humanity and frailty of your loving-wife."[19]

Theodore did not heed these warnings. His need for a confessor and a psychological pillar and prop only increased. "I am by nature so frank," he wrote, "that the attempt to hide my feelings, to cloak my shortcomings, to deny utterance to my inward sorrows, had lately driven me to despair." Obviously, Theodore could not confess to the public his perception of himself as a "whited sepulcher," but he could and did—on January 25, 1868—confess his sexual infidelity to his "espoused saint," as he addressed Elizabeth.[20]

As a part of his confession, however, Theodore insisted that Elizabeth was also guilty—guilty of rejecting him sexually and thus causing the infidelity. When she accepted his analysis of the situation, Elizabeth began to share her husband's burden of despair. She implored forgiveness for "cruelty. . . . Oh, Theodore, darling, I am haunted night and day by the remorse of knowing that because of my harshness and indifference to you, you were driven to despair—perhaps sin, and these last years of unhappiness. . . . I am the chief of sinners!"[21] Elizabeth was now prepared to accept what she had never before considered—a complete submission to her husband's will and judgment. Without her family's support she could not preserve her own identity. From now on *his* judgment would define her attitudes and actions—she vowed never to "scold" him again. "After all you have suffered through me," she wrote Theodore, "I . . . shall try to follow your wish *in every particular*."[22]

The effect of Elizabeth's capitulation and forgiveness on Theodore was to relieve him, for a time, of his guilt. Having made his confession and been absolved, he felt released, transformed, "a new creature . . . no more despondency—no more repining—no more vain regrets—no more loss of self-respect—no more groveling in the dust. . . . I am once again a man among men," he joyfully proclaimed, "and a Christian among Christians." Substituting Elizabeth for the religion in which he no longer found any solace, he wrote, "You opened for me, that night [of confession] the gate of heaven, which had so long seemed shut." Henceforth, he told Elizabeth, "You always have in your power either to crown or dethrone me, . . . you have the chief ruling influence of my life."[23] In the previous chapter we saw that Tilton worried about the power of a fickle public or an economic cycle to "crown" or "dethrone" him; in transferring that power to Elizabeth he probably considered himself on safer ground.

In a remarkable reversal, Elizabeth had been transformed from a social liability into the personification of all that was good. The simplistic religious beliefs and lack of sophistication that had always annoyed Theodore now represented her greatest virtue. She had become a model for Theodore to emulate. "Now this transformation I owe to yourself," he assured her, "to your irrepressible love and devotion, to your ceaseless prayers, and to your victorious faith." Converted from religion to a belief in salvation through Elizabeth's superior spirituality, Theodore reveled in a state of near-euphoria. "You are not only all," he wrote Elizabeth, "but more than all, than any man can need or ever can deserve. Life never seemed to me to be more full of objects and ends worth living for."[24] He rejoiced in the disappearance of his despondent moods. "I very rarely have any depression of spirits. The old claim has gone away entirely; the new day has dawned!"[25] Theodore rivaled Beecher in his hymns to the perfection and glory of womanhood.

For the moment, Elizabeth embraced, with relief if not absolute conviction, her new spiritual identity as a "saint." In exploring the implications of her new role, she moved toward a "conversion" of her own. Just as Theodore had phrased his new adoration in religious terms, Elizabeth responded in kind by comparing her husband to Christ. "I learn to love you from my love to Him; I have learned to love *Him* from loving you!"[26] Soon she had come to *equate* the two: "The Great Lover and yourself, to whom as *one* I am eternally wedded."[27] With this juxtaposition Elizabeth took a long step toward the "new marriage" in which her husband dominated her entire world.

Nevertheless, Elizabeth resented the practical ramifications of such a choice, arguing that their "ideal marriage" need not exclude "pure friendship with *many*."[28] She could not help but miss her family and the lively boardinghouse circle! However, driven by Theodore's continued insistence that they leave the "mildew" of her mother's social influence behind, Elizabeth capitulated. "I know that now, mother, children or friend have no longer possession of my heart," she assured him, "the supreme place is yours forever."[29]

By March 1868, she happily reported the completion of her transformation: "I am conscious of great inward awakening toward . . . you. . . . I shall teach my children to *begin* their loves where now I am. I cannot conceive of anything more delicious than a *life* consecrated to a faithful love. Oh, why did I sleep so long?" The word "faithful" signified to Elizabeth far more than sexual fidelity; it was a promise of emotional dependence on, and devotion to, Theodore alone—to the exclusion of all previous social and familial bonds. She agreed with Theodore that they should raise their children—as they themselves had not been—"to revere spouse more than parents."[30] After thirteen years of marriage, Elizabeth and Theodore Tilton embarked upon a new relationship—one based not on accustomed duties and responsibilities, but on romantic imagination. In a letter written a few days after her "awakening" Elizabeth summed up her new role: "This, I think, I have decided—no more chidings, scoldings! . . . I never before saw my path as clear as now—that whatever you may do, say, or be, it becometh me to be the Christian wife and mother!"[31]

But try as she would to live the role dictated by her awakening, Elizabeth indicated in her letters that she was never absolutely convinced of its validity. She repeatedly begged Theodore to reaffirm his love—to encourage her in her "conversion." Admitting her recurrent fears about her competency to manage the household, she wrote, "I would fain make the path smooth for your feet, or in other words, direct the children and the household that they minister harmony only, but I *know* I cannot, and *I am afraid!*" This fear seemed to have less to do with the actual work of the household than with her *sole* responsibility for sustaining "harmony."[32] And despite the illusion of their correspondence all through the spring— renewed vows, protestations of undying love, and mutual worship—Elizabeth, at least, remained aware that the relationship actually existed only in their "imaginations." Although she reminded him repeatedly of her human frailties, Theodore invariably became depressed and moody when she failed to live up to his expectations. But when Theodore was away from home, he wrote euphorically of his newfound happiness. Demonstrating a surprising insight, Elizabeth dismally responded, "I cannot help thinking that it [Theodore's happiness] is because I am *not* with you!"[33]

Just how little the "new marriage" had actually altered their relationship became clear when Theodore returned home in the spring of 1868. Elizabeth gave birth to their fourth child, who died in infancy.[34] But this event, which might have brought the parents together, only compounded their inability to live in harmony. Theodore again resorted to criticisms and Elizabeth once more responded with scoldings. For all their good intentions, their treatment of each other had not changed. By November 1868, Theodore realistically assessed the unbridgeable gap between ideal and reality: "It is the greatest regret of my life that I do not seem constituted so as to make you as happy as you deserve to be; but I have the best of intentions—and the worst of success." Hoping to assure Elizabeth that *she* had not the "slightest" originating share in his troubles, Theodore sadly concluded, "They are of my own making."[35]

Ironically, Theodore and Elizabeth had fallen into a trap of their own creation. Out of their doubts, insecurity, and fear, they had constructed a perfect, imaginary marriage, centered on one another. And yet, it was painfully obvious that every time they were together for more than a few days, what Elizabeth called "the old demons of ungenerosity and fault-finding" reasserted themselves with excruciating regularity.[36] Instead of enhancing their relationship, the "new marriage" only increased the bitterness of their mutual criticisms. If Theodore had been annoyed earlier at Elizabeth's lack of culture and refinement, he was now devastated by her inability to be a saint.

Even though she was incessantly reminded by both her husband and her minister of the necessity of maintaining her "sainthood," Elizabeth was not fully "domesticated." She later testified that she felt like a nonentity who had lost not only her self-respect, but her "will"—a euphemism for her sense of self. Elizabeth, at some level, had come to the conclusion that the perfect wife of Theodore Tilton's expectations could not also be a separate, vital person. (This was strikingly similar to the conclusions of Eunice Beecher.) But, ironically, the more domesticated that Elizabeth became, the less satisfactory was the marriage. Much as she desired to please Theodore, she could not. As either his social equal or his "pillar and prop," she had failed. Although the new set of values promised benefits of happiness and gratification, Elizabeth instead found herself glorified in the abstract and ignored, if not abused, in reality.

Why did these two people expend so much energy on creating the illusion of perfect togetherness? It is clear that on the deepest level, both felt, in Elizabeth's words, like nonentities. Examining their own motives, they discovered only selfishness where previously—whether in family or reform issues—there had existed a social purpose that carried with it a social identity. Turning to each other as the sole providers of a meaningful identity created a situation that was, at best, precarious. Theodore and Elizabeth's generation was caught in a limbo between a time when an individual's identity was provided by the combined social institutions of the family, community, and church, and the era when identity would be found in profession or social class. In such a state of transition and confusion, one source of comfort was the formalized but illusory romanticism of a Victorian marriage.

This inability to relate on a genuinely intimate level with a wife or husband, according to Byron Strong, was common in nineteenth-century Victorian marriages. Because, perhaps, the outside world had become so threatening, it was more imperative than ever that the marriage be orderly and calm. Often the "calmness" and "fitting together" were emphasized at the cost of the personal identities involved in the relationship. Strong adopts the term "pseudo-mutuality" to describe the intense effort exerted to create and maintain the illusion of an intimate, compatible marriage.[37] This is an apt description of the intense effort employed by Theodore and Elizabeth, especially in their letters, to fabricate the illusion of a highly romantic marriage. Unlike most couples, however, their involvement with Henry Ward Beecher brought about a series of events that made it impossible to suppress their underlying anger and hostility. In chapter eight I shall examine the effect that entering into Beecher's higher sphere had on the Tilton marriage and on Elizabeth's concept of herself as a woman. First, however, it is necessary to explore the social conflict produced by Beecher's wide-spread popularity in Plymouth Church and Brooklyn.

5

"Plymouth: The Rock upon Which Mr. Beecher Stands"

THE "BEECHER-TILTON affair" did not begin in 1866 when the minister began calling on Mrs. Tilton, or even earlier in 1860 when Beecher and Theodore Tilton became colleagues. In fact, its origins go back to conflicts initiated in 1848 when Henry Ward Beecher was called to Brooklyn to take over the pastorate of Plymouth Church. Just as changing patterns in the Tilton marriage would eventually lead to a scandal, the effect of Beecher's approach to religion on Plymouth Church had a great deal to do with the emergence of the scandal as a public event.

The 1840s were years of extremely rapid growth for the New York City area, and Brooklyn, across the East River, was part of this expansion. The small Dutch community of the 1820s and 1830s had been submerged in a mixture of new ethnic groups and commercial activity. Irish and German immigrants dominated the eastern and northern areas of the city while wealthy Yankee merchants developed Brooklyn Heights as New York's newest suburb. The ferries connecting Brooklyn with New York (the Brooklyn Bridge was not built until the 1880s) did a brisk business as commuters daily jammed their decks.[1]

The founding of Plymouth Church was part of the explosion of population and commercial expansion that characterized this period of Brooklyn's history. Later, Brooklyn would earn the designation "city of churches," and it was during the 1840s and 1850s that the majority of them were established.[2] Plymouth was an offshoot of the first Congregational Church established in Brooklyn, the Church of the Pilgrims.

Both the Church of the Pilgrims and Plymouth Church were a part of the attempt to revive Congregationalism in areas outside New England. Since the Plan of Union in 1801 had provided that churches organized by Congregationalists and/or Presbyterians outside New England would adopt Presbyterian form, Congregationalism was waning. Many New England-

ers who now populated New York City were unhappy with this arrangement: Henry C. Bowen and John T. Howard were two such individuals.

Bowen and Howard had migrated to New York City in the 1820s,
Howard from Salem, Massachusetts, and Bowen from Woodstock, Connecticut. Howard was the son of an established Salem merchant who simply moved his business to the more active city. Bowen's background was
less prestigious: he was a member of an old Woodstock family but had
been only a clerk in a small store in that town. After his arrival in New
York, however, Bowen's fortunes improved when he obtained a position
in Lewis and Arthur Tappan's prosperous silk importing business and
married Lewis Tappan's daughter. Both Bowen and Howard were well established financially by the time they took up residence in fashionable
brownstones on Brooklyn Heights.[3]

Bowen and Howard first joined the local Presbyterian church, but soon
decided to take the initiative in bringing the traditional religion of New
England, Congregationalism, to the Heights. As a result, in 1844 they
joined with others to found the Church of the Pilgrims and called as its pastor Richard Salter Storrs—a young clergyman from a family boasting a
long line of traditional Congregational ministers. It is unclear why these
men felt the need only three years later to break away and begin another
Congregational church. *The History of Plymouth Church* attributes it only to the population increase of the Heights, and "several public spirited
Christian gentlemen."[4] Hints abound, however, that when Rev. Storrs arrived in late 1846 to take up his pastoral duties, it became apparent that he
was too stodgy and conservative for some of the members.

Apparently, although Storrs was a gifted scholar and theologian, he was
not aggressive enough in attracting converts, causing revivals, and increasing membership. Bowen criticized Storrs by commenting, "splitting hairs
in theology will not save souls."[5] By early the next year, Bowen and
Howard were planning to organize another church.[6] One Plymouth member later commented the founders were "convinced that a wide and unoc-
cupied field of influence was open to them in the city of Brooklyn."[7] Indeed, Bowen especially seemed persuaded that the time was ripe to adapt
the methods of business enterprise to religious endeavor. He wrote to Beecher in 1847: "We are on the eve of the greatest events in this country.
Hundreds and hundreds of thousands from all nations are yearly landed
upon our northern and eastern shores. . . . Now is the time for the church to
awake," Bowen argued. "A more propitious time never was, when prospects were so good."[8] Most accounts of the founders of the church stress

Plymouth Church

their commitment to enterprising activities. One parishioner later wrote that the "greatest number" were "aggressive men" and "of them all," Bowen was the "most aggressive and the most of a leader."[9]

A further impetus for the founding of Plymouth Church was the prosperous economic climate of the 1840s. "Have seen much of business in this city the past fourteen years," Bowen enthused in a letter to Beecher, "but never saw anything to be compared with the present year and more particularly the present season. We hardly have time to eat and sleep and have fifty men employed all told. We could use 25 more if we had the room to show the goods." Expressing his astonishment ("I hardly know what to make of it") and attributing the unexpected prosperity to a "kind of providence favoring us with a *rich harvest*," Bowen nevertheless worried, "may it not prove a curse to us." In the same letter, Bowen explained how such prosperity could be a curse. It may, he feared, "harden our hearts and rivet them more closely to the work." Active measures, he thought, had to be taken to prevent preoccupation with economic success. "Now is the time to do *great things* to extend Christ's kingdom."[10] Like Theodore Tilton, Bowen seemed to be experiencing guilt over his worldly success.

Bowen was not suggesting, however, that he and others turn away from business and commerce, but only that they bring the methods and results of that prosperity to church affairs. This would explain his dissatisfaction with Storrs's preaching in the Church of the Pilgrims; someone who could package the traditional doctrines of Congregationalism in marketable form would save more souls. From the beginning, Henry Ward Beecher seemed the man for the job. "Your name was spoken of at the first prayer meeting," Bowen wrote to Beecher, "as the man of our choice."[11]

What was important to the founders of Plymouth Church was what Beecher had demonstrated he could do: bring in the crowds. Bowen wrote to Beecher, "God had . . . prepared you and given you the ability—the happy faculty to present truth to the conscience and heart in a way to produce an effect."[12] Some observers had already commented on the inconsistency of Beecher's theology, but the preacher's followers argued that "he preached Christ as revealed in his own heart."[13] As we have seen, the foundation of Beecher's popularity lay in his ability to project emotion, rather than to display theological logic. This talent allowed his audience to identify with him and created the magnetism for which he became so famous.

From the moment Beecher took charge of his new parish in 1848 he was a controversial figure. To a few, his theological soundness seemed doubtful, especially after the first few sermons, which caused "dissatisfaction" to some and "astonishment" to all. But Brooklynites, particularly those of New England origin, were attracted to Beecher's style; the church grew faster than any other in the "city of churches," quickly surpassing the older Church of the Pilgrims. Within ten years it was the largest in the city.[14] At Plymouth Church Beecher encountered a congregation of young men whose chances for survival in a changing world required a geographic, economic, and intellectual departure from the past. Thus, they embraced Beecher's proclamation that the "secret of true religion is that it sets at liberty," and that Jesus, "comes to every man's heart to make him free—free in thinking, free in choosing; free in tastes and sentiments; free in all pleasurable associations.[15] The theme of freedom from the rigidity of traditional institutions—family, church, or town—dominated the thinking of Beecher and his listeners.

The dynamics of this empathy between Beecher and the young men of his congregation are illustrated by a book written by one of his parishioners, Stephen Griswold, a faithful member of Plymouth Church for fifty-three years.[16] In many ways, Griswold was typical of Beecher's parishioners. Like most Plymouth Church members, he had grown up on a farm (in his case in Windsor, Connecticut). Forty percent of a random sample of the church members had similar New England origins, and another twenty-four percent were listed in the 1870 census as having come from New York (probably upstate—an area settled by New Englanders).[17] Biographies of many others indicate that a rural background was common. Typically, Griswold characterized his early years as "uneventful." In 1851 he proposed to his family that he go to New York in "search of fame and fortune —a wider horizon and a larger life." Convincing his reluctant parents that he could not be "content" to live out his days on the farm, he started out to "make his way in the world."[18]

Though Griswold does not say specifically what motivated him to leave the family farm in what he called the "beautiful valley of the Connecticut," his reference to "fame and fortune" probably reflects the unfortunate truth that New England agriculture was in such a depressed condition that it was no longer possible to survive by farming the poor stony soil exhausted by 200 years of intensive cultivation. The situation was aggravated by competition from the fertile area of western New York and the Ohio Valley; the opening of the Erie Canal in 1825 made it cheaper for New Englanders to buy western wheat than to grow it themselves. Since the early years of the nineteenth century, large numbers of young men like Stephen Griswold had been leaving New England for western farm lands or cities like New York, Philadelphia, and Boston. With its static population, unproductive farm lands, and an infant manufacturing industry, New England must have presented dismal prospects for her sons in the 1840s and 1850s.[19] Griswold made it clear that leaving home was not easy. In the summer of 1851, he wistfully reported that he arrived in New York, "a lonely country boy, with no introductions and no one to hold out a helping hand."[20]

Despite the attractions of such a glamorous metropolis as New York, Griswold and his parents considered it to be "a city of untold lawlessness and full of pitfalls, where an unsophisticated country youth like myself would be beset with many temptations on every hand, and be led away from the straight and narrow path of his upbringing by his godly parents."[21] Nor was his family alone in this assessment of urban life; one has only to read some contemporary literature to realize that the city, for all its financial opportunity, was regarded as bestial, degenerate, and dangerous.[22] Yet for a farm boy with no particular skills and no capital, the city seemed the only avenue to fame and fortune.

Being a youth in New England meant, in many cases, being closely tied to one's father both in a geographic, an economic, and a psychological sense. It involved dependence on land provided by a father when he judged the son ready to be on his own. Even after the son received his own land (often not until he was in his late twenties or early thirties), parents, brothers, and other relatives were always nearby to watch and advise. How different was Brooklyn where there were no familiar faces and no inheritance to assure a secure future. These young men, like Henry Ward Beecher himself, were on their own in the marketplace.

Griswold was successful economically, for within a week he found employment as a clerk in a business house in Brooklyn. For a short time everything seemed to go well; he was fascinated by the "hurry and bustle" of the city and adjusted to his new occupation which called into play, he said, "an entirely different line of thought." But after a few weeks, he began to feel the social isolation from his childhood home: "A few weeks of this, however, sufficed to wear away the novelty, and a full sense of my solitary condition rushed over me; I had made few acquaintances and had practically no society. I began to look around for companions, or at least for some place where I could spend my evenings, when the time dragged most heavily."[23] Griswold's reactions can only be understood if one realizes the drastic change he experienced. From a community where it was nearly impossible to be unnoticed, he had come to a place teeming with individuals who were invisible to one another.

Griswold feared his situation was desperate, even dangerous, and that he might soon be "tempted to wander into questionable or even harmful ways." At this crucial juncture he happened to attend Plymouth Church and hear Henry Ward Beecher. Despite the crowds, Griswold "received such a cordial welcome" as to make him feel "at home." He was impressed by the sermon, even though he admitted he had never heard anything like it in New England. "From this time on," he said, "I had no reason to complain of any lack of social life," and concluded, "Plymouth Church has become more to me than I can possibly express."[24] It is easy to see why the experiences of young men paralleled Beecher's quest for a new avenue to enduring success within the ministerial profession. Beecher's genius was that he articulated for this group an explanation and justification for the changes in their lives and attitudes.

Despite Beecher's popularity, divisive issues began to appear soon after he was installed. They revolved around the very nature of a Congregational church and the role of its minister. Bowen may have been interested in winning large numbers of converts, but he was also very much committed to a revival of Congregationalist polity. Plymouth Church was not, after all, a camp meeting, where the denominational orientation of the preacher did not matter. Would Plymouth Church continue as a Congregational institution or would it simply provide a platform for the effusive personality of Henry Ward Beecher himself? From the beginning, hostile observers pointed out that a Plymouth Church service was not the accustomed "prayerful worship," but a "performance" that "glorified" not Christ but Beecher.[25] Many people in Brooklyn—particularly members of the older Church of the Pilgrims—became more and more disturbed by the lack of any firm religious doctrine and moral standards in the new church and by Beecher's tendency to demand nothing from his congregation but personal loyalty. And the fact is that Beecher never did want to confine himself to ministering to a particular flock or denomination. "My ministry," he wrote his brother in 1852, "is much more a ministry to the *world* than to the *Church*."[26]

The records of Plymouth Church indicate that over the course of twenty-five years, Beecher altered the rules and character of the church to fit his own objectives. Before his arrival in July 1847, Bowen and Howard—or perhaps Bowen alone—had drawn up the Ecclesiastical Principles and Rules, the Covenant, and Form of Admission for the church. They had also chosen the name Plymouth, which signified their determination to preserve their New England heritage in the heterogeneous city of Brooklyn. The rules, covenant, and form of admission, too, reflected the standard approach to organization of Congregational bodies. Prior to Beecher's appearance, the members demonstrated their agreement with the standard forms by ordering a hundred copies printed and ready for distribution.[27]

But immediately after Beecher's installation, he proposed changes in these rules. The very first ecclesiastical principle, for example, began with the statement, "This church regards the scriptures as the only infallible guide in matters of church order and discipline, and is therefore, answerable to no other ecclesiastical body." This rule was deliberate in stressing the independence of a Congregational church from other religious bodies, *and* its dependence solely on scripture as the basis of belief, but Beecher substituted another statement: "This church is an independent ecclesiastical body; and in matters of doctrine, order, and discipline, is answerable to no other organization."[28] In his version, the scriptures are left out entirely! His opponents would say, of course, that he left them out of his preaching as well. Instead, Beecher wanted the independence of the church (himself?) to stand alone. It was still Congregationalism, but with a subtly different emphasis.

In another change having to do with the Articles of Faith, Beecher further watered down the "infallibility" of the scriptures. The original version declared that the Old and New Testaments were "given by inspiration of God"; Beecher wanted it to read simply "inspired of God." Again, this was a far less powerful version. Similarly, the Bowen draft asserted that the scriptures were "the only perfect rule of faith and practice," and Beecher substituted "authoritative" for "perfect."[29]

Beecher also modified the Article of Faith having to do with God. Bowen's original version stressed the trinity, and the Deity's commanding, somewhat frightening power: "We believe in one God, subsisting in three persons, the Father, the Son and the Holy Ghost, eternal, unchangeable and omnipresent; infinite in power, wisdom and holiness; the creator and preserver of all things; whose purposes and providence extend to all events, and who exercises a righteous moral government over all his intelligent creatures." Beecher's substitution read: "We believe in the existence of one everlasting and True God, Sovereign and unchangeable, Infinite in Power, wisdom and Goodness." Bowen emphasized God's righteous moral government; Beecher, characteristically, concludes with a reference to benevolence.[30]

In the rules for admission, too, Beecher sought to play down complicated procedures and authoritarianism. In the original rule for admission of new members, Bowen spent two long paragraphs discussing the scrutiny of applicants by an Examining Committee, gathering of testimonials, and giving notice to the congregation two weeks in advance. Beecher cut the verbiage by more than half, stating simply that application should be made to the committee with only one week's notice. No testimonials would be required.[31]

Obviously, the direction of these alterations was to make it easier to get into the church and to stay in. As Beecher's popularity grew, he loosened still further the admission standards and disciplinary functions of the church. The culmination of this trend came in 1871 when, through Beecher's influence, the church ceased to require new members to subscribe to *any* of the Articles of Faith upon admission! To join the church, all one had to do was to express the "desire" to become a "Christian."[32] A minority in the church protested, and the more orthodox ministers— Richard Salter Storrs, for example—were appalled. Church of the Pilgrims hinted darkly of disfellowshipping Plymouth Church. The *Brooklyn Eagle,* generally sympathetic to Beecher, stated that the minister had "abjured Calvinism" to give his congregation a "less rugged path to the happiness of the hereafter."[33]

A similar pattern soon became evident in matters of church discipline. The covenant of the church stressed the collective nature of Congregationalism in admonishing each member to "watch over" every other member and to "submit to necessary discipline."[34] In colonial Puritan churches, "discipline" had extended to all areas of the parishioners' lives, not just theological beliefs. Communicants were to avoid all causes of "scandal" whether in religious, economic, political, or social spheres. Therefore, in the early years of Plymouth Church, much time and attention was dedicated to the discipline of members. Many of these cases had to do with sexual immorality. But another case demonstrates just how far-reaching the church members thought their responsibility extended: in 1850, the church held a trial for dishonest business practices. Dr. Charles Rowland was accused of "falsehoods" in the conduct of his insurance business. Church members assumed that such behavior was within the purview of Congregational discipline and convicted Rowland.[35]

By 1858, Beecher was objecting to such assumptions. In that year, George Livingston, a liquor dealer, applied for admission to the church. The admissions committee, of which Beecher was a member, approved, even though the church had declared itself a temperance organization. But several members protested Livingston's admission, insisting that his occupation proved him unworthy of membership. Predictably, Beecher argued that as long as Livingston assured the church that he himself was "totally abstinent," admission should be granted. "In the present state of society," Beecher thought, "it is not possible to exclude from membership all who may be so entangled."[36] *Everyone*, in other words, somehow had to be touched by worldly corruption. Thus the church was wrong (just as Beecher's father had been) when it insisted on making judgments. Later on, the members of Plymouth Church declared that they rejected the "responsibility of authority" and accepted only the responsibility of "affection,"[37] Beecher had essentially secured his personal popularity by emasculating the traditional authority of the church.

There was resistance, however, especially in the years before 1858, to this erosion of church authority and doctrine. Bowen himself inspired two separate movements to curb Beecher's actions in the areas of church funds and music.[38] But the most extensive attempt to counter Beecher's influence came in 1856. By that time, the membership had grown to around 750—too many to "watch over" each other. Beecher, uninterested in discipline, wasn't complaining. Older members, however, were disturbed that the church was becoming, for the congregation if not the minister, an anonymous institution. A committee appointed to find a solution to the problem was chaired by Henry Bowen's father-in-law, Lewis Tappan. (Also named was an enthusiastic new member—Theodore Tilton.)[39] The report submitted by this committee decried the growing ineffectiveness and anonymity of the church: "It is better that a Church should be small in numbers, if they are living Christians, than more numerous if the members have but little knowledge of each other, and are remiss in their religious duties."[40] Of course, no one was ready to limit the number who might join, so the Tappan committee proposed a remedy: they suggested small Methodist-type group meetings in private homes "to promote the temporal and spiritual welfare of the members."[41] The committee also went so far as to recommend appointment of an assistant pastor to oversee visitation and "promote the spiritual good" of the church.[42] This was a veiled slap at Beecher who, despite his growing popularity, could not or would not personally attend to the individual needs of his flock. The committee's plan was never carried out; the greatest revival in the church's history (1857–58) doubled the membership and rendered the group idea untenable.[43]

Finally, Beecher no longer had to worry about strategies for a successful ministry—in fact, he did not have to do *anything* he did not want to do—and he quickly gave up such chores as social meetings and pastoral calls. Beecher concentrated on what he did best—preaching to thousands of admirers. Having set out to mass-produce a personalized religion, Beecher had succeeded beyond his wildest expectations.

By 1870, Beecher was secure enough to declare that "external forms" should be only of peripheral concern.[44] In fact, men of sensitivity had no need for traditional institutions. As we have seen, he believed that moral affinity, rather than institutional bonds, should act as the glue of human society. Plymouth Church had demonstrated the possibility of transforming a traditional authoritarian institution into a group voluntarily attracted to each other—and to Henry Ward Beecher—by personal affinity. The *History of Plymouth Church* written in 1873 had as its subtitle *Henry Ward Beecher*—an indication that the minister himself had become the institution!

Although the majority of Plymouth Church members had been won over to Beecher's personal approach to religion, there continued to be a small group of dissenters who feared "Beecherism." This group was able to survive in spite of Beecher's overwhelming popularity because it was led by the man most instrumental in founding the church: Henry C. Bowen. By 1870, Plymouth Church and Henry Ward Beecher may have seemed synonymous to the public both within and without Brooklyn, but Bowen had gradually begun to reject Beecher's ideas. He had come to fear Beecher's influence not only in his personal life, but in the church as well. For Bowen, this created a severe dilemma in that his economic success rested squarely (through his columns in the *Independent*) on Beecher's popularity. Thus Bowen's personal and ideological rift with Beecher is crucial to

Henry Ward Beecher was noted for his casual yet animated style of preaching. Eschewing the pulpit, he paced up and down the platform, addressing his audience in a personal, confiding manner.

an understanding of the small yet significant opposition to the minister's hegemony—opposition that was not fully purged until the public airing of the scandal in 1875.

After Beecher arrived in Brooklyn, his friends included both of the prominent founders of Plymouth Church, John T. Howard and Bowen, but it was the latter who became his closest friend and business partner. Bowen had been so anxious to persuade Beecher to accept his call to the new church that he personally raised money to pay the minister's debts and moving expenses. Authorizing the preacher to draw upon his own business firm for money, Bowen emphasized to Beecher, "We want you to be free of debt *entirely*."[45] At the same time that Bowen organized the church, he started a religious newspaper, the *Independent,* devoted to the revival of Congregationalism in New York and to the cause of antislavery.[46] Soon after Beecher's arrival, Bowen invited him to become a regular contributor, thus providing the minister with an opportunity to be heard by many more people. The two men became fast friends as well, and Beecher was often at Bowen's home—a mansion in the best section of Brooklyn Heights.

Their friendship, though strained by Beecher's changes in church policy, continued for about eight years. Church and business difficulties overlapped when Bowen discovered that Beecher was as undependable in his work habits as he was in his financial dealings. As an efficient businessman, Bowen's patience was continually tried by Beecher's inability to get columns for the *Independent* written on time. Penalty clauses for missed deadlines in Beecher's contract seemed to have no effect. As we have seen, Bowen finally had to hire Theodore Tilton to ghost Beecher's articles. In addition, Beecher's financial account at the offices of the *Independent* was often overdrawn. On two occasions between 1855 and 1864, the men submitted their differences to an arbitrator.[47]

Worse than these annoying business problems, there is evidence, which I have already mentioned, that the minister engaged—around 1855—in an affair with Henry Bowen's wife, Lucy Maria. On that occasion Bowen swallowed his pride and accepted his private humiliation for the sake of his wife and his continued economic prosperity. Bowen's financial position was extremely vulnerable around this time; his silk business had collapsed in the Panic of 1857 and in the early part of 1861 his dry goods manufacturing firm went bankrupt because of the Civil War.[48] All Bowen had left was the *Independent,* and even that was in grave financial danger. The paper was kept afloat by Henry Ward Beecher—many people bought it just to read his articles and sermons. It must have been with deeply mixed feelings that Henry Bowen, in December 1861, offered the editorship of the paper to the errant minister.

But Bowen was deeply disturbed by the wrongs Beecher had committed. Theodore Tilton claimed that on numerous occasions between 1860 and 1870 Bowen had confided tales of Beecher's adulteries—often accompanied by an "exhibition" of a "deep sense of personal injury."[49] When Beecher pleaded for forgiveness and a resumption of the old social intimacy, Bowen responded with coolness. "In the relations which now exist between us, there is no want of *cordiality, respect,* or *sympathy,*" he wrote to Beecher in 1862. More important, he reiterated that "damage" to the paper was his prime concern. "If we either of us," Bowen wrote, "make one or two or 'seventy times seven' mistakes . . . we shall forgive each other and work on for God and humanity."[50] Presumably, the success of the *Independent* precluded open hostility.

In May 1863, however, Lucy Bowen's death revived all her husband's frustration and bitterness. It was at this point that Bowen wrote to Tilton that *one* word from him could cause a *"revolution"* in Plymouth Church and drive Beecher from his pulpit.[51] But only six weeks later, Bowen wrote to Beecher in England that although he mourned the death of his wife, he hoped the past could now be "buried" and their friendship restored.[52]

There were contradictions, but these responses were genuinely ambivalent rather than hypocritical. Bowen, like Tilton, came from humble origins. Even after he obtained Lewis Tappan's considerable financial backing through marriage, prosperity eluded him until well into the 1860s. Like Tilton, he too was flattered by association with the rich and famous— collecting autographs of such notables as President Grant and Senator Roscoe Conkling.[53] Fame was a very high recommendation in Henry Bowen's estimation, and Beecher had as much of that as anyone in America. Later, Bowen excused his concealment of Beecher's sexual adventures by arguing that the minister had appeared "repentant."[54] This perhaps is only a partial version of the truth; Bowen, like others in the Gilded Age, believed that fame, power, and money signified innate good qualities that demanded respect. Bowen's ambivalence reflected his conflicting values —Beecher's behavior deserved contempt, but at the same time his public stature seemed proof of ultimate worthiness. Bowen floundered between the two. As we shall see, many people in Brooklyn and Plymouth Church had similar contradictory attitudes toward Beecher. Nonetheless, Bowen and Beecher could never return to their former intimate and trusting friendship.

Beecher turned to new friends for the admiring adulation he needed from his associates. One of these was the other primary founder of Plymouth Church, John T. Howard. Unlike Bowen, Howard had never objected to Beecher's alterations in rules and discipline. Thus, after Beecher's break with Bowen, Howard and his family became the preacher's chief advisers on political and economic matters. It was a delicate situation, for the Howards were Democrats although most members of Plymouth Church were Republicans. Howard's son Joseph was at one time city editor of the Democratic *Brooklyn Eagle*.[55] Although Beecher preferred to remain noncommittal on political issues, the Howard influence was apparent in many of the pastor's political utterances. For example, Beecher continually attacked President Lincoln for his lack of "social refinement" and "personal magnetism," while making excuses for the corruption of New York's Democratic mayor, A. Oakey Hall, Boss William Tweed, and the Tammany Ring.[56] Nonetheless, Beecher remained Republican because that was what most of his followers were; and his sermons continued to appear in the *Independent*, a newspaper committed to the Republican party. In his usual style, Beecher managed, through the early 1860s, to preserve a precarious balance.

Tilton was also a part of the circle that surrounded Beecher. When the two became close friends in 1861, Tilton was so overcome by the attentions of such a man that he extended unconditionally the adoration that Beecher so craved and appreciated. Tilton, however, was an idealistic young man and before long he noticed that Beecher never seemed to preach in public the radical ideas he expressed in private. Moderation was Beecher's lifelong instinct—don't "scare" your listeners, he had once written to his brother—but it was a theme Tilton never comprehended.[57] In 1860, for instance, the two men disagreed over the distribution of some church funds. Tilton objected to supporting an organization that was "soft" on slavery, although Beecher was quite content to continue the funding.[58] This issue was settled without a personal rift between the two men, but their next clash—over politics—caused a serious split. By fall of 1866 most Republicans had turned against President Andrew Johnson's lenient policies on Reconstruction, and Tilton was in the forefront of Johnson's critics.[59] Beecher, however, to his friend's surprise and dismay, came out in the *Independent* with a statement, "the Cleveland letter," which urged leniency toward the South and support for Johnson.[60]

At this point, Beecher's usually safe moderation backfired. Because most Republicans were closer to Tilton's views than Beecher's, there was a general consternation at his sympathy for the southern "traitors." Even Bowen had to endorse Tilton's editorial policy and allow the scathing editorials that Tilton rained on Beecher's head. Beecher found himself beset on every side by unaccustomed public criticism. "The mail has groaned and travailed in pain with woe-smitten letters," he lamented to a colleague. "One would think I was in Purgatory, and that all ministers were come to lament over me, or rather to suggest that Purgatory was too good for me."[61]

Beecher was hurt by the criticism—especially from Tilton and the *Independent*. After writing a public letter of retraction and apology, the minister notified Bowen of his intention to withdraw the right to all his articles and sermons from the *Independent*.[62] "Toward me," he complained, "the feeling [at the *Independent*] is not grief but ferocity."[63] The tenuous alliance between Beecher and Bowen was now, in 1866, at an end. Beecher had made a powerful enemy—one who would play a crucial role as the scandal emerged.

As a result of this debacle, Beecher, in the fall of 1866, approached his friends the Howards, suggesting they might help him launch a new religious newspaper of his own.[64] Delighted at Beecher's break with Bowen, they immediately formed a publishing company that would be devoted exclusively to the minister's writings. Besides signing him on to a contract for a two-volume biography of Christ, the Howards began making arrangements to purchase a religious weekly, the *Church Union*. With their encouragement, Henry Ward Beecher also signed a contract to write his first novel—a project that was to bring him and Elizabeth Tilton together.

Henry Bowen could only fulminate inwardly. Bowen had brought Beecher to Brooklyn, paid his debts, and given him the forum on which his popularity was built. Now, this same man had seduced his wife, robbed the *Independent* of the Beecher name, its most important asset, and reduced Plymouth Church to a mass of sycophants and sentimental gush. But Bowen had no intention of giving up. He still thought of Plymouth Church as "his" church (he later told a reporter that he had been there before Beecher and he "intended" to be there after him).[65] The *Independent* increased in circulation even without Beecher, thanks to the growing popularity of Theodore Tilton. So Bowen continued his denunciations of Beecher to Tilton and a few friends, but said nothing publicly.

After 1866, as personal conflict and economic rivalry intensified within the church, the existence of "parties" caused Beecher considerable anguish. Each of these parties pressured the minister to espouse its particular view—making it difficult for Beecher to achieve what he desired above all else: universal approval and love.[66]

The first of the three parties consisted of younger men—journalists and reformers like Theodore Tilton. These men wanted Beecher to take an even more liberal religious position, and a more radical political and social stand. They were not happy with Beecher's habit of flirting with radical positions without making definitive declarations. A characteristic example of Beecher's infuriating equivocal radicalism was his involvement in what became known as the MacFarland scandal. In 1869 New York papers were full of this intricate affair. In December of that year, Beecher had been asked to perform a marriage ceremony between a divorced woman, Mrs. MacFarland, and her lover, Thomas Richardson. At the time of the marriage, Richardson lay on his deathbed, having been shot by Mrs. MacFarland's husband. The issue centered on whether it was moral for a divorced woman to remarry. In addition, many people questioned whether the divorce was legal at all, because it had been granted in Indiana, a state notoriously lenient in its divorce laws. If the couple had not really been divorced, Beecher would be a party to bigamy. The minister, however, in accordance with his own beliefs in the romantic basis of marriage, performed the ceremony.[67] Tilton, in the *Independent,* applauded the minister's decision. [68] But most church members were appalled. This was carrying liberality too far. Capitulating to the majority, Beecher backed down and issued an apologetic statement. By this time, however, Tilton and his radical allies in the church were vocal in their criticism.

A second party led by Henry Bowen and his friends believed that Beecher's tremendous influence was subverting the traditional principles not only of Congregationalism, but of the Republican Party. They interpreted both these institutions as founded on inviolable principles. For this conservative group there was a "right" way to think and believe that transcended popularity. Although they had admired Beecher's aggressive style in winning converts, they were now afraid that he had gone too far. This was the minority of twenty-five that had voted in 1871 against Beecher's elimination of the Articles of Faith as an admission requirement for church membership. One reason for their small numbers was that many of them had become so disturbed by Beecher's preaching that they had returned to the Church of the Pilgrims or joined the newly founded Clinton Avenue Congregational Church. Those few who remained in Plymouth Church were, like Bowen, among the oldest, most prestigious members. They could not be ignored with impunity. Now, worried over the "man-worship" apparent in Beecher's religious services, they criticized his willingness to abjure both religious doctrine and party distinctions. [69] Like Beecher's father, this group accepted change only within the limits of tradition.

The resemblance of the interior of Plymouth Church to a theater did not fail to draw criticism from its opponents. Beecher's dramatic style, the lack of a pulpit, and the noisy responses of his audiences were shocking to orthodox Congregationalists. (Courtesy American Antiquarian Society, Worcester, Mass.)

The third faction, consisting of Beecher's most ardent disciples, was the largest. It was led by the Howard family, Benjamin Tracy, and Thomas Shearman. Tracy and Shearman would eventually act as lawyers in the trial of 1875: Tracy was also to figure prominently in the Brooklyn political struggles that became entangled with the scandal. Both Tracy and Shearman, fiercely loyal to their minister, saw no distinction between Beecher and the church. In fact, in church meetings, Shearman and Tracy consistently sanctioned Beecher's personal control over church policy.[70]

Benjamin Tracy, in particular, exemplifies the kind of parishioner who remained loyal to Beecher. Born in a small upstate New York town, Tracy was first apprenticed to a private law office, then served in the Civil War. After the war he settled in Brooklyn and, as a reward for his loyalty to the state Republican machine, was appointed United States District Attorney. Like the majority of Beecher's parishioners in 1870, he was young—in his mid-thirties—and a recent arrival in Brooklyn. Awed by the confusion and anonymity of city life, Tracy had written to a friend that he needed the position of United States Attorney, not for any "pecuniary compensation" but because it would serve to "distinguish" him from "the great mass of mankind by which I am surrounded."[71] The Tracys in Plymouth Church were struggling with the same anonymity that threatened Tilton but they found an easier solution—one that more closely resembled Beecher's. Rather than holding themselves to the highest standards in both private and public life, Tracy's decision was to pursue morality only within the private sphere. Thus, Beecher's judgment that "private" character was more important than public behavior served to justify business or political practices that had once been morally or ethically reprehensible. Beecher, for example, excused Boss Tweed's public corruption on the grounds that the political and social system made corruption inevitable. What was important was Tweed's unimpeachable behavior as a good family man and loyal friend.[72] In the same vein, Tracy was once quoted as saying that "lying is justified" in defense of a good friend.[73] Thus, Tracy's "ideology" centered on personal loyalty and friendships rather than identification with any specific political or religious theoretical constructs.

The large numbers of church members who sympathized with the Howard-Tracy-Shearman faction could only make Henry Bowen more and more of an outcast. By January 1870, Beecher's new religious paper, the *Christian Union,* began to be published, further threatening the *Independent*'s circulation. Beecher had changed the name from the *Church Union* to signify disdain for organized religious bodies, announcing in the initial issue that he intended to put aside any discussion of the "external forms" of society. What mattered, said Beecher, was not an individual's beliefs, intellectual attainments, morality, or principles, but rather, his "heart."[74]

For Bowen, it seemed an overwhelming defeat. Although he had made a peace of sorts with Beecher early in 1870 in which the minister had once again allowed his sermons to appear in the *Independent,* the *Christian Union* promised to be formidable competition. Because of his animosity toward Beecher he was no longer welcome in Plymouth Church. In January 1870, Henry Bowen, although retaining membership in Plymouth Church, shifted his focus from the religious to the political arena, creating an interplay of religious and political factionalism in Brooklyn that was to transform the scandal into a symbol for social and cultural conflict.

6

The Scandal and Local Politics:
The "Radical Rumpus"

IN JANUARY 1870 Henry Bowen bought the controlling interest in Brooklyn's Republican newspaper, the *Union*. In doing
so he enlarged the economic and ideological rivalry between
him and the Howard-Tracy faction in Plymouth church from
the church itself to Brooklyn politics. Joseph Howard had been city editor
of the Democratic *Eagle* and his family was still connected with that paper.
During the late 1860s and early 1870s, there was an intense rivalry between the two political parties and the papers that represented them. Indeed, when the Beecher affair erupted, a small weekly newspaper claimed
that it was this journalistic-political rivalry that lay at the root of the
scandal![1]

Although the Brooklyn *Sunday Press* was certainly wrong in asserting
that the scandal was entirely the result of such a rivalry, it was accurate in
pointing out the connection between the newspaper war and the public
disclosure of the scandal. Not only was the affair used in the political mud-
slinging, it helped shape the outcome of a crucial political contest. However, what is more important, the ideology of the contending factions in
Brooklyn, together with their attitudes toward Beecher and the scandal,
reveal profoundly contradictory beliefs concerning the basis of leadership
and social organization in family, church, and party. It was these compet-
ing sets of social values that, no less than the sexual affair between Henry
Ward Beecher and Elizabeth Tilton, created the scandal. It is therefore imperative that we understand the development of these opposing ideas in
Brooklyn political alignments.

In the years since Henry Ward Beecher's arrival in 1848, as Brooklyn
had been transformed from a Yankee-Dutch village into the country's
third largest city, it had also come to be dominated by an immigrant machine government.[2] The voting strength that sustained the Democratic machine rested primarily with the Irish, who constituted about a third of the
population. The aldermen and most local elected officials were politicians

under the control of the local boss, Hugh McLoughlin. Originally a foreman at the Brooklyn Navy Yard, by the 1860s McLoughlin was in undisputed command of the Democratic machine—and as such, was openly recognized and supported by the city's largest daily newspaper, the *Eagle*.[3]

Founded in 1841, the *Eagle* was so assured of its pre-eminent position and widespread circulation that its attitude toward Brooklyn's Republican-Protestant minority on the Heights was one of amused toleration.[4] Perceiving no threat from Beecher, *Eagle* editor Thomas Kinsella befriended the minister and wrote sympathetically about him in the paper.[5] In any case, Kinsella found it easy to support the minister, because, much as Beecher might criticize corruption in the abstract, he made it a policy never to interfere directly in local politics.[6]

Until the 1870s, many of the New Englanders who lived on Brooklyn Heights were satisfied with maintaining this distance from local politics. Refusing to acknowledge the growing resemblance of Brooklyn to New York City, Brooklynites claimed that their city had managed to maintain a small-town atmosphere which excluded the evils of New York—crowding, poverty, prostitution, corruption. At the same time they were proud of the commercial and industrial productivity that had increased to equal if not surpass that of New York City. Brooklyn, they insisted, boasted the best of two worlds; the sobriquet "the city of churches" indicated the superior moral virtue of their city.[7]

In reality, however, this idea of Brooklyn applied only to the suburban community of Brooklyn Heights. While this small area of the city did retain its upper-middle-class New England character, elsewhere a burgeoning immigrant population, with its resultant poverty and ethnic hostilities, had created urban problems very much like New York's. The Republican newspaper, the *Union*, however, customarily ignored local issues and politics before 1870, preferring to focus on national problems such as the Civil War and Reconstruction. This left the concern for development of services in the rapidly expanding city—roads, sanitary collection, police and fire departments, and schools—to Hugh McLoughlin and his "saloon keeper" aldermen.[8]

During the first four months of the *Union* under Henry Bowen's supervision (January-April 1870) this national orientation continued, and the paper was not particularly successful. Despite editorial appeals to all good Republicans to subscribe, most residents of Brooklyn, Democrats and Republicans alike, still read the *Eagle*. *Eagle* editor Thomas Kinsella wrote contemptuous editorials ridiculing the "amateur" newspaper.[9] Finally Bowen made a shrewd decision which ensured the success of the *Union*,

Henry C. Bowen

but at the same time laid the groundwork for the public exposure of the long-simmering personal conflicts within Plymouth Church: he hired Theodore Tilton as the paper's editor. From a business perspective it was a wise choice. Following the defection of Beecher in 1866 from the *Independent,* Tilton—surprisingly—had made that paper more popular than ever before. His highly personal, sometimes caustic style had increased circulation. Though his sympathetic treatment of social radicalism disturbed some readers, his professional ability was undeniable.

Immediately upon becoming editor in 1870, Tilton made a dramatic shift in the paper's editorial policy. Abandoning the long-standing tradition of ignoring local issues, he set out to reform corrupt machine politics in Brooklyn. Bowen heartily applauded his new editor's attacks on the Democrats and Boss McLoughlin; it was a different matter, however, when Tilton began to criticize "spoilsmen" and "patronage" politics in the Republican Party as well. Bowen was outraged. Ironically, Tilton had moved from faulting Beecher's opportunism to hinting that Bowen was guilty of the same methods in politics! An overt split between the two eventually took place when Bowen's friend, E. D. Webster, ran as a Republican for Congress in the mid-term elections that November. Bowen naturally insisted that the *Union* support his candidacy; Tilton defiantly refused.[10]

Not alone in his defiance of Bowen, Tilton was supported by a newly formed group of Republican reformers. The "Liberals," as they called themselves, objected to Webster because he was the "known and recognized dispenser of federal patronage in this city."[11] The Liberal Republicans of Brooklyn patterned themselves after the national reform movement of the same name that had been organized by Carl Schurz in Missouri. Appalled by the increasing political corruption—both national and local—they railed at the selfish personalism that was rapidly beginning to dominate the political climate. Liberals hoped to restore principles and ideology to politics. Concluding that too much energy had gone into preserving radical military Reconstruction in the South, they thought the party should shift its attention to fighting corruption in government. They were also impatient with the tendency of many Republicans to ignore the pressing issues of the day and to rely on the "bloody shirt" to win elections.[12]

Dominated by merchants and professional men hitherto aloof from local politics, the Liberal Republican organization of Brooklyn declared its intention of fighting for reform in the local arena by nominating the "best men" and emphasizing honesty and educational qualifications rather than blind party loyalty.[13] In short, they proposed to restore ideology to politics. This was a particularly appealing concept for Theodore Tilton; it was reminiscent of the principled stand taken by the abolitionists. In 1870, however, there was no such clearly defined principle at stake. In the context of Brooklyn politics, the Liberals' claim to power based on their superior education and moral character sounded suspiciously elitist. Indeed, it was recognized as such by Boss McLoughlin who insisted that even though these were personally "good" men, they had never done anything for the city of Brooklyn.[14]

The members of Brooklyn's elite who had rallied to the Liberal Republican banner now set out to change that image. Claiming that Bowen's Republican organization had become more interested in dispensing federal patronage than in winning local elections, this group nominated an alternative to Webster as a candidate for Congress.[15] Tilton agreed to support him in the *Union*.[16]

Now threatened by Tilton's popularity, Kinsella of the *Eagle* observed with relish the editor's defection to the rebellious wing of the Republican Party. The *Eagle* lent its wholehearted support to the Liberals, denouncing Bowen and Webster as the "great carpetbaggers."[17] When Webster and the Liberals' candidate were defeated in the November 1870 election, local Republicans were more than ever divided, confused, and disorderly.[18] The

Union became the butt of ridicule from the spectacle of its editor and owner at odds with each other. As Republican recriminations and subsequent
jockeying for power within the party ensued, Kinsella and the *Eagle*
looked on with amusement and delight.

Although the Liberals had failed in the election and in unseating Bowen,
they had broken the ground for another group of younger Republicans
who would challenge and eventually usurp Bowen's power. This faction
was led by Benjamin Tracy, Beecher's future lawyer as well as his close
friend and supporter in Plymouth Church. As we have seen, the forty-four-
year-old Tracy was a relative newcomer to Brooklyn, having arrived in
1866 from a small town in upstate New York. As far as can be ascertained
from Tracy's public or private papers, he was primarily and exclusively
committed to his own interests and power. Even his sympathetic biographer describes him as a "personal" politician who never felt bound by party principles and platforms.[19] Despite Tracy's recent entry into Republican
politics his prospects for replacing Bowen were considerably enhanced
after the bolt of the Liberals and the defection of Tilton.

Essentially, then, the three factions that had worried Beecher so much in
Plymouth Church had now been roughly replicated, in both personnel and
ideology, in the larger framework of Brooklyn Republican politics. Tilton
and the Liberals were temporarily united as idealists who hoped to unite
public and private spheres in social and political institutions based on ideology and honesty; Bowen and his faction were older men who had been
willing to back, even emulate Beecher's personal approach to religion and
politics, but were now fearful that too many traditions had been eroded;
Benjamin Tracy and the regular Republicans seemed nearly identical to the
largest group in Plymouth Church who sought to extend to politics the system of personal loyalties Beecher stood for in the church.

Now under attack from two sides—the idealists and the practical politicians—Bowen decided in mid-November 1870 to bolster his position with
a personal visit to President Grant. The issue involved the appointment of
a new assessor in Brooklyn. If Grant could be persuaded to appoint
Bowen's choice instead of one advocated by Tracy, his credibility might be
restored.[20] When Grant refused his request, Bowen returned to Brooklyn
empty handed. For a time, however, in early December it looked as though
Bowen might retain a semblance of his old power. On December 7, at the
first post-election meeting of the Republican General Committee, Bowen
mustered enough support—including Tilton's, whom he seems to have
persuaded to return to the fold—to dominate the meeting.[21]

It is impossible to say with certainty why Tilton supported Bowen at this point, but it was probably related to his contract renewal. Bowen had just informed him of his removal as editor of the *Independent*.[22] Even though he was slated to remain as editor of the *Union*, Tilton saw the possibility of losing both positions; it was at this same time that he was under great pressure to pay the mortgage on his new house.[23] Agreeing to support Bowen once again, Tilton signed his new contract on December 20, 1870.[24]

This renewal of Tilton's backing did not improve Bowen's situation significantly, however. By December 22, he angrily accused the Liberals of conspiring with the Tracy faction *and* the Democrats to oust him from the General Committee. Further, Bowen charged that the Tracy group was envious and wanted to "control the Federal patronage," thus implicitly conceding that his own power rested on that control.[25] Feelings on both sides ran high when that same day the Republican Committee met to select delegates for the coming year; the meeting was unusually well attended. Tensions built to a final shocking climax when a close friend of Bowen's struck a Tracy partisan a smashing blow in the face![26] This violence—the *Eagle* called it the "radical rumpus"—sprang from panic; Bowen's faction was clearly losing out to Tracy's.

In this charged atmosphere, a confrontation took place between Bowen and Tilton that combined the sexual scandal, Plymouth Church factionalism, and political conflict. Four days after the incidence of violence, Bowen summoned Tilton to his home. He had heard, Tilton said later, some "prejudicial" rumors. Later, at the trial, Beecher's lawyers would suggest that the meeting concerned Tilton's illicit relations with several married women, but it seems more likely, from the recent political differences between the two, that Bowen was still worried over Tilton's sympathy with the insurgent Republicans. Apparently this issue was at least partially resolved —most likely by Tilton's reassurances of loyalty—and the conversation turned to the treatment of Plymouth Church in the *Union*. Noting the damage done to the *Independent* by Beecher's absence from its columns, Bowen suggested that Tilton "make more of Plymouth Church" in the *Union*. Tilton first refused, but when Bowen insisted, his pent-up agitation surfaced: Beecher, he told his employer, had seduced Elizabeth! After her confession six months ago, he told Bowen, he had promised to protect her and had said nothing to anyone, including Beecher. Yet, just a few weeks ago, the minister had had the audacity to advise Elizabeth to seek a divorce! Now in a state of feverish excitement, Tilton declared that he could not be expected to write favorably about Plymouth Church.[27]

Angered by political setbacks, Bowen saw he had an opportunity for revenge in another arena: Plymouth Church. Now he could strike at Beecher with more than rumors; here was concrete evidence of gross sexual immorality. Hastily changing his tactics, Bowen persuaded Tilton to write a letter demanding that Beecher resign from Plymouth Church. Although not signing the letter, Bowen assured Tilton of his support: he even offered to deliver it personally.[28] In the excitement of the moment, Bowen perceived a real chance to prove something against Beecher with no risk to himself, an opportunity to rid Plymouth Church—*his church*—of Henry Ward Beecher. In addition this would have the happy effect of discrediting the rival *Christian Union,* and possibly, or at least so Bowen must have hoped, undermining Benjamin Tracy's growing influence in Brooklyn politics.

But the later events of that same day and the next indicated that Bowen had made a hasty and unsound judgment. Upon receiving the threatening letter, Beecher did not seem to be intimidated. Further complications arose when Tilton threatened to reveal Bowen's role in the composition of the letter to Beecher.[29] If this happened, Bowen himself could be the one ruined. Consequently, the day after delivering the letter, Bowen attempted to retreat. He "excitedly" called on Tilton at the *Union* office. With "unaccountable emotion" and "livid with rage," Tilton said, Bowen threatened in a "loud voice" to "deprive" Tilton of his position and have him "ejected" by force from the office.[30]

However, an agitated Bowen did not wait to find out whether Tilton would keep quiet, but immediately dismissed him from both the *Independent* and the *Union.* Tilton's worst fears were now realized. He had been manipulated, humiliated, and finally, fired. In desperation, Tilton blamed Henry Ward Beecher for the loss of his wife, his job, and his reputation. It was now Tilton's turn to act in panic. On December 29, 1870, he angrily insisted that Elizabeth produce a written version of the confession she had made verbally six months before. Assuring her that he would not make the document public, Tilton said he only wanted to enlist the minister's influence in winning reinstatement. The next evening Moulton appeared at Plymouth Church and informed Beecher that the affair with Elizabeth was now documented with written evidence. With Moulton's offer to arbitrate began the conspiracy to cover up the scandal, which is examined more closely in chapter 9.[31]

For Henry Bowen, the results of this imbroglio were disastrous. His enraged outburst and dismissal of Tilton signified not only the strain of the previous few months, but also his defensive position. With his future as Republican party leader in jeopardy, the success of both the *Independent* and the *Union* in doubt, and the overwhelming popularity of Henry Ward Beecher virtually ostracizing him from the church he had created and considered his own, Henry Bowen had lashed out bitterly and irreparably. Despite attempts to make peace with Beecher, Bowen's actions continued only to identify him with an anti-Beecher position that further damaged his influence and reputation. In April 1872, he was persuaded by Moulton —as part of the cover-up—to sign a document known as the Tri-Partite Covenant. In this secret agreement, he, Beecher, and Tilton agreed not to spread rumors about each other; Beecher promised to reinstate Bowen in the church and Bowen was to pay Tilton $7,000 compensation for breaking his contracts.[32]

It was in the midst of this renewed effort by Bowen to re-establish his credibility that Victoria Woodhull published her version of the scandal in *Woodhull & Claflin's Weekly*. Eagerly the Democratic *Eagle* seized the opportunity to blame Henry Bowen—denouncing him for originating unfounded rumors about the preacher. When, in April 1873, some friends of Beecher's decided to publish the Tri-Partite Covenant in the hope it would vindicate the minister, the *Eagle* stridently insisted this document proved Henry Bowen's sole culpability.[33] Finally, as the *Eagle* day after day labeled Bowen "cadavorous, malign, and malicious," the editor, in a dramatic capitulation to his challengers sold the *Union* to the Tracy group![34] This faction had succeeded in eclipsing Bowen's leadership within the party as well as Plymouth Church! Bowen's downfall had been his precipitate action in forcing the scandal issue; it proved to be the mechanism that finally drove him out of Plymouth Church and Brooklyn politics. Officially refusing to give up his pew at Plymouth Church (he would not admit to defeat by Henry Ward Beecher) Bowen actually attended Storrs's more orthodox Church of the Pilgrims.[35] Ironically, Bowen's return to orthodoxy would soon be replicated by many of the same Plymouth Church members who were denouncing him in 1873 and 1874.

With Bowen and Tilton removed from direct participation in Republican party politics, two opposing groups emerged with a new clarity—the Regulars and the Liberals. Led by Benjamin Tracy, the Regulars were the largest and most powerful. Throughout the first half of the 1870s, Tracy's group engaged the powerful Democratic machine in a contest for control of Brooklyn's local government. This was, however, purely a power struggle; there were no real ideological issues at stake. In fact, the underlying similarities between the Republican machine and its Democratic counterpart were far more striking than the surface differences. Both were organizations centered around personal loyalties and reciprocal obligations; both valued loyalty above public honesty and public morality; and both sought power for its own sake.[36] In short, they represented the kind of politics Henry Ward Beecher spoke for when he excused Boss Tweed's corruption as less important than his personal loyalty.

There were good reasons for Beecher's tolerant attitude toward both Boss Tweed and Boss McLoughlin. Most obvious was Beecher's friendship with John and Joseph Howard, who were involved in both the New York and Brooklyn Democratic machines. But more than Beecher's friendship with the Democratic Howard family links the minister to machine politics. There is, for example, the striking similarity of Plymouth Church itself to a political machine. We have seen how the church began as a traditional institution organized around principles that, theoretically at least, it had the power to enforce. Beecher's personal success, however, negated the older traditions and transformed the institution into a religious "machine" for the support of the minister himself. This change became blatantly apparent later when the adultery case came to trial. The members of the church —many of them unconcerned over his guilt—closed ranks behind Beecher and proceeded to crush the opposition. As we shall see, Tilton was exiled from America; Bowen and his friends summarily excommunicated; and Beecher and the financial interests he represented protected.

Political machines, too, had in many cities replaced the principles or issues around which party politics had once revolved. The personal power of the bosses overshadowed party ideals in much the same way that Beecher's popularity overshadowed the principles of Congregationalism. The following description of a city boss could be applied to Beecher: "His road was charted not by signs of moral principles but by political expediency, for the boss tiptoed around Burning Issues with uncanny dexterity."[37] If Boss McLoughlin was a political entrepreneur, Henry Ward Beecher was a religious entrepreneur. Both men were interested in blind obedience and unquestioning loyalty from their constituents. Considering these parallels between Plymouth Church and political machines, it becomes easier to understand Beecher's identification and support for the "machine" faction in both Republican and Democratic parties. Both operated on the basis of personal "affinity."

The minority of Liberals, then, were confronted with the task of challenging not only the Democratic immigrant machine, but the Regular majority of their own party. If anything, the Liberals were more indignant at the spectacle of their own party's operating with the same disregard for honesty and principle that characterized the immigrants. The capitulation of fellow Republicans to personalism and power hunger seemed more reprehensible. In a stunning rejection of their own party, the Liberals, in 1872, chose to form an alliance with the local Democratic machine! This action mirrored the national alliance between Liberals and Democrats in support of the presidential campaign of Horace Greeley.[38]

After Greeley's ignominious defeat, however, and the collapse of the national movement, the Brooklyn Liberal party, still a viable organization, faced a new dilemma. Admitting their discomfort with the Democratic alliance, Liberals argued bitterly over whether the party should continue to ally with the Democrats or rejoin the Republicans. Clearly, the majority of Liberals identified historically with the Republican party, yet objections to the "obnoxious leaders" of the Regulars (Tracy and friends) prevented such a reunion.[39]

It was in the midst of this political impasse that the scandal broke and became national news. All through the summer of 1874, Brooklynites read and talked of little else than the guilt or innocence of Henry Ward Beecher. When the minister appointed several leading members of Plymouth Church to investigate the charges, Benjamin Tracy was chief among them. To the Liberals, this was further confirmation of the corruption of Beecher, Tracy, and the whole Plymouth Church "crowd." In addition, it gave them ammunition to use against Tracy. As the Congressional elections of 1874 approached, Brooklyn Liberals demonstrated their rejection of Tracy and the Regulars. Nominating their own candidate for Congress, they boldly set out to win Boss McLoughlin's support! As a result, the Democratic convention, reported the *Eagle,* was attended by "men of a character which is rarely represented at political conventions." The Liberals, the *Eagle* announced, had won a "startling political coup" when Boss McLoughlin endorsed the Liberal candidate.[40]

For purposes of understanding the public disclosure of the scandal, the Liberal victory itself is less important than what it revealed about the nature of religious and political conflict in Brooklyn.[41] When the Liberals decided to nominate their own candidate for Congress, they submitted to him a petition declaring their support. This petition, containing the signatures of ninety leading Liberals, was published in the *Eagle* on October 26, 1874.[42] This document, with its identification of Benjamin Tracy's opponents, reveals a striking and unmistakable connection between the opponents of "machine" politics and the opponents of Beecherism. Of the ninety Liberals who signed this petition, fully one-third were also members of Beecher's rival church in Brooklyn—the Church of the Pilgrims.[43] Considering the number of churches in Brooklyn, this is a remarkable fact.

This revelation of the congruence of political and religious opposition to Plymouth Church suggests some explanations for previously puzzling aspects of the scandal. In March 1874, Storrs and the Church of the Pilgrims had called a Congregational Council to investigate the internal affairs of Plymouth Church. The council was sharply criticized because it had the effect of highlighting and legitimizing Victoria Woodhull's earlier accusations of Beecher. Why, wondered many, would Richard Salter Storrs desire to add any credence to the ravings of such a disreputable woman? After all, it had been a year and a half since her "bombshell" article; the press had tacitly agreed to ignore her charges and Plymouth Church had quietly "dropped" Tilton from its membership roll.[44] It seemed, at best, out of character for the distinguished Reverend Storrs, despite his generally known criticism of Beecher, to become voluntarily mired in such a sordid affair. For not only did the council bring the matter once again to the public attention, it precipitated the "scandal summer" of 1874. As a response to the council's deliberations, a friend of Beecher's publicly called Tilton a "knave" and a "dog."[45] This insult motivated Tilton to abandon the ongoing cover-up and defend his reputation by confirming Woodhull's accusation of adultery. The whole affair was finally out in the open, not because of Victoria Woodhull, but because of the persistence of Storrs and his church in publicizing it.

The role of the Church of the Pilgrims in making the scandal public has long been ignored by historians who tend to find the flamboyant Woodhull a more dramatic subject than Richard Salter Storrs. This has also necessarily obscured the question of Storrs's motives in calling the council. However, the evidence provided by the Liberal petition—that Beecher's religious as well as Tracy's political opponents were roughly identical —suggests deep-seated patterns underlying the determination of this group to persist in their anti-Beecher efforts, risking the label of scandalmongers. It suggests that Storrs and his parishioners were disturbed by more than a single outrageous incident of adultery. During the council, attacks on Beecher's social philosophy and the stunning success of Plymouth Church were rife.

We now turn to an analysis of these attacks on Beecherism as they emerged in the Congregational Council and in a somewhat more veiled form in the trial. In an examination of the collective characteristics of members of two rival churches, I also will attempt to define the social origins of the conflicts.

7

Two Churches: Money, Power, and Social Conflict in Brooklyn

A N UNDERSTANDING OF the conflict between Beecher's Plymouth Church and Storrs's Church of the Pilgrims as it emerged in the Congregational Council of 1874 is important in any attempt to define the fundamental issues of the scandal. Because most historians have accepted at face value the terms of the debate in the civil trial of 1875, they have neglected to examine closely the role of the Church of the Pilgrims and the council, or to scrutinize carefully the rhetoric of the trial itself. Failure to do either can easily leave one with the impression that the trial served as a forum for a debate over social radicalism—the "woman question," Free Love, or the abolition of marriage.

In fact, although Victoria Woodhull hoped her "bombshell" revelation of 1872 would force Henry Ward Beecher into a position of leadership in what she saw as an inevitable social revolution, there was little chance that such a thing would actually happen. Whatever his private beliefs about affinity and Free Love, Beecher was far too shrewd to associate with the notorious Woodhull. Beecher had been burned once in the arena of social radicalism; he had learned his lesson from the public outrage that resulted in 1869 after he married Mrs. MacFarland to her lover. If the minister had previously harbored any notions as to public readiness for Free Love, this incident disabused him of them.

Theodore Tilton, too, after the scandal became public, attempted to appear as conventional in regard to marriage and religion as Beecher. Although admitting he favored more "lenient" divorce laws, Tilton insisted that this change, far from destroying marriage, would simply strengthen the institution by ensuring that *all* marriages would be based on spiritual affinity. He had always, he insisted, opposed the "evil" of Free Love. Although Victoria Woodhull never testified, Beecher's lawyers called a parade of admitted spiritualists, mediums, and even one communist in an effort to show that Tilton was part of their "circle." The culmination of this strategy came when Stephen Pearl Andrews testified amidst the hoots and laughter of spectators.[1] Indeed, the strategy of *both* sides was to appear absolutely conventional in religious and moral beliefs, while attempting to associate the opposition with such disreputable ideas as spiritualism, Perfectionism, and communism. Thus, few people genuinely believed that proof of Beecher's guilt would mean the downfall of Christianity or the abolition of marriage. No, in Brooklyn, as in the nation, both marriage and Christianity were actually undergoing revitalization in the 1870s.

The issue central to the trial, which was prefigured in the Congregational Council of March 1874, was the source and nature of power—religious, political, and social. This question, as we have seen in the recent political

Plymouth Church. The architecture of Plymouth Church and Church of the Pilgrims expresses the difference in temperament between the members. The simple, expansive lines of Plymouth Church invited openness, sociability, and equality, while the imposing stone and spire of Church of the Pilgrims evoke a somber awe for the dignity and tradition of the past.

Church of the Pilgrims

struggles, had a particular significance for the Brooklyn of 1875. In the heterogeneous and anonymous urban environment of New York and Brooklyn, who should exercise leadership? It was around this issue that Liberal Party and orthodox Christians united in their criticism of Beecher and the machine politicians. The Reverend Richard Salter Storrs and his parishioners (who now included Henry C. Bowen) worried about the growing impotence of Congregational institutions resulting from the personalization of religion by Henry Ward Beecher. The Liberal political reformers (a disproportionate number of whom belonged to the Church of the Pilgrims) had become frightened that political power was being usurped by "machines" that were, in reality, based on personal loyalty and reciprocal obligations. Principle and honesty, it seemed, had become out-dated. The question, as they perceived it, was one of principle and law ver-sus personal power.

Indeed, the arguments addressing this question were the only ones treated seriously at the trial; they were subsumed under the euphemism "character," or in another variation, the "great man" theme. Further-more, this was the only theoretical issue on which lawyers for the defend-ant and the plaintiff substantially disagreed. Briefly stated, Beecher's lawyers made it clear that their client's established fame and popularity should render actual refutation of Tilton's charges unnecessary. All the jury needed to decide, insisted Beecher's lawyer, William Maxwell Evarts, was whether the depraved action was consistent with Beecher's reputa-tion. "I prefer," said the lawyer, "to find in character the refutation of false evidence."[2] Actual facts were not necessary! Evarts was clearly trading up-on Beecher's monumental stature in the eyes of the American public.

Evarts's point was not that Beecher's "noble" nature had prevented him from committing adultery—although he used that argument, too—but rather that his mistakes should be forgiven. In his final summation, Evarts half-jokingly quoted a "lady" admirer of Beecher's who had written that "for a man who had done so much good . . . a little aberration of this kind . . . instead of being excused, should be justified."[3] This idea, of course, had been a common one implicit, if not explicit, in his preaching—the exemp-tion of individuals in the higher sphere from conventional morality. Most of Beecher's parishioners seem to have agreed. One commented, "Whether the insinuations [of adultery] have any foundation or not . . . I shall, as long as I live, look up to him."[4] (Indeed, as we have seen, Henry Bowen, at an earlier date, demonstrated his agreement with this view by keeping quiet about Beecher's seduction of his wife.)

Tilton's lawyers, predictably, disagreed. "The struggle this day," one of them argued, "is between the law and a great character and a great church." Simply because Beecher was popular did not guarantee his inno-cence or place him above the law. Tilton's lawyer hoped to win the case by removing some of the aura that surrounded Beecher as a minister and a hero. The importance of the trial, Tilton's lawyer concluded, was in decid-ing whether society would allow Theodore Tilton to be "hounded to his ruin" by a system of "influence and denunciation and clamor."[5] The real issue, the lawyer insisted, was not Beecher's heroic quality, but rather the support he enjoyed from the wealthy members of Plymouth Church. Defense of Beecher amounted to nothing more than a defense of the raw economic power of his parishioners.

For Tilton then, but even more dramatically for the members of the Church of the Pilgrims, the trial revolved around the legitimacy of Beecher's power and influence. Should his mass appeal be permitted to generate its own definition of right? Did Beecher's ability to inspire loyalty in masses of people justify his influence? Could the wealth of Plymouth Church buy innocence? Was Beecher's sheer magnetism, charisma, and physical appeal sufficient to make him infallible in the public eye? And did this mean that there was no longer any respect for tradition or education in American society? Or, as the leaders of the Church of the Pilgrims and the Liberals of Brooklyn hoped, did there still exist some intellectual and moral standards that might form the foundations of society? If there were not, reformers like Tilton and traditionalists like Richard Salter Storrs were doomed to impotence. For quite different reasons, each of these groups felt impelled to mount a public assault on Henry Ward Beecher and Plymouth Church.

The trial was a challenge, not merely to Beecher, but to society itself for the arbitrary and capricious manner in which it treated leaders. In a single stroke, Tilton had been stripped of his livelihood, his reputation, and his social status; just as he had once felt that his success was undeserved, so now he knew that his ruin was unwarranted. Henry Ward Beecher was merely an example of the irrationality of popular sentiment. This may help explain why Tilton felt compelled to press charges against Beecher when he must have known that the facts about his own personal life would also come to light. With his reputation and influence in shambles, Tilton's rage for revenge overwhelmed his need to conceal his own sexual indiscretions. In a similar way, Storrs and his flock were willing to risk being labeled "scandal-mongers" in order to destroy Beecher's power.

On one level, Tilton's frustration with the Plymouth pastor made perfect sense to Richard Salter Storrs, the members of the Church of the Pilgrims, and the Liberal Republicans of Brooklyn. It was not that they had any sympathy with Tilton, for he as well as Beecher had violated their moral code, but his experience with the irrationality of "popular sentiment" mirrored their own plight in Brooklyn society.

Storrs himself epitomizes the kind of man who was frustrated by the ascendancy of personalism and emotionalism in Brooklyn. Born in Braintree, Massachusetts, the neighbor of such illustrious families as the Adamses, the Quincys, and the Hancocks, Storrs carried on a ministerial

The Reverend Richard Salter Storrs

tradition of four generations. After graduating from Andover Theological
Seminary, he had been called in 1846, at the age of twenty-five, to the
Church of the Pilgrims in Brooklyn Heights. There he soon gained a reputation for unruffled dignity, tempered orthodoxy, and a scholarly manner.[6] Unlike Henry Ward Beecher, Storrs treasured the authority conferred
on Congregationalism by its long history. Although his theological doctrine was clearly "liberal," his scholarly, dignified, and tradition-bound
manner labeled him "orthodox."

By 1875, Storrs's Church of the Pilgrims had grown to 720 members,
largely New York merchants and their families who formed the stable,
loyal core of the church. It would seem to be a success story—except for
the incredible mushrooming of Plymouth Church after the advent of
Henry Ward Beecher. Within five years of his arrival in 1847, Beecher had
attracted the same number of parishioners that Storrs would attract in
thirty![7] Beecher rarely wrote a sermon—he usually preached from one-
page outlines—but he elicited a remarkably spontaneous, emotional response.[8] Storrs was not a jealous or vindictive man, but he did want to

learn how to be more successful at his calling—so he began to preach without notes. The response of his congregation was less than enthusiastic—he could not seem to communicate his thoughts without a written manuscript. After sporadic attempts, he gave up the technique entirely and accepted his limitations.[9] Neither the liberalizing of this theology nor the exhibition of his logical mind produced a response similar to that inspired by Henry Ward Beecher.

Although Storrs accepted and developed his own style, he seemed later to regret the lack of spontaneity, "where no pervading and animating spirit transforms what is written into a quickening personal message . . . and where the element, however indefinable, which changes words into powers, and makes sentences surprise us with fine inspirations, is palpably wanting."[10] Nevertheless, Storrs was a "gentleman" in every way. He had been raised and steeped in the traditional orthodoxy of New England, yet had managed to adapt to the confusion of urban life with intelligent dignity. But it was increasingly frustrating to see Beecher's vulgar emotionalism exert such influence upon Protestants of Brooklyn. His parishioners seemed also to share his ambivalence of revulsion and envy at the power commanded by popular demagoguery and money. From Storrs's perspective, those were the only two things that accounted for the success of Beecher and those like him.

In his opening speech to the council, Storrs dealt directly with the issue of "scandal-mongering." Vigorously denying that his action was motivated by envy or jealousy, he explained that the issues at stake transcended the sordid nature of the scandal. "The case itself was remarkable," he said, "but the principles involved in it are more remarkable still." In essence, Storrs contended, Congregationalism was a system that necessarily depended upon historical tradition. Its rules, usages, and laws had to be "believed, by those who live in it and love it." Although Plymouth Church called itself a Congregational church, it had not acted in accordance with Congregational principles. If Plymouth Church represented Congregationalism, said Storrs, then "that which our fathers knew, and loved, and honored, no more exists . . . the system has already gone to pieces."[11]

This rhetoric may seem excessive in terms of the single error on the part of Plymouth Church of dropping Tilton; yet it makes perfect sense when considered in the light of Beecher's rejection of *all* religious tradition, doctrine, and principle—and his reliance on his own personality to create a following. From Storrs's perspective, Plymouth Church was in reality no church at all. Tilton's attorney thundered out what genteel Storrs could only hint at. What goes on at Plymouth Church, he charged, ". . . is not an

orderly, spirit-broken, prayerful worship; it is not a service which holds up
Christ and Him crucified; but it is a performance which exhibits Beecher
and him glorified. Throughout all his sermons are scattered minutes of
noisy applause and laughter."[12] Beecher, according to Storrs, had already
dissolved his church as an "organized body," making it into an "incoherent assembly in attendance upon a particular ministry."[13]

The leading Liberal Republicans of Brooklyn, who were also Church of
the Pilgrims members must have agreed, for as we have seen, they were in
the midst of a political struggle to rid the city of parties based on "bossism." And Storrs, obviously aware of the political activity of many of his
parishioners, extended his criticism beyond the religious sphere. "The
same principle [of social organization]," he continued, "applies everywhere, if it is admitted as proper anywhere." Thus, if Beecher's flouting of
the rules, usages, and laws of Congregationalism were carried into other
areas, "it would dissolve human society itself, and chaos would result."[14]
Richard Salter Storrs and his parishioners must have felt, from their perspective in Brooklyn, that the basic institutions of American society were
on the road to disintegration!

What this emotional rhetoric about impending social and ecclesiastical
collapse suggests is its personal basis. Although Church of the Pilgrims
members were not—like Tilton—in immediate danger of actual "ruin,"
they were overwhelmed and personally threatened by the success of the
Benjamin Tracy group. Worse, from the perspective of the Liberal Republicans and the Church of the Pilgrims, Plymouth Church, as well as the men
who had come to dominate Brooklyn politics, were of low, undisciplined,
and uneducated social background—upstarts whose lack of education, refinement, and regard for tradition threatened to destroy the social order.
Although disturbed by the gains of immigrant politicians, the Liberals
were even more directly threatened by those native-born Americans whose
new wealth enabled them to pose a more immediate danger to the "gentlemen" of the old school.

In this context, Storrs's allusions to the lack of "discipline" and "standards" in Plymouth Church surely referred to the fear of social amalgama-
tion encouraged by Beecher's mass appeal. The most flagrant example of
this disregard for necessary social distinctions, many of Beecher's critics
felt, was Plymouth Church's system of pew rental.

The practice of assigned seats in church had a long history in New England. Throughout the colonial period, the seat any individual occupied in
the church was a clear indication of his status within the community. Up to
the Revolutionary period, seating was usually done by a committee ap-

pointed by the town or church; in the seventeenth century the committee simply assigned seats with no instructions or written criteria from the town—presumably everyone knew the social rank of each member. In the eighteenth century, however, when social status in New England was becoming somewhat more fluid, committees often recorded their criteria in order of importance. The criteria usually included age, wealth, and the still undefined social rank. Even then, however, there were often arguments over whether to define social rank by birth or by wealth.[15]

Now, in Plymouth Church, there was again no more debate over how to "seat" the church. Each year, during the first week in January, Plymouth Church held a "pew auction." A professional auctioneer was hired to make it an evening of entertainment as well of church business. Anyone, church member or not, was eligible to bid for a pew; the highest bidder in each round chose any pew in the church for the coming year. The front and center pews went for the highest premiums because they were traditionally the most prestigious.[16] In colonial New England, sitting in the front would indicate a generally acknowledged social status; in Brooklyn, it indicated the accumulation of a great deal of money.

There was wide criticism of this practice, not just from Storrs, but from many churches in Brooklyn. It was said to be the clearest indication that Plymouth Church had abandoned all spiritual standards. Money should not buy religion, status, power; that in itself was scandalous! Yet it was the openness with which Plymouth Church flaunted the power of money that was particularly revolting to the Church of the Pilgrims. They, too, had their own pew rental system in which higher prices were paid for the more prestigious pews, but it was done in private, discreetly.

In probing the ideological and temperamental differences between Storrs and Beecher, one is also struck by the social and economic disparity between the membership of the two great Congregational churches of Brooklyn: Plymouth Church and the Church of the Pilgrims. Is it possible to systematically establish the underlying differences between these two groups, which superficially, to a later generation, seemed so similar? Contemporary observers noted that the Church of the Pilgrims had a reputation for a membership of "marked intellectual ability, high social influence and financial strength."[17] In contrast, Plymouth Church was characterized as a "cross-section" of America, or the "great middle class."[18] Were these contemporary impressions correct and did they, in reality, form the basis for social conflict in the scandal? Or was it true as some recent historians have asserted that Plymouth Church was the stronghold of wealth and status in Brooklyn Heights?[19]

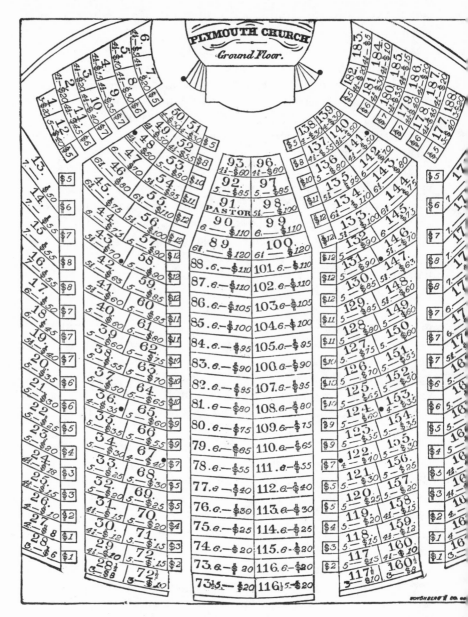

Unembarrassed by the direct connection between religion and money, Plymouth Church, in 1872, proudly published its pew-rental chart.

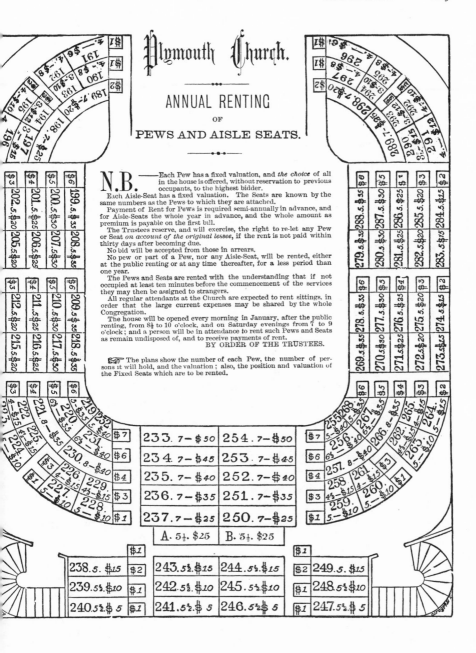

Plymouth Church.

ANNUAL RENTING

OF

PEWS AND AISLE SEATS.

N.B.——Each Pew has a fixed valuation, and *the choice* of all in the house is offered, without reservation to previous occupants, to the highest bidder.

Each Aisle-Seat has a fixed valuation. The Seats are known by the same numbers as the Pews to which they are attached.

Payment of Rent for Pews is required semi-annually in advance, and for Aisle-Seats the whole year in advance, and the whole amount as premium is payable on the first bill.

The Trustees reserve, and will exercise, the right to re-let any Pew or Seat *on account of the original lessee*, if the rent is not paid within thirty days after becoming due.

No bid will be accepted from those in arrears.

No pew or part of a Pew, nor any Aisle-Seat, will be rented, either at the public renting or at any time thereafter, for a less period than one year.

The Pews and Seats are rented with the understanding that if not occupied at least ten minutes before the commencement of the services they may then be assigned to strangers.

All regular attendants at the Church are expected to rent sittings, in order that the large current expenses may be shared by the whole Congregation.

The house will be opened every morning in January, after the public renting, from 8½ to 10 o'clock, and on Saturday evenings from 7 to 9 o'clock; and a person will be in attendance to rent such Pews and Seats as remain undisposed of, and to receive payments of rent.

BY ORDER OF THE TRUSTEES.

☞ The plans show the number of each Pew, the number of persons it will hold, and the valuation; also, the position and valuation of the Fixed Seats which are to be rented.

A comparison of the members of the Church of the Pilgrims and Plymouth Church does bear out the class differences described by contemporary observers. With the help of a group of undergraduates, I was able to locate approximately one-third of the members (in 185 families) of both churches in the Brooklyn City directories and the federal census schedules. The results of the comparison appear in Tables 1–4.[20]

Table 1 compares the average value of real estate and personal property. It is apparent from this table that Storrs's church is far above Beecher's in both categories: the average real estate value of Storrs's members is *triple* that of Beecher's members and the average personal estate of the Church of the Pilgrims is *quadruple* that of Plymouth Church. This evidence must be qualified, however, because in urban areas in 1870 many people may have simply refused to state their property values at all. For example, some members of both churches whom other evidence shows to be wealthy have *no* property listing at all. This discrepancy is most likely explained by the fact that the higher one's social status the less one would feel compelled to reveal information to the census taker.

Table 2, which categorizes the occupations of church members, confirms the fact that Storrs's members were primarily from the upper class and the upper-middle class of Brooklyn. Merchants, manufacturers, and professionals such as lawyers and physicians made up sixty percent of the church. This is a remarkably homogeneous and stable group both in occupation and geographic location. Table 3 shows that fifty percent of Storrs's members lived in Brooklyn but actually worked in New York. (Small wonder they took so long to awaken to the necessity of assuming an active role in Brooklyn politics!) Table 3 also demonstrates that sixty-four percent of the members resided in the Brooklyn Heights section of the city. Not only were the members of the Church of the Pilgrims isolated by their connections with New York from their home city, they were insulated, as well, from the surrounding rings of lower-class and immigrant areas. (See map, page 108.)

In marked contrast to the wealth and homogeneity of the Storrs group were Beecher's parishioners. Here, there was a wide diversity of occupational levels, from merchants to a large percentage of white-collar workers and artisans. The latter two groups, in fact, make up almost forty-five percent of the church. Far from being upper class or even securely middle class, these men were closer to the lower fringes of the middle class. Not only were they a heterogeneous occupational group, but only twenty-five percent of them commuted from Brooklyn to New York. (Perhaps this is one reason that they provided more support for the regular Republicans

Table 1   Economic Status, 1870

	Beecher's church		Storrs's church	
	number	*percent*	*number*	*percent*
Number in sample	130		55	
Number found in census	52	40%	42	76%
Families with no property listing	30	58%	13	31%
Families with some property listing	22	42%	29	69%
Average real-estate value	$19,000		$ 77,000	
Average personal property value	$45,000		$201,000	

Source: United States Census, Ninth Census, 1870, Population Schedules, 1870, Brooklyn, New York, Wards 1–12, 20, 22.

Table 2   Occupational Status, 1870

	Beecher's church		Storrs's church	
	number	*percent*	*number*	*percent*
Merchants and				
Dealers	34	26%	19	35%
Manufacturers	1	1%	3	5%
Professionals	9	7%	11	20%
Small businessmen	14	11%	3	5%
Agents and brokers	9	7%	5	9%
Clerks, bookkeepers	12	9%	3	5%
Artisans and				
Skilled laborers	36	28%	4	7%
Unskilled laborers	3	2%	0	0%
Widows	8	6%	4	7%
Other	4	3%	3	5%
Total	130	100%	55	102%

Source: 1870 Census, Brooklyn, Brooklyn City Directory, 1869–1870

Table 3   Church Cohesiveness, 1870

	Beecher's church	Storrs's church
Percent living on Brooklyn Heights (Wards 1 and 3)	28%	64%
Percent living in newer well-to-do wards (9, 11, 20, 22)	20%	8%
Total percent living in wealthy wards	48%	72%
Percent living in middle-class, mixed, or lower-class wards (2, 4, 5, 6, 7, 10)	38%	20%
Other	14%	8%
Percent who live in Brooklyn but work in New York City	25%	50%

Table 4   Geographic Origins, 1870

	Beecher's church	Storrs's church
New England & New York	64%	87%
Other States	1%	6%
British Isles	35%	7%

Source: 1870 Census, Brooklyn.

than the Storrs group did.) Plymouth Church members generally lived and worked in Brooklyn itself; but more than that, they were scattered throughout the city as Storrs's group was not. Table 3 shows that more than a third (thirty-eight percent) of Plymouth Church members lived in mixed, middle- or lower-class wards. Most historians have treated Beecher's church as strictly a Brooklyn Heights institution, but, in fact, Table 3 shows a surprisingly low figure of twenty-eight percent lived on the Heights; while in contrast, the majority of Storrs's parishioners (sixty-four percent) did live there. It is Storrs's church, not Beecher's, that was more representative of the elite Heights.

Although this portrait of the two groups is revealing, it can also be somewhat misleading. It is a static profile, and Brooklyn society was anything but static. Beecher's parishioners may have been less elite than Storrs's, but many of them were moving up—and they were doing so without any style. After all, approximately a quarter of Beecher's church members *were* rich

—more wealthy, in fact, than Storrs's members. One staunch Plymouthite, H. B. Claflin, received "a larger income from trade" than anyone else in Brooklyn; he also owned the "costliest" residence, having spent "more money than has ever before been expended on a private residence in Brooklyn." Henry Bowen had built a fine white mansion on Willow Street, importing Italian marble, and hiring a sculptor to carve the heads of his children on the furniture. In contrast, a prominent member of Storrs's church and a Liberal Republican leader, Simeon B. Chittenden, was noted, according to a Brooklyn paper, for a "substantial, but rather old-fashioned house on Pierrepont Street."[21] Thus, the homes of Bowen and Claflin might be described as nouveau and ostentatious, while Chittenden's was "substantial" and "old-fashioned"—a graphic illustration of the difference between the contending groups in Brooklyn.

In addition, one occupational category—the professional—further emphasizes the fundamental differences between the two groups. Professionals made up twenty percent of the Church of the Pilgrims, while Beecher's group contained only seven percent. Further, the way in which these professionals prepared for their careers was very different. No quantitative comparison can be made because this kind of background information cannot be obtained from the census but must be located in city and county local histories. However, one indication that Storrs's professionals were of higher social status may be the very fact that more of his members than Beecher's have biographical sketches in Henry R. Stiles, *History of Kings County* (1884). Of those who are included, a few examples are revealing. Two Plymouth Church lawyers, Benjamin Tracy and Thomas Shearman, came from relatively poor backgrounds—Tracy from a small upstate New York town and Shearman from England—and both entered their profession through apprenticeship rather than college training.

The professionals in Storrs's church, on the other hand, had the social advantage and education that Plymouth Church members lacked. One of the leading members of the Church of the Pilgrims was Lucien Birdseye, a lawyer who, according to Stiles, "entered life under auspicious circumstances." Birdseye's father had also been a lawyer and was a representative to Congress well able to send his son to Yale and set him up in a practice in New York. Another member of the Church of the Pilgrims, Francis E. Dana, was the third generation of his family to become a lawyer. He had been born in Brooklyn, attended private schools and Columbia College before studying law with his father. In 1869, Dana married the daughter of Reverend William Ives Budington, minister of one of the wealthiest Congregational churches in Brooklyn. His home in one of the newer "hill" sub-

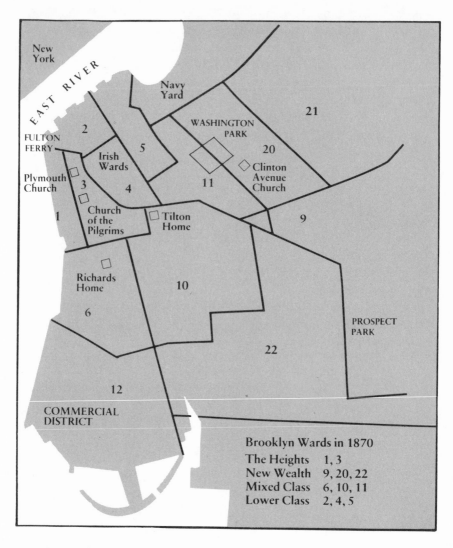

Ward Map of Brooklyn, 1870

urbs, reports Stiles, was "the abode of refinement and culture."[22] Another Storrs member, J. Carson Brevoort, a civil engineer, is also representative. Born in Brooklyn, he was educated in Switzerland and France and served as private secretary to Washington Irving in Spain. Upon his return, he settled in Brooklyn to manage the estate of his father-in-law and act as president of the Long Island Historical Society.[23] These were men who benefited from family influence and resources and, like Richard Salter Storrs himself, could treasure their heritage.

In the light of this collective difference in social origin and education, Beecher's emphasis on *rejecting* a family background if it restrained mobility is understandable. His claim that emotion and intuition were far superior to education encouraged the majority of his parishioners who lacked such advantages. His vindication of aggressive self-interest and forgiveness of occasional moral lapses was surely a comfort to men like Henry Bowen and Benjamin Tracy, whose survival depended upon shrewd calculation and experience in daily business and political struggles. Beecher's parishioners had good reason to be attracted by the positive side of the Gospel of Love and the doctrine of moral affinity that rationalized their efforts to advance socially. In portraying love as a social force (rather than as sexual attraction), Beecher was urging that all personal and social relations be based on the mutual emotional attraction of like natures. Love and affinity, then, were to define not only romantic liaisons, but were also to justify new social class alignments! Theodore Tilton had done that when he rejected his ties with his wife and her family and established affinities with reformers and intellectuals. In this case, moral affinity was a mechanism for social advancement.

Indeed, Beecher's parishioners were mostly young men and women— their average age was thirty-four in 1870—who had migrated to Brooklyn from rural New England and upstate New York towns; the church records indicate a high turnover of membership as these young men came to the city, joined the church, and then, failing to "make it" (as many did), moved on.[24] The wealthy segment, by and large, was the one that prospered in the city and stayed on to demonstrate their gratitude to Beecher. Thus, these were the men who were on the ascendant in Brooklyn, or had reason to hope they soon would be. They, most of all, could appreciate the social freedom Beecher preached because it meant improvement in their "place, business, and repute."[25]

In stark contrast to the Plymouthites were the Liberal Republicans and members of the Church of the Pilgrims, for whom the mobility of mid-nineteenth-century society threatened displacement. Men like Storrs and

Chittenden could not claim the power that came from a mass appeal, but only a status rooted in family standing, education, and historical tradition. And more and more, this tradition was being undermined by the power that wealth could buy. For example, many of the families of Storrs's church had been in Brooklyn Heights since the 1840s when the community was created. As Table 3 shows, sixty-four percent of them lived on the Heights; significantly, only eight percent had moved out to the newer wealthier sections near Washington and Prospect Parks. Storrs's members were proud of their community—it was relatively cohesive and congenial (except for the tourists who gathered every Sunday at Plymouth Church!) and they preferred to keep it that way. However, as two Brooklyn newspapers noted in 1874, the Heights was beginning to decline as a neighborhood. Some commercial enterprises were invading the area and there was a "gradual exodus" of the residents to the new "hill" areas.[26] It was not Storrs's parishioners who were moving out, but Beecher's; Table 3 shows that a higher ratio—twenty percent—of Plymouthites had already moved to these newly developed areas. The "high intellectual achievement and social standing" of the Church of the Pilgrims was not preventing the gradual erosion of their community as well as their power and influence. The world, they must have thought, was being taken over by the likes of Benjamin Tracy, Boss McLoughlin, and Henry Ward Beecher.

Thus, the conflict between these two social groups in Brooklyn during the 1870s was not so much a limited conflict over a single issue but rather a much broader one, in which each group failed to understand the goals and fears of the other. The irony is that Beecher and his parishioners never hoped to eclipse their friends and neighbors at the Church of the Pilgrims. Indeed, they hoped the accumulation of money would raise them to the level of respectability and refinement historically enjoyed by the Storrs group. For Storrs's members, however, the challenge was to retain or recapture the influence that they perceived was due their superior status and education.

Moral affinity and social freedom, to these men, smacked more of social humiliation and defeat than of opportunity. Therefore, their concern was different from that of Plymouth Church members; they were anxious to reestablish social order and social control. Beecher's doctrine of affinity could, they thought, only lead to social chaos. To them, the parallels Storrs had suggested between the erosion of authority in family, church, and polity was a valid one. The very basis for organization of these institutions had been altered by Beecherism. Plymouth Church had become an "incoherent assembly"; the family a spiritual commune; and the Republican party a "machine" in which there was no attention paid to "principle." It was in such a broad context that Storrs and his parishioners perceived Beecher's adultery not as a single instance of hypocrisy but as representative of a widespread trend toward disguising lust for sex and power with the rhetoric of love and purity.

What Storrs, because of his social background, recognized so readily, however, was not obvious to the men and women of Beecher's congregation. For them, the Gospel of Love stood for freedom, honesty, and upward mobility; a change in that perception would require a more dramatic demonstration of its pitfalls. The scandal, on both its private and public levels, proved to possess just such resonance and ultimately led to a subtle withdrawal from the tenets of the Gospel of Love. It is to that retreat on the part of Beecher's adherents we now turn. In a final examination of the Tiltons' "new marriage" and the ordeal by trial of Plymouth Church we discover a paradigm for the truncated dreams of self-respect and autonomy promised by the Gospel of Love.

8

The Higher Sphere:
Nesting on Brooklyn Heights

WHEN THEY BECAME personally acquainted with Henry Ward Beecher, Elizabeth and Theodore Tilton began to confront those aspects of the minister's ideology that he obscured from the public. Although Beecher preached openly about "higher" and "lower" spheres, and the unnecessary restraints conventional morality imposed on those who were already on the higher plane, he refused to acknowledge his belief in what were essentially the doctrines of Free Love. Beecher did, however, obliquely justify this less than candid approach in 1868: "Those who are on the lower plane—namely the plane where they act from rules—are strongly inclined to believe that those who go higher and act from principles are . . . abandoning right and wrong."[1] In a world in which traditional institutions and morality were being undermined, what was right and what was wrong? And who could make that judgment? The Tiltons were about to confront these questions in a personal struggle.

Not long after Theodore Tilton began working with Beecher at the *Independent,* he had been introduced to the higher sphere. It was Henry Bowen who, in 1862, first informed Tilton of some of the activities going on in this sphere. According to Bowen, Beecher was "guilty of adultery, a practice begun in Indianapolis and continued in Brooklyn."[2] True or not, the information shocked the young idealistic editor. His own upbringing had been as uncompromisingly rigid in its moral standards as in its religious outlook; he recalled his father's counsel on the subject of the great dangers of "undue intercourse" with women.[3] The knowledge of Beecher's indiscretions troubled Theodore more and more as time passed, particularly as he recognized his own weakness in the face of sexual temptation. Elizabeth later testified that her husband talked to her of "Mr. Beecher's wrongdoings with ladies . . . night after night, and day after day." He seemed, she said, "to be worried on that subject."[4]

Although shocked at Bowen's revelations about his idol, Tilton was not prepared to dismiss Beecher as a hypocritical sinner. After all, the minister had been a loving friend, almost a father. The conflict within Tilton manifested itself in 1865 when he let slip to a mutual friend that Beecher had exhibited "certain loose conduct with women."[5] When Beecher reproved him for this gossip, Tilton, full of regret, wrote a letter affirming his unshaken love and faith in his mentor.[6]

The ambivalence this situation engendered considerably aggravated Tilton's existing anxiety over his tenuous social and economic status. He desperately wanted Beecher's friendship—it enhanced his own and the world's image of him—and he wanted to believe in Beecher. Yet the strength of his old values caused doubt. Thus, he behaved toward Beecher in vacillating fashion; continuing to urge the minister to make frequent visits to Elizabeth when he was away on lecture tours, but at the same time fearing the consequences of these calls.

Recognizing that Elizabeth might, despite the "new marriage," be overwhelmed by the famous minister's attention, Theodore became suspicious. "If you should appear to me," he wrote his wife in 1866, "anything less than the ideal woman, the Christian saint that I know you to be, I shall not care to live a day longer!"[7] The jealousy intensified as Elizabeth's letters were more and more filled with glowing references to Beecher. Rebuking her for not accompanying him on one of his lecture tours, Theodore admonished his wife in 1866, "Leave home, children, kith and kin, and cleave unto him to whom you originally promised to cleave. You promised the *other* man to cleave to *me* and yet you leave *me all alone* and cleave to him."[8]

Yet there was a part of Theodore that envied Beecher's apparent sexual freedom and found his arguments for it compelling. The idea that love could not be bound by "mechanical" ties such as blood or marriage vows seemed appropriate to his own situation. As much as Theodore worked at convincing himself that Elizabeth was a "saint," her social and intellectual inferiority annoyed him. Their "new marriage," with its imperatives of "soul-loving" and "affinity," never seemed to approach reality. Was it right, Theodore began to wonder, to be legally chained to someone with whom one had no spiritual bond? What is to be the legal status and the social fate of persons, he questioned, "who find themselves married, but not mated."[9] In the new concept of marriage, the absence of romantic love challenged the validity of the marriage itself.

Thus it was that Theodore, with Beecher as his role model, began to explore his sexual responses to other women. Bessie Turner, a maid in the Tilton household, testified at the trial to an incident that illustrates Tilton's attempts to imitate Beecher. Theodore had come to her room at night, she said, and "stroked" her "forehead and hair . . . putting his hand in my neck." In an effort to quiet Bessie's resistance, Tilton argued, "Why, those caresses, those are all right; people in the best society do all those things, and it is pefectly proper." When Bessie objected further, she later testified, Theodore went on to insist that an affinity between a man and a woman justified its physical expression. Indeed, Tilton said, he himself knew of "ministers that caressed girls and married women—it was all perfectly right and proper and beautiful."[10] This comment makes sense when one recalls Theodore's obsession with social class—his desire to join Henry Ward Beecher's circle.

It is possible that his arguments were intended as much to convince himself as Bessie, for many of his letters to Elizabeth indicate that as much as he tried, Theodore could not bring himself to believe his own rhetoric. But when the lecture tours created an opportunity, Theodore, as we have seen, actually had a sexual affair. The results were devastating. "I once thought myself," he wrote, "a good, true, and upright man. But now . . . I find myself a constant sinner."[11] Although Tilton could emulate Beecher's sexual experimentation, he could not justify it with the minister's arguments. These ambivalent attitudes soon began to create an obsession with sexuality.

While Tilton struggled with the relationship between sexual affinity and social class, Beecher had begun, in the fall of 1866, to call on Elizabeth. Because she was bewildered and intimidated by her husband's constant shifts from adoring worship to verbal abuse, and suffered from social isolation, Elizabeth felt flattered and comforted by the minister's friendship. In the years before her personal acquaintance with Beecher, Elizabeth recalled that at "the mention of his name . . . or better still, a visit from him, my cheek would flush with pleasure." It was, she said, a reaction common to "all his parishioners of both sexes."[12] This was the period when Beecher, writing his novel, was in need of "uncritical praise."[13] Thus Beecher took the chapters of *Norwood* to a "sympathetic" woman who he knew regarded him with "artless familiarity" and "entire confidence."[14]

Elizabeth believed that Beecher had come to her because he really respected her critical abilities. In sadly ironic fashion she later testified to the church committee, "He [Beecher] brought out that in me which Theodore never did . . . assertiveness . . . self-respect . . . I felt myself another woman."[15] In the early months of their friendship, Elizabeth wrote guilelessly to her husband, "I have lived a richer, happier life since I have known him." Yet the same letter hints at the real cause of the rise of Elizabeth's self-esteem—the attention of such a famous and respected man. She hoped that *his* recognition of her would improve her relationship with her husband. "And have you not loved me more ardently," she asked Theodore, "since you saw another higher nature appreciated me?"[16]

As we have seen in her response to the "new marriage," Elizabeth was often more insightful than her husband. This quality was now evident in her relationship with Beecher. Although Elizabeth always contended that, unlike her husband, the minister respected her intellectually, she soon began to understand that the two men had attitudes in common. "I realize that what attracts both of you to me," she wrote Theodore, "is a supposed purity of soul you find in me."[17] Innate "purity" was her unique attribute, rather than her intellect or personality. The basis of that purity, however, Elizabeth had yet to discover.

In addition, although flattered by his attention, Elizabeth was not entirely convinced the minister deserved such admiration. When Theodore related to her the stories of Beecher's sexual adventures, she lamented the "lack of Christian manliness in this beloved man." Writing to Theodore in December 1867, Elizabeth proposed to use her own newly discovered spiritual "purity" to help Beecher see through his "delusion" and rebuild his "Christian manliness." Implying that as early as 1867, Beecher had been making sexual advances, Elizabeth wrote Theodore, "If I, by God's grace, keep myself white, I may bless you both. I am striving." Despite the minister's persuasive arguments, Elizabeth still considered herself sexually bound by her marriage vows; whatever her feelings for Beecher, her duty to Theodore required fidelity. Thus by neither giving Beecher "silly flatteries" nor succumbing to his sexual advances, Elizabeth hoped to demonstrate "the honor and dignity of her sex." In fact, for two years after the minister began to "solicit" her to be a "wife," Elizabeth refused, insisting that no amount of "fascinations" would cause her to "yield" her "womanhood."[18]

But we have seen that when Elizabeth and Theodore's "new marriage" collapsed in bitter arguments in the fall of 1868, Beecher's pursuit of Elizabeth was unwittingly encouraged and reinforced by Theodore himself. It was he, after all, who had convinced Elizabeth of the importance of "soul-loving." Mutual "affinity," he had argued, should transcend legal sanctions, or indeed, any humanly conceived law. When love prevailed, he insisted, a marriage existed; when love disappeared, a divorce had taken place.[19] After the death of their child in August 1868, it was obvious that much as they might extol each other in letters, when they were together, there was neither love nor affinity. Rejected by her husband and mourning over the death of her child, Elizabeth turned increasingly to Beecher for solace and the bolstering of her "self-respect." It is not clear just how much she confided to Beecher about the volatile state of her marriage, but it is likely that she did not hide very much. Indeed, her letters to Theodore often referred to conversations she and Beecher had concerning him. Beecher and Tilton both testified later that Elizabeth could always be depended upon for "truthfulness."[20] Elizabeth began to give consideration to Beecher's sexual overtures and his justification for them.

In the context of Beecher's implicit quasi-perfectionism, it is readily believable that he justified the affair to Elizabeth as "high religious love" though it violated conventional morality.[21] For "morality," he said in a sermon in 1872, "is founded upon external convenience, and not upon the requirements of things relating to man's whole nature."[22] Beecher often stressed the necessary integration of man's physical and spiritual needs. "The abstract (i.e., platonic) doctrine of love would be well enough," he argued, "if men were nothing but spectators."[23] Obviously, Beecher did not intend to be a spectator in love; for its fullest and best expression, his spiritual love for Elizabeth needed to be accompanied by physical love.

Beecher used the same arguments in a sermon in 1872. "God has never put a faculty into the mind of a man," he insisted, "which is not in its own sphere and degree, right."[24] (Beecher indicated later to Moulton that his love for Elizabeth fell within the right sphere.) In another sermon of the same year, he argued, "Whoever loves rightly loves upward ... and ... loving that object, loves God."[25] Beecher believed that his own spiritual nature was naturally drawn to Elizabeth's spiritual nature; this love—existing as it did in a "higher sphere"—should never be subject to mere human law. Later on, in justifying the affair to Frank Moulton, Beecher argued in the same vein: that their sexual intercourse was as "natural and sincere an expression of love . . . as words of endearment" and would be justified "on the ground of our love for each other." The minister insisted that, "God would not blame them."[26] This was probably the explicit and personal manner in which he put it to Elizabeth. However, the ideas are essentially the same. In Beecher's private system, moral affinity or spiritual love had replaced institutional obligations as the basis for human relationships—at least for those on the "higher, nobler plane."

In short, Victoria Woodhull was entirely accurate when she claimed Beecher as a covert believer in Free Love. Woodhull simply said that all individuals had the right to decide for themselves who they would love—that no laws should govern such personal decisions. This belief coincided with Beecher's conviction that morality, fear, or law had no place in the lives of those who have reached a high religious sphere. The real difference between Woodhull and Beecher lay in the judgment of who was entitled to this freedom of choice. Woodhull was a radical because she advocated for everyone what Beecher reserved for a select few. Only in this way, Beecher seemed to think, could the higher as well as the lower spheres be protected.

Beecher insisted to Elizabeth that their affair would have to be concealed from everyone even though it had the sanction of God. According to Tilton, Beecher used the term "nest-hiding" in reference to the affair. In *Norwood,* Beecher explained his concept of a nest: "It would seem as if, while her whole life centered upon his love, she would hide the precious secret by flinging over it vines and flowers, by mirth and raillery, as a bird hides its nest under tufts of grass, and behind leaves and vines, as a fence against prying eyes."[27] The preacher clearly believed that individuals of a higher nature *ought* to be free from social convention—only an ignorant and misguided public opinion prevented it. Nest-hiding was his solution. The moral elite may break what Beecher called the "constraining bonds" but with discretion—those still in the lower spheres should not be allowed to get the wrong idea.[28]

Elizabeth was finally persuaded. "She was an extremely sympathetic woman," Theodore said later, "taking the ideas of others readily."[29] Elizabeth's testimony that she felt free of sin even after the affair indicated an assimilation of these ideas. Refusing to admit that she had violated her marriage vows, she embraced Beecher's assurances that she remained "spotless and chaste."[30] At the trial, Tilton himself was convinced of his wife's sincerity, saying she would never have surrendered to anyone but Beecher.[31]

As in the affair with Lucy Bowen, the minister managed to place the blame on the woman and transform his private anxiety into a public advantage. In a characteristic inversion of reality, Beecher considered Elizabeth the guilty party. Because her sexuality tempted his sincere need for love and approval, *she* was at fault. Later he indicated to Emma Moulton that Elizabeth was to blame for the adultery scandal—after all, she had sinned by confessing! "I don't understand how *she could have done it to me,*" he said.[32]

On November 22, 1868, a month after the affair with Elizabeth began, Beecher delivered a sermon in Plymouth Church entitled "Love of Money." Its ostensible subject was the dangers young men were exposed to as their original simplicity and honesty were corrupted by the accumulation of money. But—considering the timing of the sermon—it can also be read as a description of Beecher's own feelings about the plight of an innocent

man confronted with sexual temptation: "Let us follow the young man into the market. He has simplicity, and beauty, and purity, and honorable intentions. He goes . . . without intention of harm." But this "purity" is corrupted when the young man begins to make "gain" unexpectedly fast. This
very success intensifies the danger, argued Beecher, for "he has gone out
into life a little way, and already the harpies are upon him." "Harpies,"
after all, are female—and represented a much greater threat to Beecher's
career than the accumulation of money. And they are clearly employing
worldly allurements to seduce the innocent into a life of vice, playing upon
a simple trusting nature. For Beecher's congregation, this temptation was
money, although for the minister himself—in November 1868—it was
sex. The mixing of allusions in this sermon to money and sex also suggests
their close relationship in the minds of Beecher and his listeners. The injus-
tice of the temptation inspired Beecher to a high emotional pitch. "And
when I see young men surrounded by certain harpies," Beecher cried, "I do
know that . . . the fatal fire begins to burn within."[33]

Not only did Beecher shift responsibility to the "harpies" with these arguments, but he went on to convince himself that this surrender to temptation *enhanced* his stature with God! In another sermon delivered two
months after the affair began and titled appropriately, "The Value of Deep
Feelings," Beecher explained how such a capitulation might bring about
God's grace. "If a man had had such a struggle with himself that he is profoundly impressed with the might of evil in him," Beecher said, and had experienced a "revelation" that he is "utterly undone" and "helpless," then
the result would be to create "vividly and most powerfully" a sense of
God's grace. More than that, however, the intensity of the suffering would
further elevate the "gift of God's grace."[34] Beecher not only excused his
behavior, he argued that it would work in his favor!

For Elizabeth, the year and a half of her affair with Beecher—before she
confessed to her husband—was relatively happy. She basked in the great
man's attentions and even recovered some of the will and self-respect she
had felt herself losing as the "new marriage" developed. A new confidence
prompted her to engage in some activities outside her home. She began to
teach a Sunday school class of unwed mothers at a church mission and became active—partly because of Theodore's involvement—in the Brooklyn
Equal Rights Association, a women's suffrage group. Her letters to Theodore became less frequent and less obsessed with introspection. Writing of
her class at the mission school, she said, "They all love me, I *feel* it—because I, too, love everyone." "Already, in many things," she wrote with a
new confidence in 1869, "I am a changed woman."[35]

Indeed, there is evidence to support Elizabeth's hopeful assessment. Secure in the "self-respect" provided by Beecher's attention, Elizabeth's timidity gave way to confidence. In contrast to her previous and later disapproval of the public men and women Theodore cultivated, she became one of them, acting as corresponding secretary of the Equal Rights Association and editing a poetry column for the *Revolution*.[36] Elizabeth Cady Stanton, Susan B. Anthony, Laura Curtis Bullard, and other leaders of the women's movement began to meet at her home when Theodore was away. Although Elizabeth insisted in letters to her husband that she was simply "representing" him, the tone of her correspondence makes it clear that this may have been the most rewarding period since her marriage.[37]

Theodore, meanwhile knowing nothing of Elizabeth's affair with Beecher, seemed to sink more and more into a sea of emotional cross-currents. Guilty over his loss of occupation, his capitulation to the "mercantile world," and his own sexual infidelity, he alternately attempted to justify his actions with radical ideas of Free Love and affinity and to castigate himself for lack of self-control. He manifested his disillusionment with himself in an obsession with the purity and superiority of women.

Theodore's belief in the superiority of women surfaced in correspondence he carried on with the well-known author and reformer, Lydia Maria Child. Apparently in response to a question from Tilton, Child tried to persuade him that women were not innately superior, they were simply socialized differently. In fact, the real problem, she said, was that woman's nature was "repressed" by "false customs."[38] This was not what Theodore wanted to hear; more and more he wrote of women as a more divine form of creation. During his long "winter of meditation," as he pondered Beecher's "looseness" with women and his lack of control over his own sexuality, he feared that the irrepressible male sexual urge would automatically preclude the attainment of spiritual perfection. Even Christ's divinity came into question because he was a man—therefore a sexual being. Would it be "profane," Tilton wondered, to consider whether Jesus might have loved a woman, "perhaps passionately?" Could a man—even Christ—love sexually and still be pure and noble? "I believe," Tilton concluded, "that this fact would have so completely humanized Him in the eyes of all the world that He never would have been regarded as God."[39] Perhaps Theodore was expressing his own fear that once people knew of his passionate sexual nature, they would reject him as a writer, editor, or poet. Because women lacked male sexual passion, Theodore wrote to Elizabeth, "I see in you, and in a few women more greatness, such as Christ would have called great than in all the motley, rushing company of brave and hardy men whom I encounter day by day." Not only did Theodore conclude that women were better than men but that they should be set apart. He even suggested that they marry each other rather than having to be linked to corrupt men![40]

Expressing his desire to be more like Elizabeth or other good women, Theodore became increasingly frustrated with his lack of progress. "I trust I am growing less and less selfish," he wrote from Ohio in March 1868, "for I wish to walk in the way in which *you* are going."[41] His envy of women's superior purity is apparent in the following letter: "But you and Mrs. Bradshaw [Elizabeth's closest friend] and the Saints, are far ahead of us all in the pilgrimage toward Zion. . . . Henceforth I wish to join you, and the company of the good, the pure, the prayerful, the self-denying, the Christ-loving."[42] Theodore was probably referring not only to women's lack of sexual passion but also to their noninvolvement in the market place. What Theodore never seemed to realize, however, was that Elizabeth had been *forced* into the confinement that insulated and protected her from the competitive and threatening world in which he himself had to operate. Unlike her husband, she did not have to compete in the market place for money and status while at the same time remaining "pure" and "self-denying." All Theodore perceived was the fact that she *was* removed from the world; he did not understand that this alone might be the source of what he thought of as "purity." Indeed, it was without her consent that Elizabeth had been maneuvered into a position where she did not have to accomplish anything to command his love and respect. All she had to do was to continue to *be* insulated from the world. It was a state that Theodore desired very much for himself but could not achieve. It caused him to be jealous and envious of his wife, indeed of all women. Eventually, as we shall see, the jealousy and envy turned violent.

The spring and summer of 1870 were crucial for Brooklyn's "higher sphere." Tilton's idealization of women had resulted in his and Elizabeth's active involvement in the women's movement. Since the split between the conservative and radical wings of the movement in the fall of 1869, Tilton had been lobbying to reunite the two groups; in the spring of 1870, with the support of Anthony and Stanton, he started the Union Suffrage Association and was himself elected its president. In numerous editorials in the *Independent,* he argued that the more conservative wing (its president was Henry Ward Beecher!) could now join *his* organization and forget its quarrels with the radical group.[43]

Through Tilton's work with the suffrage associations, he had met the new editor of the *Revolution,* Laura Curtis Bullard. Bullard came from an upper-class Rhode Island family and had been chosen by Stanton to take over the editorship.[44] Tilton thought he had finally discovered a true affinity with a woman who was his equal in intellectual ability and social standing. With an arrogance already demonstrated in dealing with Elizabeth, Theodore now appropriated Bullard as his possession. Tilton actually considered himself the head of both the women's movement and the *Revolution*, perhaps with good reason—Bullard moved the editorial offices of the newspaper to Brooklyn in order to make them more convenient for Tilton. Writing to a friend, Tilton referred to the suffrage organization as a "movement of mine."[45]

Whether Tilton and Bullard ever had an affair is impossible to determine, but there were many rumors to that effect. In January 1871 the *Brooklyn Eagle* reported that the two had "eloped" to Europe.[46] Also, though not conclusive, Theodore's lines to a friend are suggestive: "The *Revolution* is (as perhaps you have heard) in what is equivalent to my own hands, 'to have and to hold.' "[47] Further evidence that Theodore had persuaded Elizabeth, at least for the moment, to accept this affinity is a letter she wrote to a friend (almost certainly Bullard) that same month. In this letter, she expressed the hope that God would "perfect in us *three* the beautiful promise of our nature" (my italics), but lamented how difficult it was "to *bring out* these blossoms of our heart's growth—God's gifts to us—to human eyes. . . . Our pearls and flowers," Elizabeth commented cryptically, "are caught up literally by vulgar and base minds that surround us on every side."[48] Elizabeth had learned her lessons on "nesting" from Beecher with some conviction!

During this same time, Tilton's suspicions of an affair between Elizabeth and Beecher grew. Elizabeth recalled in her testimony at the church trial that he became obsessed with the idea that things would improve between them if she would only admit the affair. According to the servant Bessie, Tilton's attitude was one of jealousy—not of Beecher, but of Elizabeth; he seemed very upset when *any* of their friends, male or female, liked Elizabeth better than him.[49] Throughout the spring of 1870, Tilton persuaded, cajoled, and demanded that Elizabeth admit to adultery with Beecher. If she did so, he insisted, he would forgive her and they could reconstruct their marriage.[50] Finally, on the evening of July 3, 1870, Elizabeth made the trip from their summer home in Monticello, New York, to confess the affair.[51]

Elizabeth's hopes that the confession would improve her relationship with Theodore were soon dashed. Their initial conversation, to be sure, was tender and loving, with Theodore promising to keep the secret and to help heal her "wounded spirit." At first, he even encouraged his wife to continue the affair with Beecher! A friend later reported that during the summer of 1870, the editor attempted to persuade his wife "to save her health and life by accepting some 'affinity' other than himself."[52] Beecher himself testified that on one occasion in the early summer of 1870 when he offered to take Elizabeth riding and she declined, Theodore "playfully reproached her" and thereupon she agreed to go.[53]

At the same time, however, Theodore's anger at Elizabeth intensified. Her surrender to Beecher, said Theodore, proved she had a "sensual" effect on men. He accused her of attempting to seduce every man who paid a social call at the house. In violent rages he claimed that only the first of their four children was his. Elizabeth, stunned by the intensity of his accusations, recalled: "He said I had a sensual influence; I used to become impregnated with this idea of his myself while under his influence, and I wondered if it was so, and would think it over and over; he would often talk to me in that way by the hour, and try to persuade me that it was true. . . . I was perfectly sure that no man ever felt that way toward me."[54] If this harassment was a "hard thing to live under," Elizabeth soon discovered that it could be worse. Theodore began to insinuate to friends that he had a "dreadful secret" concerning his wife and Beecher. In September 1870 when Elizabeth could no longer endure such humiliation, she escaped to the home of a friend in Ohio where she wrote pleading letters to her husband. "Oh, Theodore, Theodore! What shall I say to you? My tongue and pen are dumb and powerless, but I must force my aching heart to protest against your cruelty." In desperation she reminded her husband that he had guilty secrets as well: "Theodore, *your* past is safe with me, put away never to be opened—though it is big with stains of various hue."[55]

But Theodore was not moved by such appeals. On the very day Elizabeth returned from Ohio, he renewed his harassment, according to Bessie Turner's testimony, with reminders of her infidelity with Beecher. Moreover, he said, she was in the habit of "having her bosoms [sic] and legs fondled by many men."[56] The servant claimed that when she came to Mrs. Tilton's defense, Theodore, in a rage, knocked her down.

If it is difficult to understand such contradictory behavior in one individual, it must be pointed out that at this point—December 1870—Theodore was under severe pressure in his professional life. Just a week before the violent scene with his wife, Tilton had joined the insurgent Liberal Republicans in defiance of Bowen's desired policy for the Brooklyn *Union*. In consequence, the publisher was threatening to remove him as editor of the *Independent* and the *Union*. His attack on Elizabeth for her promiscuity and her inferior cultural attainments may have been exacerbated by guilt and anxiety in both personal and professional areas. No longer dealing with his wife as a real person, he had projected onto her all his own "passions whirling within."

Three years later Theodore Tilton himself described the situation with penetrating accuracy. He did so not in a letter or in trial testimony, but under cover of fiction—in a novel he wrote as the scandal was breaking, which appeared in 1874 under the title *Tempest Tossed*. Two of the principle characters are Anthony Cammeyer, a man (in the most classic Beecher tradition) once innocent and honest, but now corrupted by selfishness and greed, and Lucy, the woman who loves him unfalteringly despite all his faults. One vivid scene, portraying a conversation between Anthony and Lucy, is so genuine and intense, and so reminiscent of Theodore's own long introspective letters to Elizabeth, that it was surely inspired by them. The young man is "violently seized by the wild feeling which, of late years, had many times mounted into a horrible possession of his mind—the same unaccountable rage which had occasionally impelled him to pace up and down his solitary room—to gnash his teeth—to clench his hands—and to threaten violence, sometimes against others, oftener against himself." All through this scene, the man is angered by Lucy's calm and loving forgiveness of the horrible sins he had committed. "The base trickster," wrote Theodore, "scowled at her like a madman—clenched his right hand —sprang toward her where she stood—and was about to fell her to the earth—but her calm, undaunted, and defiant look paralyzed his cowardly arm."[57]

At this point in the narrative, Theodore addressed his readers directly to explain such extreme behavior: "The close student of human nature will hardly need to be reminded in reviewing Cammeyer's apparently uncharacteristic behavior that the chief part which Lucy played in this drama of incipient madness was merely to be the mirror in which this defeated villain saw himself revealed in such hideous lineaments that he was now again unpoised at the self-contemplation—as he had often been before."[58] Theodore had, in fact, once written to Elizabeth, "The more I compare myself to you, the worse I seem."[59]

Having been threatened with actual physical violence, Elizabeth at last had had enough. On the same day that she returned from Ohio—when Bessie was knocked down—she gathered up the four children and went home to her mother. Mrs. Richards innocently tried to help by requesting that Henry Ward Beecher pay a pastoral call![60] The minister, understandably worried about becoming involved in the Tiltons' marital troubles— though he did not yet know that Elizabeth had confessed to Theodore—

The artist who depicted Eunice Beecher in Frank Leslie's Illustrated Newspaper *(above) probably reflected the common view of her as a sour, joyless old woman. Indeed, she seems to be an example of what an insensitive woman could do, both to her husband and her marriage. However, as the photograph on the left suggests, she may have been more victimized than villainous. (Drawing: Courtesy, American Antiquarian Society. Photo: Beecher Family Papers, Yale University Library)*

sent his wife, the formidable Eunice Beecher, to advise Elizabeth.[61] Despite Mrs. Beecher's advice—and her husband's concurrence—that she divorce Theodore, Elizabeth was still convinced that his erratic behavior was a result of his loss of religious beliefs, and decided that her duty required one more attempt to help him recover from his "morbid state of mind."[62]

But Elizabeth's severest ordeal—in which she finally internalized Tilton's and Beecher's definition of her—was only beginning. Granted, she had for several years been subjected to increasingly intense emotional pressures—pressures related to Theodore's treatment of her, to her own inability to handle the situation, and, ultimately, to a conflict between the traditional morality in which she had been raised and the amorphous rhetoric of affinity and "soul-mating" to which she had recently become attached. But through all this, she had never concluded that her problems lay entirely within her own character. The relationship with Beecher had produced such positive results in her own life that she did not see how—provided it was kept from "vulgar and base minds"—it could possibly harm anyone, even her husband.

A month after she returned home, around Christmas 1870, however, a

crisis arose that would leave Elizabeth feeling not only bewildered, but utterly crushed and submissive. The precipitating cause was Theodore's dismissal, in late December, from his position as editor of the *Independent*.
This prompted Theodore to insist on a written version of the confession
Elizabeth had made six months before. Assuring her that he would not
make use of it unless absolutely necessary, Theodore pointedly cited her
wifely duty to help him keep his job. Elizabeth, ill and "wearied by importunity," acquiesced in the request.[63]

Learning of this development from Moulton that same evening, Beecher
confronted Elizabeth with a demand for a written retraction. Her later description of this scene with Beecher conveys something of her anguish.
When Beecher arrived, Elizabeth said, she was "lying very sick" (actually
she was recovering from a miscarriage). He berated her, insisting that she
had "ruined him." Why, he wanted to know, had she done such a thing?
Guilt-stricken by her minister's accusations, Elizabeth agreed to sign a
statement—composed for her by Beecher—that would clear him of the
charges, and he left in triumph. Tilton, upon learning what Beecher had
done, demanded a recantation of the retraction she had given Beecher. A

weak and defeated Elizabeth signed this third statement, "in order to repair so cruel a blow" to her "long-suffering husband."[64]

Immediately following this night of confrontations, Beecher and Tilton
—with the help of Frank Moulton—had a temporary reconciliation,
agreeing to cover up the scandal. But on every occasion when Theodore's
reputation was impugned or his finances met with a setback, he threatened
to expose Beecher, leaving the minister in a constant state of anxiety
and fear of public disgrace. Frightened of scandal, Beecher altered his earlier advice that Elizabeth divorce Theodore and now insisted that she
must "do her part" in the policy of silence and make a happy home for
Theodore.[65]

As for Elizabeth, although she bitterly protested that all of these plans
were being pursued without reference to her feelings, the somewhat comic
maneuverings were less important than her desperate need to understand
what had gone wrong. Her efforts to fulfill her duty to her husband in spite
of his insults and accusations, while at the same time affirming her integrity through affinity with a man who revived her diminished self-respect,
had ended in disaster.

Frustrated at the failure of either the moral injunctions of her youth or
the nebulous guidelines of affinity to provide an explanation of suffering,
Elizabeth turned to a new authority—the popular novel. Beecher once said
that had Elizabeth been a Catholic and lived in another age, she would
have been given to ecstatic visions, and indeed, she now found the explanation for her plight in a "heavenly vision" which came to her as she read a
sensational novel of the day, *Griffith Gaunt* (1866), by the English author,
Charles Reade.[66] In a letter to Theodore, she explained the novel's profound effect upon her. "Today through the ministry of Catherine Gaunt, a
character of fiction, my eyes have been opened for the first time in my experience, so that I see clearly my sin."[67]

It is easy to understand why the story spoke so directly to Elizabeth.
Catherine Gaunt, a fictional heroine with whom she identified, is an eight-
eenth-century gentlewoman, beautiful, devout, and rigidly honest. She is
married to Griffith Gaunt—a morbidly proud and jealous man, obviously
similar to Theodore. Though she loves her husband, Catherine forms a
close relationship with her priest—a man whose warm and sensitive nature is uncannily reminiscent of Elizabeth's descriptions of Henry Ward
Beecher.

Catherine and the priest never become sexually intimate, but she spends
a great deal of time in his company and Griffith becomes suspicious. At
first, Catherine stubbornly defends her right to the priest's friendship. But

In Frank Leslie's Pictorial History *of the scandal, an artist re-created the scene in Elizabeth's bedroom as she wrote for Beecher her letter of retraction. (Courtesy, American Antiquarian Society)*

in one scene that was surely significant to Elizabeth, Catherine and the priest walk in the garden discussing religious subjects with an emotional intensity that is innocent, yet laden with sexual undertones. Reade makes unmistakably clear that, although their words and intentions are "pure," mutual sexual desire is the "real" level of communication. Here, in the guise of fiction, Elizabeth encountered precisely what Theodore had told her about herself![68] Intentions are irrelevant; women are sexual creatures.

Elizabeth, then, was not so fortunate as Beecher in the lessons she learned from their relationship. Although the minister's parishioners sanctioned his self-exoneration and thus unwittingly encouraged his lack of responsibility, Elizabeth had to face more severe consequences. From her experience with Beecher, she learned something that was implicit in the concept of the "new marriage" her husband had articulated, but which hitherto had not been clear to her: the spiritual influence that was now her exclusive sphere rested, in reality, on the power of sexuality. Elizabeth had finally internalized Theodore's conviction that *all* her relations with men must necessarily be founded upon an inviting sensuality. Catherine's repressed sexual desire for the priest, and Elizabeth's own warm response to Beecher, reinforced the notion that a woman's appeal must, inevitably, be rooted in sexual attraction. Therefore, she concluded, "a virtuous woman should check instantly an absorbing love."[69] With the acceptance of this innate sensuality, it followed that *she* was the cause of all the recent troubles. It did not matter that she had been "misled" by her pastor, he was still a "good man." "I am the one that is to blame," she told a friend, "I invited it."[70] The "sin," it turns out, was her unwitting use of her sexuality to tempt Beecher! The affinity she thought she felt was, in reality, her sexual desire! She had learned that, for women at least, affinity was not a separate spiritual sphere but rather was firmly rooted in sexuality. There was no way to escape the implications. Elizabeth's identity was defined solely by her sexual nature.

Elizabeth's world was inexorably constricting. As a result of her awakening, she had foregone the identity provided by her parental community. Now she was driven to reject the many possibilities opened to her through the world of freedom and affinity. In essence, Elizabeth had retreated from her experiments with social freedom to a more confining concept of marriage than the traditional one. Not only must she now fulfill her duty to her husband, she had to somehow achieve a spiritually exclusive and perfect union as well. The impossibility of the task should have been staggering. Yet Elizabeth embraced the new ideal as well as the revelation of her guilty sensuality with "profound thankfulness that I am come to this sure foundation, and that my feet are planted on the rock of this great truth. . . . When you yearn toward me," she assured Theodore in June 1871, "be assured of the tried, purified, and restored love of . . . Elizabeth."[71]

Tragically, Elizabeth had finally been convinced that from her sexuality alone emanated both her weakness and her spiritual power. For Elizabeth as well as a generation of women, it must have been a thoroughly devastating discovery. Moreover, the only way for women to achieve social status, respect, and influence was to manipulate that sexual power in such a way as to appear innocent of its presence. Only this can explain the elaborate etiquette of Victorian relationships between the sexes.

In many ways, Elizabeth, in her woman's sphere, had learned something that Theodore and the members of Plymouth Church had learned from Henry Ward Beecher in the economic and social spheres. Money, they were afraid, had become the real basis for power and influence in Brooklyn, but because they themselves desperately wanted to believe that an individual's worth was not based on money, they vigorously denied its omnipotence. Men insisted they had no ambition to acquire money and status —as Theodore did. Similarly, just when they became convinced of its domination in their lives—women denied any hint of their sexual natures. But money and sex were undeniably the driving forces in Victorian America. This was a paradox that was to shape the responses of the members of Plymouth Church to the participants in the scandal.

9

Theodore Tilton As Scapegoat: Retreat from the Gospel of Love

FOR ELIZABETH TILTON, the ultimate significance of the Gospel of Love was the narrowing of her social identity to a sexual one. She finally internalized what old-fashioned moralists like Storrs had argued all along, that the Gospel of Love was nothing more than a rationalization for selfish indulgence—whether in acquisition of power and money, or sexual passion.

For most Plymouth Church members, however, the issues were not so clear. Like Tilton, they had benefited from the Gospel of Love—they were not as threatened by it as many Church of the Pilgrims members had been. Therefore, when Beecher's case became public, they instinctively defended their minister. Yet, like Tilton, they too harbored mixed emotions as well as doubts about both Beecher and his gospel, feelings that became more apparent as details of the scandal and cover-up emerged. In this chapter we return to the December night when Beecher learned that Elizabeth had confessed, this time to follow the implications of the attempts by Moulton, Tilton, and Beecher to conceal the affair, and the reaction of Plymouth Church to it.

After the stormy confrontations of December 30, 1870—Theodore with Beecher, Beecher with Elizabeth, Theodore with Elizabeth—Moulton negotiated a peace between Beecher and Tilton. The minister wrote a letter of apology that begged Tilton's forgiveness; later he entered into a "partnership" to recuperate and "restore" the "bankrupted" Tilton. "We are all in the same boat together," Beecher said later at the trial. "He had his reasons why he did not want matters to come out about his family, and I had my reasons." However, this agreement came too late to save Tilton's editorial career. Bowen, in a state of agitation over his failure to play off Tilton against Beecher, had summarily fired Tilton from both the *Independent* and the *Union*. Appeals to the embittered Bowen to rehire Tilton came to nothing.[1]

Moulton, as manager of the cover-up, now had two problems. One was to keep the sex scandal from becoming public. The other, more difficult one was to restore Tilton's economic security and professional career. The first clearly depended on the second, for if, as Moulton said, Tilton remained without "place, business, or repute," he would have nothing to lose in producing the evidence that could ruin Beecher. For three and a half years—from January 1871 to June 1874—Moulton succeeded in keeping the scandal from widespread public knowledge.

What becomes remarkably clear in any examination of the cover-up is how completely it was motivated by the desire to preserve Henry Ward Beecher's public image—irrespective of his guilt or innocence. Ordinary people all over the country might have been shocked to learn of Beecher's sexual adventures, but those in the inner circle—whether Tilton's or Beecher's friends—were primarily interested in protecting his reputation. Both Moulton and his wife believed Beecher guilty from the beginning; Tilton had made use of Elizabeth's confession not to expose Beecher, but to save his own editorial career. The adulteries engaged in by both Beecher and Tilton were a matter of common speculation, yet the strongest condemnation one intimate of both men could muster was that they had behaved in "reckless" or "impulsive" ways.[2] Among the inner circle there seemed to be a consensus that Beecher's reputation must be protected regardless of the truth—that his sin was not great enough to warrant the condemnation that would result from public knowledge of the affair. General Benjamin Butler, a friend of Frank Moulton's, is reported to have said: "I don't care who is right and who is wrong. This exposure will work harm. . . . The thing to be advised in the case was to keep it hidden and that advice I strongly pressed."[3]

The assumption that the public had no right to know of Beecher's or Tilton's private exploits was the basis for what Beecher came to call the "policy of silence." In characteristic fashion, Beecher justified the concealment of these matters from his own church as well as the public by insisting that they were not able to "judge of the motives and influences which have acted at various stages of a history, essentially private and domestic . . . and which . . . should have had the privilege of seclusion."[4]

This idea that one's personal life should also be *private* was relatively new to those raised in New England communities where all areas of one's life were routinely subjected to public scrutiny. In short, personal life was not equated with private; indeed, privacy and solitude were always deeply suspect. As part of the Gospel of Love, Beecher sought to alter this negative image of the private self. A theme in many of his sermons is the novel idea that an individual's "hidden" self was not necessarily a destructive force, but could, in fact, be the source of purity. This hidden self, indeed, according to Beecher, formed the basis for moral affinity in the higher sphere. The public, as a collective identity, could not be expected to understand the inner principles of individuals of such sensitivity. The public—like Beecher's father—was too quick to be judgmental and punitive. A change in popular sentiment, as Tilton had discovered, could rob prominent figures of their reputation and livelihood in arbitrary and capricious ways. Therefore, justice was more faithfully served by preventing the masses of people from knowing the actions of those on the higher plane. "Public sentiment," said Beecher, "refuses to be just and earnest."[5]

The practical result of this attitude as far as Beecher was concerned was that there were no institutions or laws to which private disputes among higher-sphere individuals could be safely appealed. Mere public suspicion was synonymous with judgment and conviction. Thus, both Beecher and Tilton turned to a "mutual friend," Frank Moulton, for private arbitration. Although recognizing Tilton's "impulsiveness" and Beecher's sometimes "morbid gloom," Moulton attempted to mediate in a private manner—one that had gained acceptance as traditional institutions became less effective. It was what Tilton termed "social obligation."[6] Thus Beecher agreed to help finance a newspaper, the *Golden Age*—a vehicle intended to restore the editor's professional standing, and Moulton negotiated the Tri-Partite Covenant.[7]

Indeed, this private method of stifling the rumors worked so well that Moulton, Tilton, and Beecher considered it the only way to deal with Victoria Woodhull when she threatened to expose the scandal. Woodhull first published hints in the *New York World* in May 1871, six months after Elizabeth's written confession, that she knew of the affair. Although names were omitted, Beecher and Tilton recognized themselves immediately. After hurried conferences at Moulton's house, Tilton was assigned to placate Woodhull. They agreed, Tilton testified later, that "as part of the method by which we should deal with Mrs. Woodhull . . . we would become personally acquainted with her; that we would treat her as a gentleman would treat a lady, and that we would in that manner put her under obligation to us—social obligation, kindly obligation."[8]

This emphasis on reciprocal personal obligation was, of course, similar to the way in which Plymouth members operated in both church and politics. Beecher had eroded the tenets of Congregationalism in favor of personal loyalty to himself, and "machine" politics had come to be based on personal loyalties and reciprocal obligations. Responsibility and morality were now defined by an individual's faithfulness to these personal obliga-

This artist's conception of Theodore Tilton preparing a public statement depicts him as a tortured romantic hero; a view not unlike the one he held of himself. (American Antiquarian Society)

tions rather than to a shared system of theology or ideology. These personal, private loyalties circumvented ideas of public responsibility; they were, indeed, the essence of the Gospel of Love.

Thus, at the beginning of the cover-up, Tilton reaffirmed to Beecher his eternal friendship and loyalty. The only reason he would ever use the evidence against the minister, he insisted, was to retaliate in the event Beecher "betrayed" him first. Because this was well after Elizabeth's confession, Tilton was not referring here to Beecher's seduction of his wife, but rather to a possible betrayal of their friendship. In the novel he wrote in 1873,

Discord among the Angels. (Frank Leslie's Illustrated Newspaper,
October 24, 1874.

Tilton expressed his ideas about friendship—ideas he clearly learned from
Beecher. "How often he and I talked of friendship and its obligations!
How strenuously he maintained it to be a holy tie!—an unwritten oath!
—an unsworn marriage of man with man! What a friend to his friends
was Rodney Vail! He would have made any sacrifice for *them*—any sacrifice for *me*. I will be worthy of such a friendship, and reciprocate its obligations."[9] Indeed, when Beecher himself testified at the trial, he echoed
these sentiments, stating he knew of "no more horrible evil in this world
than to betray or hurt a friend. . . . in being unfaithful to the highest honor

of obligations.''[10] The "unfaithful" in this quote refers not to the adultery with Elizabeth, but to accusations that Beecher had not done enough to restore Tilton's career. What is remarkable in all this is that both men considered their personal loyalty to each other far more important than sexual morality.

Had Tilton been persuaded of the necessity of concealing affinity in the higher sphere, the scandal might never have become public. But he was not fully convinced, and his acquaintance with Woodhull further undermined Beecher's influence. As we have seen, Tilton had already adopted, at least superficially, some socially radical ideas in regard to love, sex, and marriage, and he—unlike Beecher—felt compelled to justify them in public. Like Beecher, he used these ideas to justify his own behavior, but in contrast, he was driven to seek public approval for them as well. Thus after Tilton's initial reluctant contact with Woodhull, he began to be charmed by her personality and impressed by her dedication to social freedom. Through the summer and fall of 1871, Tilton and Woodhull spent several days a week discussing her ideas as preparation for writing the biography that was intended to place her under "social obligation." In the *Golden Age,* the paper that had been established by Moulton and Beecher, he began to advocate her ideas on Free Love. More and more, Tilton came to feel that Woodhull's philosophy had much in common with Beecher's. Later, at the trial, Beecher was asked, "Did you ever know anybody who took hold of it [Free Love] seriously who was not ruined by it?" His answer was extraordinarily revealing of his method of skirting cautiously around his true feelings as he refused to state them directly. "No, sir; provided they were susceptible of ruin. I have had women write to me that if I did not send them $10 they were ruined, and I wrote in reply that they were ruined before.''[11] Tilton, already troubled about Beecher's and, indeed, his own, hypocrisy, came to see Woodhull as a courageous figure.

The admiring biography Tilton wrote reflected his enthusiastic approval. He began the sketch by announcing his admiration for her as a woman "whose position, as a representative of her sex in the greatest reform of modern times, renders her an object of peculiar interest to her fellow-citizens, and whose character (inasmuch as I know her well) I can portray without color or tinge from any other partiality save that I hold her in uncommon respect. . . ." Tilton concluded by asserting that "to see her is to respect her—to know her is to vindicate her . . . she [is] one of the sincerest, most reverent, and divinely gifted of human souls.''[12] When it was published in the fall of 1871 by the *Golden Age,* Moulton complained that Tilton had gone too far. "So many statements in it seemed extravagant," he later said, "that the effect . . . on the paper [the *Golden Age*] would be dis-astrous."[13] It soon became apparent that Moulton was right. Tilton's first lecture tour after the publication of this biography was a failure. Beecher described it this way: "The winter following [1871–72] Mr. Tilton re-turned from the lecture field in despair. Engagements had been cancelled, invitations withdrawn, and he spoke of the prejudice and repugnance with which he was everywhere met as indescribable."[14]

Tilton, however, believed that this public rejection emanated not from the biography of Woodhull, but from rumors of personal immorality stemming from his dismissal from Bowen's newspapers.[15] The solution, he thought, was for Bowen to write a public letter indicating that their differ-ences did not involve morality but were only "political and theological."[16] Bowen complied, but the *Golden Age* and Tilton's career continued to decline.

This situation was frightening for Beecher, because the success of his "policy of silence" was contingent upon Tilton's renewed prosperity. Changing tactics, he urged the editor to "make a prompt repudiation of these women and their doctrines." "I told him," Beecher testified at the trial, "that no man could rise against the public confidence with such a load."[17] Apparently, Beecher was willing to abandon "obligations" when it came to his own reputation! As usual, the minister was much keener than Tilton in his perception of the public temper. In September 1871, Wood-hull planned a speech on social freedom at Steinway Hall in New York. She threatened to make the scandal public unless Beecher appeared on the platform to introduce her. But this Beecher could not bring himself to do; Woodhull later reported that "he said he agreed perfectly with what I was to say, but that he could not stand on the platform . . . and introduce me."[18] At the last minute before the speech, Tilton hurried up onto the stage in Beecher's place and Woodhull apparently decided not to carry out her threat.

Eventually Tilton did break with Woodhull, but it was not on Beecher's advice. In the fall of 1872 Woodhull informed Tilton that she planned to fabricate embarrassng stories about leaders of the women's movement whom Tilton admired—including Susan Anthony and Elizabeth Cady Stanton; this was too much for him and he ended their friendship.[19] At the same time, his support of Horace Greeley, the Liberal Republican and Democratic candidate for President, angered Woodhull because she had proclaimed herself a presidential candidate.[20] Thus it was Tilton's and Beecher's rejection of Woodhull that finally persuaded her to expose the scandal.[21]

Although the revelation caused something of a stir in the press, most newspapers dismissed the accusations as unfounded rumors and respected Beecher's condescending refusal to respond. Indeed, it was Tilton who was penalized for his involvement with Woodhull. More lecturing engagements were cancelled and some of the businessmen Moulton had persuaded to back the *Golden Age* withdrew their support.[22] With investors pulling out of the *Golden Age,* Beecher, in desperation, mortgaged his house to give Theodore $5,000. At the trial, Beecher explained it this way: "The situation was that of a man that had been bankrupted in every way, and whom we were endeavoring to recuperate and restore. The devices were, among others . . . soothing the prejudices against him and of preventing men's talking to his disadvantage, and everything else that would help him to become a man again—a man, I mean, that had overcome distrust and become apparently, again, a man."[23] Beecher's gesture, however, did not help. As his position worsened, Tilton's resentment deepened: he was suffering for espousing Free Love, while Beecher's popularity increased! Tilton began to put together a document called the "True Story" which, he testified later, was intended for a few "personal friends" who wanted a "frank explanation" of what they had found "erratic" in his behavior for the past two years.[24]

Having provided the radical Woodhull with the details of the scandal, Tilton proceeded to give the same ammunition to Beecher's conservative enemies in Brooklyn. He showed his "True Story" to Richard Salter Storrs. Later, Tilton claimed that he went to Storrs because he considered him a friend of Beecher's who might be able to offer some advice, but given the long-standing animosity between the two ministers and their churches, it is difficult to believe that Tilton did not know exactly what he was doing. When Beecher discovered what Tilton had done, he cried, "Oh Theodore, of all people, why did you go to him?"[25]

Beecher was to become more and more frustrated with Tilton's "inexplicable" and "uncontrollable" behavior.[26] In a letter to Frank Moulton, Beecher complained that "with such a man as Theodore Tilton, there is no possible salvation for any that depend upon him."[27] Beecher had come to a point in his life where he might have regretted the part he had played in weakening social institutions. In this situation, he had no other recourse than to plead with his former friend to be more prudent and to beg Frank Moulton to exercise more control over Tilton. Private obligations, he was learning, did not always work.

Tilton's prospects continued their headlong plunge. In the spring of 1874, just as the first Congregational Council assembled, Tilton was forced to sell the *Golden Age*.[28] Thus when one of Beecher's friends, Leonard Bacon, referred to Tilton as a "knave" and a "dog," he was in the worst possible mood to deal rationally with such a public insult. In spite of the fact that Beecher was equally appalled by Bacon's statement, Tilton published his response on June 21 in the "Bacon Letter." In it, Tilton insisted that he had remained loyal to Henry Ward Beecher even after the dishonor brought by the minister upon his family. But now, however, he had no intention of "sacrificing" his own honor for the sake of Beecher's. "You have put me before my countrymen," he wrote Bacon, "in the character of a base and bad man."[29] As we have seen, Tilton's concern with his newly achieved social status and reputation often prompted him to feel guilty; he wanted to believe his motives were pure and unselfish—his loyalties and personal obligations unsullied by passions such as lust for status, sex, or money. With the Bacon Letter, his sensitivity to his public reputation finally won out over personal loyalty to Beecher.

This letter initiated the long, hot "scandal summer" of 1874 when the bonds of moral affinity and social obligation that had formed the basis for the cover-up completely broke down. Beecher appointed a church investigating committee made up of his supporters and denounced both Moulton and Tilton as blackmailers and conspirators.

The public response to the scandal gradually altered as more and more information became available—primarily the testimonies taken during the church investigation. At first, many in Brooklyn sympathized with Tilton; some of the documents he published seemed conclusive. Beecher's letter of apology of January 1, 1871, for example, asking Tilton's "forgiveness" and pleading that he would "humble" himself before the "wronged" husband, although not admitting guilt outright, made little sense if Tilton's charges were false. In the same letter, Beecher had further insisted that Elizabeth was "guiltless," and "bearing the transgressions of another." "I humbly pray," Beecher concluded, "that He [God] may put it in the heart of her husband to forgive me."[30] Later in the summer when Frank Moulton appeared before the Investigating Committee, he stated categorically, "Both Mrs. Tilton and Mr. Beecher admitted in language not to be mistaken that a continued sexual intimacy had existed between them, and asked advice as to the course to be taken because of it."[31]

However, as more of the testimony emerged, particularly that of Eliza-

Henry Ward Beecher dictating his "Letter of Apology" to Frank Moulton. (Frank
Leslie's Illustrated Newspaper, *February 20, 1875)*

beth Tilton, it appeared that Theodore had not been the innocent victim he
seemed. His wife claimed he had been physically abusive and had himself
committed adultery. This information, along with evidence that Tilton
had conspired with Beecher and Moulton to cover up the affair, led significant segments of the public to condemn what the *Chicago Tribune* called
the whole "Plymouth Church crowd."[32] The *Brooklyn Sunday Sun* declared that it "believed in Mr. Beecher's guilt, in Mr. Tilton's guilt, in his
meanness and cowardice; and it believes in Mrs. Tilton's guilt."[33] "The

reasonings," editorialized the *Sun* at the end of the summer, "of a Tilton, of a Victoria Woodhull carried into practice would Bohemianize mankind."[34] "One by one the great newspapers dropped from [Beecher]," noted one observer, "not in hostility, but in sorrow."[35]

Despite all this evidence, at the end of its investigation, Plymouth Church declared in the official report: "We find nothing whatever in the evidence that should impair the perfect confidence of Plymouth Church or the world in the Christian character and integrity of Henry Ward Beecher."[36] Many people were puzzled by such apparent disregard for the evidence. Elizabeth Cady Stanton theorized in the *Chicago Tribune* that many of the businessmen defending Beecher were doing so for economic reasons—to protect their financial investments in Plymouth Church, in the newspapers that published his sermons, and in the firm that produced his books.[37] Granted Plymouth Church and Henry Ward Beecher were big business, but this willingness to allow the great man his "errors" was widespread, even among church members who had no direct or indirect interest in marketing the Gospel of Love. For this reason, it becomes crucial to investigate the vociferous support for Beecher despite a consensus as to his guilt.

It seems strange that Theodore Tilton was denounced by the church for "monstrous perfidy." The remarkable point here is that this condemnation was not for adultery, but for betrayal of a friendship. In a confidential communication, Oliver Johnson, a close friend of both men, expressed Plymouth Church sentiment when he wrote that Tilton, "according to his own story" had "condoned" and "forgiven" the adultery and "passed his word that he would forever keep it a secret from the world." Despite the willingness of Theodore's friends—including Beecher—to conceal from the world his own "reckless wickedness," Johnson went on, he had violated that trust and "took counsel of those who ministered to his vanity and inflamed his passions." Thus he was led to a betrayal of a "sacred" obligation which Johnson characterized as a "game of treachery, perfidy, and folly that is without parallel."[38]

The issue, then, was not betrayal of the marriage bond, but betrayal of a "social obligation." A marriage bond was, after all, a mere legal instrument, but betrayal of a social obligation based on affinity was of a much higher order. Beecher had pursued the moral course by keeping silent about an embarrassing domestic problem and by making every effort to shield both Tilton and his wife from public exposure. More than that, he had actively helped Tilton find a new job and loaned him money. Tilton, on the other hand, had betrayed his benefactor; moreover, he had done so in the grip of a selfish passion. Not only was he, said Oliver Johnson, a "knave" but he was a "fool" who could never be lifted from the "pit into which he has plunged headlong," even if he should win the court case.[39] For someone who had committed no greater sin than Beecher himself, that of adultery, it is ironic that Tilton was labeled a "monster," while Beecher's transgression was excused. Beecher could be forgiven, Tilton could not. Why?

Beecher had acted out of weakness, his lawyer admitted at the trial, but Tilton's behavior was a result of "a passionate love of self."[40] The significant point at issue here is the resonance of the word "passion" for a nineteenth-century audience. In that era, passion referred to a lack of self-control and implied the acting-out of a lust for worldly pleasures such as sex, status, or money. Passion, then, held the negative connotation that "obsession" might hold today. Thus, although Beecher himself had advocated that young men love and trust themselves, his lawyer's addition of the word "passionate" condemned Tilton for letting that attention to self-interest run wildly out of control.

There was, Beecher's lawyers argued, a vast difference between weakness and a passionate or aggressive self-centeredness. The former, although not condoned, might be understood and excused because it arose from a sensitive and generous nature. Beecher himself had often reiterated the difficulties people of such finer sensibilities encountered in dealing with a harsh world. The aggressive self-centeredness exhibited by Tilton was frightening because it was both a quality required for survival in an urban impersonal world *and* the solvent of the bonds of affinity that, following the breakdown of traditional institutions, were the only bonds uniting autonomous individuals. The tension constantly present in Beecher's preaching—and in Tilton's life—was now reflected in the adultery trial as well. The ironic twist was that it was Theodore Tilton who was on trial for his "passionate love of self." In their summing-up speeches, Beecher's lawyers Evarts and Tracy condemned Tilton in rhetoric reminiscent of the preacher's own. A word painting of terrifying dimensions, rather than rational argument, illustrated the horrors of ambition and self-love. From similar backgrounds, Evarts pointed out, Beecher and Tilton had embarked upon the "same career." In much the same way, they had been "wrapped up in Christian faith and Christian duty." But, unlike Beecher, Tilton's "morbid self-worship" had caused his "alienation from faith and duty," and ended in the "evil" gratification of the selfish appetites, regardless of any disaster to those who were "nearest . . . and dearest."[41]

Although to the uninitiated this may sound like a description of Bee-

Beecher's acquittal seemed assured as he confidently took the stand to testify in his own behalf. (Frank Leslie's Illustrated Newspaper, *April 17, 1875*)

cher's behavior, the minister's parishioners, on the contrary, perceived Beecher as a generous, warm-hearted individual who had been *victimized* by the calculating and selfish people surrounding him. It was an image Beecher had fostered and it was one with which his struggling young parishioners could easily identify. By contrast, Tilton's apparent selfish preoccupation inspired betrayal and erratic, violent behavior. Identification with Tilton was frightening rather than comforting; in fact, the hysterical condemnation of him may have been a way of projecting profound fears about the Gospel of Love onto its most ardent disciple.

In a remarkable speech during the trial, Benjamin Tracy dramatized Tilton's life story as a step-by-step descent into the maelstrom of "passionate egotism." Significantly, this descent was brought about by the very values that had for twenty-five years been the basis of the Gospel of Love. In Tracy's narrative, Tilton is described as a kind of mirror-image of the young men who followed the steps of Beecher's moral evolution to the higher plane. This, he seemed to be saying, is what happens when an individual loses control of his own moral evolution. "A staunch new vessel, launched upon an honorable voyage, sailing with prosperous winds over unruffled seas, has been transformed into a pirate by the wickedness of her commander, and wrecked by his folly, and now lies a stranded and battered hulk, the object at once of the curiosity and abhorrence of mankind."[42] For middle-class Victorian Americans, ever conscious of their social status, the prospect of becoming the object of curiosity and abhorrence conjured up the worst horror. It was indeed the opposite of the universal admiration bestowed on Henry Ward Beecher.

The difference between Beecher and Tilton, Tracy said, was that although Beecher had become an eminent clergyman, he had "left neither his simplicity nor his independence behind." He was still, in fact, a "genuine, true-hearted, unaffected man," even in the "midst of all the refinements and luxuries of city life." He had not been led astray by ambitious pursuit of success. Tilton, by contrast, as a boy was "bright and ambitious," said Tracy, and therefore he lacked the unselfish aims which were the "prime elements" of "noble manhood." Tilton, unlike Beecher, did not remain "unaffected" by the "gay, fascinating people" who surrounded him and "became inflated with success, and fancied himself a monumental genius . . . the foremost man of his time."[43]

This emphasis on the achievement of success without ambition as the key to Christian manhood reveals the psychological tightrope upon which Beecher's aspiring middle-class church members had to walk. After all, one of the basic elements of the Gospel of Love was the acceptance of self-interest as valid. "On one side," preached Beecher in a sermon in 1868, "we ought to be careful about our motives, and seek to act from high ones; but on the other side we ought not to be morbid and over-cautious in such a way as to take all satisfaction from human conduct."[44] "You must," he reiterated, "trust yourself." The point of the sermon "Motives of Action" had been that self-interest was not necessarily wrong. Yet in Theodore Tilton, Beecher's parishioners perceived a case where the aggressive pursuit of self-interest had resulted in a "master passion" leading ultimately to his plunge to the "bottom of the abyss."[45]

On a fundamental level, Tracy and the parishioners for whom he spoke found the "master passion" image the most frightening. Self-interest might be acceptable, they and Beecher would say, as long as it did not become an obsession. This, in fact, was the point of Beecher's sermon on the "Love of Money." Here, he went to great lengths to explain that it was not the money itself that was evil. "Wealth is a great power and a great blessing," Beecher said, "when it is held in a truly manly—that is Christian way . . . we are not to understand that *money* is the root of all evil but the *love* of it . . . bestowing love idolatrously upon material gain." It is only, Beecher insisted, when men sacrifice every "virtue and scruple for it [money], that it becomes dangerous—these men are likely to end their lives in suicide or in-

sanity!"[46] Thus Beecher justified the possession of fame, money, or material gain by reasoning that it was not those external goals that were evil, but
simply the internal *ambition* or passion for them. "The plaintiff [Tilton],"
explained Tracy, "presents the most impressive instance that has ever
come within my observation of the remorseless power and the destructive
effect of a *single absorbing master passion*. An all-dominating, selfish egotism is the basis of his character."[47]

Thus, in spite of his weakness and errors in judgment, Henry Ward Beecher was still idolized by his congregation because they believed that he
had achieved for himself what he promised them: fame and fortune without loss of "simplicity," and integrity. This assessment, of course, had little
to do with Beecher's real character, but rather with the idealized image he
projected to his audience so successfully. Beecher's very charm, boyish-
ness, and lack of sophistication, which so horrified his ministerial colleagues, served to heighten his idolization by these farmers' sons trans-
planted to the city.

Tilton, however, stood for the darker side of the Gospel of Love. In his
eagerness to achieve the same upward mobility as Beecher, he had, it
seemed, violated the bonds of affinity. Plymouthites were fearful that betrayal of such private political and class affinities would lead to a severing
of the only ties that bound them to humanity. For the young men of Tilton's generation this tension between individualism and loyalty to others
had particular importance. Because of the break from family and community—both in a geographic and a psychological sense—they were more
acutely sensitive to the need for a new set of loyalties or affinities than most
members of the Church of the Pilgrims. But as they adopted the Gospel of
Love with its emphasis on aggressive self-interest as a necessary prerequisite to success, the pursuit of such a goal increased the need to violate the
very affinities that had created social bonding in an impersonal urban environment. One measure of just how deeply these contradictions pervaded
their inner lives was the vehement denunciation of Theodore Tilton for following Beecher's advice in pursuing wealth and fame. In complaining that
Plymouth Church had treated Tilton with "epithets and denunciation,"
his lawyer made a telling point when he cried, "If Henry Ward Beecher is
innocent he needs no such clamorous and foul defense."[48] In short, the reason Plymouthites defended Beecher so vehemently (indeed violently) and
denounced Tilton so viciously was that Tilton had indeed carried Beecher's philosophy to its logical, and—perhaps—inevitable conclusion!

And yet the members of Plymouth Church remained loyal to Beecher
until his death in 1887. The year of the great trial, they voted to raise his

salary by $100,000 in order to pay for lawyers' fees. A year later, in 1876, they called a second Congregational Council to clear Beecher's name in a way the trial had failed to do. Carefully choosing the participant churches for their loyalty to Beecher, this council, unlike Storrs's Council of 1874, proclaimed its complete support for any action taken by Plymouth Church.[49] This included approving the excommunication of church members who had testified against the minister in 1875: Henry Bowen, Emma Moulton, Frank West, and Mattie Bradshaw.[50] At the same time, Plymouth Church generously rewarded Elizabeth Tilton for maintaining all through the councils and trial that Beecher was innocent. Several church members set up a private teaching arrangement for Elizabeth so that she could be paid for tutoring their children.[51] As long as she remained a loyal part of Beecher's circle, she was well supported. Like the political machines to which it bore a great similarity, Plymouth Church scrupulously took care of its faithful adherents.

When, however, Elizabeth Tilton bolted from the protective fold in 1878 with a strong, nonambiguous statement of her own and Beecher's guilt in the affair, Plymouth Church was just as determined in its rejection.[52] She, like Moulton, Bowen, and Bradshaw, was swiftly excommunicated. Elizabeth Tilton grew old in Brooklyn, a virtual outcast, sustained only by the devotion of her daughter and a small radical group known as the Christian Friends.[53]

Thus, in a process begun by Beecher in 1847, Plymouth Church completed the transition from a traditional authoritative institution with a specific theology and creed, to an amorphous group organized almost solely around the personal charisma and charm of Henry Ward Beecher. The triumph of that organizing principle came with the final purging of all dissenters from the Beecher cult. The trial had succeeded as nothing else had in welding Plymouth Church into an even more efficient machine than Brooklyn's political parties. On the surface, it seemed that Beecher's ideas of affinity, love, and loyalty had proven completely successful in winning over his parishioners.

On another more subtle level, however, the trial was not the triumph of Beecherism it seemed. It was, rather, the beginning of a retreat by Plymouth Church members from the full implications of the Gospel of Love. At the same time that Beecher's parishioners demonstrated their personal loyalty to the minister, the adultery trial shocked them into a perceptible withdrawal from the implicit dangers of the Gospel of Love. The minister, although he remained popular, was no longer taken quite as seriously; his sermons and books declined in sales until the Plymouth Church-owned firm of J. B. Ford went bankrupt, and his lectures were often frequented by curiosity seekers rather than admiring parishioners.[54] The once respected minister became the butt of satire and ridicule in weekly magazines such as *Puck's.*

The change can also be observed in more indirect ways, for example, the shifting political alliances of the church members. Just as Henry Bowen had been attracted to Beecher, then repelled by his excesses, Plymouthites, while still proclaiming their personal faith in their minister, began to retreat to more socially and politically conservative attitudes. Within ten years after the scandal, many Plymouth Church members, including Beecher himself, bolted the Republican party to join the Independent Republicans in supporting Grover Cleveland. Gerald McFarland, in his book *Mugwumps, Morals, and Politics,* notes the prominence of Beecher and Plymouth Church in that movement.[55]

Beecher historians have argued over the motivation for that support— whether it was the minister's empathy with the scandal in Cleveland's private life or a genuine commitment to reform—but that is not the most significant point.[56] What the defection to Cleveland really signified was the shift toward a greater conservatism. Although Mugwumps reflected a "reform" impulse in their attacks on corruption, they were most concerned with the restoration of ideology, principle, and strong social institutions. Mugwumps, then, sought to check the decline of hierarchy and authority in such fields as the ministry, law, and medicine.[57] This description is also a reasonably accurate one for the earlier Liberal movement—a movement highly antagonistic to Beecher and his church.[58] Thus, Plymouth Church members made a dramatic 180-degree turn from the Liberal bolt of 1874 to the Mugwump movement of 1884. In a short period, Plymouthites seem to have turned from affinity to ideology.

This shift was also reflected in Beecher's own writings and sermons. As Clifford Clark notes, Beecher's book *Evolution and Religion,* published in 1884, stresses the necessary role of institutions in "curbing" individualism.[59] Whether prompted by a general public shift in attitudes or Beecher's own evolving ideas, there was a marked change from his earlier anti-institutional emphasis.

A retreat from the Gospel of Love had other ramifications as well—ramifications that illustrate changing social attitudes toward women and ministers. The response of a number of Plymouth Church members to Elizabeth Tilton was similar in many respects to their reaction to Henry Ward

Beecher. Elizabeth was thought to be "pure," "truthful," and "pious"; her vacillating "weak" behavior, the consensus said, stemmed *not* from devious insincerity, but rather from simple innocence. Ironically, she was thought to be innocent of her own sexual nature that was, in fact, the guilty party. When Theodore insisted during his testimony that Elizabeth could commit the sin of adultery and at the same time retain her "purity," Beecher's congregation understood. It was a paradox Beecher had often described in his sermons. A higher sensitive nature, he said, was by definition closer to God, but it was also more unsuspecting and therefore vulnerable. The weakness inherent in purity was, in fact, an open invitation to victimization. Herein lay Elizabeth's dilemma—a condition that required not censure but protection—protection that would take the form of insulation from the harsh and dangerous world of sexuality, power, and politics. The Beecher trial occurred at the peak of the women's movement in the nineteenth century. Not until the 1970s would America again produce as outspoken a radical as Victoria Woodhull. It is no coincidence that Elizabeth Tilton rejected a vision of sexual and personal autonomy at the same moment that the majority of American women rejected Woodhull and her social revolution. External social pressure as well as internal psychological pressure left very litle choice.

The most important aspect of this feminine "domestication" was that women were now to accept reverence and protection at the price of any real political, economic, or social power. Ambition and innocence were thought to be incompatible in one person. Theodore Tilton, in particular, demonstrated the folly of uniting ambition with tenderness and sensitivity. Men striving to achieve both could probably be expected to experience the same anxiety and erratic behavior exhibited by Tilton. Conversely, it was commonly assumed that a woman's involvement in the competitive market place could drive her insane, or, at the least, result in physical illness. This, then, was the rationale for keeping women's superior sensitivity and vulnerable sexuality insulated from a world that could only corrupt. In effect, she had to be protected from herself in a way that had never been explicit in the Gospel of Love or the Free Love movement. Both those social models had been predicated upon man and woman's ultimate perfectability, but the new conservatism was based upon a rather gloomy view of human nature—both male and female. It was positive in the sense that the conservative reformers believed in uplift through social institutions and social environmental engineering, but it was negative in rejecting alternate lifestyles and personal freedom. Certain groups of individuals especially were subject to more control and protection than others—because they were now more vulnerable. One such group was obviously women. The scandal trial—and particularly the behavior of Elizabeth Tilton—had demonstrated that women, even pious, honest women, were not equipped to handle their own sexuality and the emotions associated with it in a world of temptation. We have already traced the morphology of Elizabeth's personal capitulation to this idea. The second set of people directly affected by the trial were ministers.

Henry Ward Beecher was exonerated by Plymouth Church because his motivation, his "integrity" emerged intact in their eyes. But this did not mean Plymouth Church members continued to think of him as strong or trustworthy. The report of the Plymouth Church Investigating Committee stated: "If this were a question of errors of judgment on the part of Mr. Beecher, it would be easy to criticize, especially in the light of recent events. In such criticism, even to the extent of regrets and censure, we are sure no man would join more sincerely than Mr. Beecher himself."[60] Beecher, they said, was known to be a man of impulsive temperament and generosity, thus, easily taken advantage of. These characteristics rendered him, like Elizabeth Tilton and women in general, vulnerable to unscrupulous individuals. Thus, Beecher was still honored for his sensitivity, even his exalted ideals, but his shrewdness or strength of character were now in doubt. He was never again taken quite so seriously in political or economic matters. By the time of his death, although still popular in some circles, he could no longer be called a major social force in American life.

Ironically, Beecher's role in the erosion of traditional authority in religion, his softening of the doctrines of Congregationalism and his identification of ministers and women as belonging to a higher sphere ultimately served to remove both those groups from the world of decision-making and power. In their retreat from the Gospel of Love, Plymouthites demonstrated their sympathy for innocence and simplicity by relegating people imbued with those characteristics to a protected and separate world: the nonthreatening and private world of church and home.

Essentially, the Gospel of Love was a social philosophy constructed by Henry Ward Beecher to make sense and order out of a society that had experienced a shattering breakdown of social institutions. Beecher's ideas did not cause this disintegration of family, church, and polity—they merely justified and rationalized that breakdown while at the same time substituting a system of social bonding between individuals who had been most affected by it. Acceptance of the Gospel of Love as a rationale for individualism and mobility, however, opened the door for experimentation with a personal freedom unrestrained by entrenched institutions. The disruption in the mid-nineteenth century of traditional institutions such as church, slavery, and political parties also brought into question the validity of marriage, so that at that time there was more questioning of the role of women and the institution of marriage than at any previous time. Most historians have dismissed that questioning as either heroic or lunatic. But as we have seen, these anti-institutional movements came to affect the lives of large numbers of middle-class men and women. Theodore and Elizabeth Tilton experimented directly with sexual affinity, but one suspects that most people demonstrated their attraction to these ideas by adopting the standards of romantic love within their own marriages. The enduring legacy of the Gospel of Love is, in fact, this overly romantic and sentimental notion of love and sexuality. Stripped of its implications for personal autonomy, the Gospel of Love came to represent an oppressive hypocrisy in its denial of sexuality and ambition. Instead of justifying those two, as Beecher had striven so tortuously to do, his parishioners ended up denying them altogether as motivating forces.

The dangers in the Gospel of Love lay not so much in the actual inability of human beings to deal with personal freedom, but in the perceptions of Beecher's followers that they did not possess sufficient internal discipline to suppress what Beecher had termed the "passions whirling within." Thus, they began to alter their opinions on the viability of personal loyalty and affinity. As we have seen, by 1884, many of them deserted "machine" politics for various conservatively oriented reform movements. In the late nineteenth-century "search for order," described by Robert Wiebe, Beecher's followers abandoned the Gospel of Love as a stabilizing force in the political and economic spheres.

The trial of Henry Ward Beecher signified an important turning point in that process. For Storrs's more orthodox church members, as for the early Liberal Republicans, it merely confirmed their long-held fears of the social chaos inherent in the Gospel of Love. Inasmuch as the scandal allowed them to pursue more successfully their goals of re-establishing strong intellectual, professional, and moral standards that would curb social experimentation and diversity, this group prefigured the progressive movement of the end of the century.

But more significant was the effect of the trial on the parishioners nurtured and steeped in Beecher's Gospel of Love. Not that this single instance of immorality caused a complete rejection of Beecher's ideas, but the trial did serve to create a mirror for collective psychic anxiety associated with changing values. Theodore and Elizabeth Tilton dramatized the internal turmoil created by the loss of social institutions and their replacement with

Beecher's new notions of romantic love and quasi-perfectionism. Tilton became something of a martyr to the struggle; unable to compete in the market place because of the obstruction of the Plymouth Church "machine," he ended up in Paris, an impoverished, changed man. Elizabeth, as we have seen, accepted her new role as subservient wife and mother but because of the scandal was never able to live it out; in that way she was atypical of a whole generation of middle-class women. It is no accident that Victoria Woodhull left America in 1876. She eventually married an English nobleman and repudiated all her scandalous views on Free Love. She, like Beecher's parishioners, accepted marriage as a necessary prerequisite for social stability and the protection of women. The Gospel of Love, it seems, had proven too dangerous a doctrine for any but the powerless.

Notes

I INTRODUCTION

1. *Woodhull and Claflin's Weekly,* 2 November 1872.
2. John B. Ellis, *Free Love and Its Votaries* (New York, 1870), p. 442.
3. Ibid., pp. 9–10.
4. For the career of Victoria Woodhull, see Johanna Johnston, *Mrs. Satan: The Incredible Saga of Victoria C. Woodhull* (New York, 1967); Emanie Sachs, *"The Terrible Siren," Victoria Woodhull 1838–1927* (New York, 1928); M. M. Marberry, *Vicky: A Biography of Victoria C. Woodhull* (New York, 1967); and for a sympathetic contemporary view—Theodore Tilton, "Victoria C. Woodhull: A Biographical Sketch," *Golden Age Tract No. 3* (New York, 1871).
5. *Woodhull and Claflin's Weekly,* 2 November 1872.
6. James Parton, *Famous Men of Recent Times* (Boston, 1893), p. 349.
7. For contemporary studies of Beecher's influence and popularity, see Lyman Abbott, ed., *Henry Ward Beecher: A Sketch of His Career* (New York, 1883); Joseph Howard, Jr., *The Life of Henry Ward Beecher* (Philadelphia, 1887); John R. Howard, *Henry Ward Beecher: A Study of His Personality, Career, and Influence in Public Affairs* (New York, 1891); Thomas W. Knox, *The Life and Works of Henry Ward Beecher* (Hartford, 1887); John Henry Barrows, *Henry Ward Beecher: The Shakespeare of the Pulpit* (New York, 1893).
8. *Woodhull and Claflin's Weekly,* 2 November 1872.
9. The source of the newspaper accounts was primarily the verbatim reports of the Plymouth Church investigation which continued for most of July and August 1874. The testimony was originally supposed to be secret but was routinely leaked to the press. Immediately after this church trial, many sensational books and pamphlets on the scandal were hurried to press in order to cash in on public fascination with the affair. Most of these contain identical documents, testimonies, and letters that had been lifted from newspapers. Any of them can be used as a basic sourcebook—but the one I found valuable and readily available was Charles F. Marshall, *The True History of the Brooklyn Scandal* (Philadelphia, 1874). It contains Victoria Woodhull's original statement, brief biographies of the principal characters, public statements of Henry Ward Beecher, Theodore Tilton, Elizabeth Tilton, and Francis Moulton, their cross-examinations before the church committee, the final report of the committee, and numerous lengthy quotes from newspaper articles and editorials. Indeed, in some ways, the church investigation of 1874 revealed more than the later civil trial, for Elizabeth Tilton testified here as she did not in the civil case. The only extensive body of documentation not included in Marshall's *True History* is Elizabeth's and Theodore's letters to each other, which were first published in the *Chicago Tribune* on August 13, 1874. The following summary of the scandal is taken mostly from statements and testimony before the Plymouth Church Investigating Committee (PCIC) and the Tilton letters—many of which were published later in the trial transcript.

Additional contemporary works on the scandal include: *The Beecher-Tilton Investigation: The Scandal of the Age* (Philadelphia, 1874); *The Beecher-Tilton Scandal: Complete History of the Case from November 1872 to the Present Time* (Brooklyn, 1874); John E. P. Doyle, *Plymouth Church and Its Pastor, or Henry Ward Beecher and His Accusers* (Hartford, 1874); Edmund Fairfield, *Wickedness in High Places* (Mansfield, Ohio, 1874); *The Great Brooklyn Romance: All the Documents in the Famous Beecher-Tilton Case, Unabridged* (New York, 1874); Leon Oliver, *The Great Sensation* (Chicago, 1873); [Treat, Joseph], *Beecher, Tilton, Woodhull: The Creation of Society* (New York, 1874); Francis P. Williamson, *Beecher and His Accusers* Philadelphia, 1874).

10. Elizabeth Tilton (hereafter ET) to Theodore Tilton (hereafter TT) 25 January 1867, in *Theodore Tilton vs. Henry Ward Beecher, Action for Crim. Con.*, 3 vols. (New York, 1875), 1:499 (hereafter *Trial*).

11. TT, "Sworn Statement," 20 July 1874, Plymouth Church Investigating Committee (hereafter PCIC), in Marshall, *True History*, pp. 116, 115.

12. "Mr. Moulton's Last Statement," *New York Daily Graphic*, 11 September 1874, in Marshall, *True History*, p. 479.

13. Theodore Tilton, "Victoria C. Woodhull: A Biographical Sketch."

14. "Dr. Bacon's Speech," 2 April 1874, in Marshall, *True History*, pp. 40–42.

15. TT to Dr. Leonard Bacon, 21 June 1874, ibid., pp. 42–43.

16. ET testimony, 31 July 1874, PCIC, ibid., p. 197.

17. "Report of the Committee of Investigation," 28 August 1874, ibid., pp. 405–33.

18. Henry C. Bowen to the Examining Committee of Plymouth Church, 4 February 1876, in the *Independent*, 10 February 1876, p. 3.

19. Paxton Hibben, *Henry Ward Beecher: An American Portrait* (New York, 1927), p. 284. Beecher's most recent biographer, Clifford Clark, believes that the minister did retain his "central" position in the community.

20. Ibid.

21. Sachs, *"Terrible Siren,"* p. 90.

22. Robert Shaplen, *Free Love and Heavenly Sinners* (New York, 1954).

23. William G. McLoughlin, *The Meaning of Henry Ward Beecher* (New York, 1970), pp. ix, x.

24. Ibid., p. xii.

25. Paul A. Carter, "God and Man in Brooklyn: The Reputation of Henry Ward Beecher," *The Spiritual Crisis of the Gilded Age* (DeKalb, Ill., 1971), pp. 109–32.

26. Clifford E. Clark, Jr., *Henry Ward Beecher: Spokesman for Middle-Class America* (Urbana, 1978), p. 225.

27. Key works on family history are: Philippe Aries, *Centuries of Childhood: A Social History of Family Life* (New York, 1962); John Demos, *A Little Commonwealth: Family Life in Plymouth Colony* (New York, 1970); Michael Gordon, *The American Family: Past, Present, and Future* (New York, 1978); Peter Laslett, ed., *Household and Family in Past Time* (Cambridge, 1972); Edward Shorter, *The Making of the Modern Family* (New York, 1975).

28. Hibben, *Beecher: An American Portrait*, p. 276.

29. Shaplen, *Free Love*, p. 38.

30. A. McElroy Wylie, "Mr. Beecher as a Social Force," *Scribner's Monthly* 4 (October 1872): 754.

2   HENRY WARD BEECHER

1. Henry Ward Beecher to Robert Bonner, 3 January 1866, quoted in Thomas W. Knox, *The Life and Works of Henry Ward Beecher*, p. 253.

2. William G. McLoughlin, *The Meaning of Henry Ward Beecher,* pp. 85, 91–92. Mc-Loughlin's book is limited to an exploration of the ideas presented in *Norwood.*

3. HWB testimony, *Trial,* 2:735.

4. ET testimony, PCIC, quoted in Marshall, *True History,* p. 192.

5. Paxton Hibben, *Beecher: An American Portrait* (New York, 1927), p. 50.

6. For the Beecher family see HWB testimony, *Trial,* 2:729; Barbara Cross, ed., *The Autobiography of Lyman Beecher* (Cambridge, 1961); Constance Rourke, *Trumpets of Jubilee* (New York, 1927); Kathryn Kish Sklar, *Catherine Beecher: A Study in American Domesticity* (New Haven, 1973); Charles H. Foster, *The Rungless Ladder: Harriet Beecher Stowe and New England Puritanism* (Durham, N. C., 1954); Lyman Beecher Stowe, *Saints, Sinners, and Beechers* (Indianapolis, 1934); Robert Merideth, *The Politics of the Universe: Edward Beecher, Abolition, and Orthodoxy* (Nashville, 1968); Stuart Henry, *Unvanquished Puritan: A Portrait of Lyman Beecher* (Grand Rapids, Mich., 1973); Marie Caskey, *Chariot of Fire: Religion and the Beecher family* (New Haven, 1978); Milton Rugoff, *The Beechers: An American Family in the Nineteenth Century* (New York, 1981).

7. HWB, *Trial,* 2:729.

8. Harriet Beecher Stowe, n.d., quoted in Abbott, *Henry Ward Beecher: A Sketch of His Career,* pp. 14–15.

9. HWB Autobiography, in Joseph Howard, Jr., *The Life of Henry Ward Beecher* (Philadelphia, 1887), p. 589.

10. Ibid., p. 587. Marie Caskey, *Chariot of Fire: Religion and the Beecher Family* (New Haven, 1978) contains good evidence on this point.

11. *Christian Union,* 15 January 1870, p. 36.

12. Ibid., 8 October 1870. Also quoted in Hibben, *Beecher: An American Portrait,* p. 50.

13. HWB to Harriet Beecher Stowe, 28 March 1833, Beecher Collection, Amherst College.

14. HWB, "Moral Affinity the True Ground of Unity," 6 December 1868, *The Plymouth Pulpit: Sermons Preached in Plymouth Church, Brooklyn, New York* (London, 1894), ser. 1, pp. 286–89.

15. HWB Diary, Beecher Papers, Box 47, Folder 2, Yale.

16. HWB Autobiography, Howard, *Life,* pp. 586, 587.

17. Hibben, *Beecher: An American Portrait,* p. 27.

18. Lyman Beecher to H. Humphrey, 30 September 1830, Beecher Collection, Amherst College.

19. Quoted in Hibben, *Beecher: An American Portrait,* p. 14.

20. Ibid., pp. 31–32.

21. Madeleine B. Stern, *Heads and Headlines: The Phrenological Fowlers* (Norman, Okla., 1971); Stephen Nissenbaum, *Sex, Diet, and Debility in Jacksonian America* (Westport, Conn., 1980), pp. 147–49.

22. Hibben, *Beecher: An American Portrait,* p. 43; Rugoff, *The Beechers,* p. 130.

23. HWB, *Eyes and Ears* (New York, 1862), p. 25. Quoted in ibid., p. 43.

24. HWB Autobiography, Howard, *Life,* p. 588.

25. The *National Union Catalogue* of the Library of Congress lists thirty-nine editions published between 1844 and 1912.

26. HWB, *Lectures to Young Men* (New York, 1873), pp. 68–69.

27. HWB, *Yale Lectures on Preaching* (New York, 1872), p. 146.

28. HWB Autobiography, Howard, *Life,* p. 589.

29. HWB, *Yale Lectures on Preaching,* p. 11. Quoted in Hibben, *Beecher: An American Portrait,* p. 86.

30. Daniel C. Calhoun, *Professional Lives in America 1750–1850: Structure and Aspiration* (Cambridge, Mass., 1965); Ann Douglas, *The Feminization of American Culture* (New York, 1977), pp. 17–49.

31. On the importance of land in shaping relations between fathers and sons, see Philip Greven, Jr., *Four Generations: Population, Land, and Family in Colonial Andover, Massachusetts* (Ithaca, 1970), pp. 125–72, 222–38.

32. HWB, "Through Fear to Love," 16 February 1873, *Plymouth Pulpit*, ser. 5, pp. 451–61.

33. See Douglas, *The Feminization of American Culture*.

34. Noyes L. Thompson, *The History of Plymouth Church (Henry Ward Beecher) 1847–1872* (New York, 1873), pp. 181–82, 202–3.

35. Ibid., pp. 202–3.

36. Henry Ward Beecher, *The Life of Christ* (New York, 1871), p. 345.

37. Cited in Thompson, *History of Plymouth Church*, p. 223.

38. Eunice Bullard to HWB, Winter 1834–35, Beecher Papers, Box 7, Folder 308, Yale.

39. HWB to Eunice Beecher, 27 September 1847, ibid.

40. Hibben, *Beecher: An American Portrait*, p. 86.

41. Eunice Beecher, *From Dawn to Daylight: The Simple Story of a Western Home* (New York, 1859), p. 39.

42. Ibid., pp. 292–93.

43. Eunice Beecher to HWB, 20 September 1843, Beecher Papers, Box 7, Folder 308, Yale. In this letter Eunice lets her husband know that she is aware of his perception of her as a whimpering complainer.

44. Eunice Beecher, *From Dawn to Daylight*, p. 293.

45. HWB Sermon, *Independent*, 27 October 1859. Quoted in Hibben, *Beecher: An American Portrait*, p. 144.

46. Henry C. Bowen to HWB, 31 July 1863, Beecher Papers, Box 9, Folder 345, Yale.

47. Henry Bowen's Statement to the Examining Committee of Plymouth Church, 4 February 1876. In the *Independent*, 10 February 1876, p. 3.

48. Plymouth Church Records, Book 39, Minutes of the Board of Trustees 1856–1900, Plymouth Church, Brooklyn, New York.

49. Henry C. Bowen to Theodore Tilton, 14 June 1863, Beecher Collection, Box 1, Library of Congress. Later, after the Congregational Council at which Bowen admitted he knew Beecher to be an adulterer, Bowen still insisted that it was not his wife who had been involved. He would not reveal names but said he knew of several women whom Beecher had seduced.

50. HWB testimony, *Trial*, 3:127.

51. HWB to J. P.Clarke, January 1858, Beecher Collection, Houghton Library, Harvard.

52. HWB, "The Seducer," in *The Beecher-Tilton Investigation*, p. 75.

53. "Mr. Beecher's Initiation into Free Love," unsigned manuscript, 1872, Woodhull Collection, University of Southern Illinois Library, Carbondale.

54. Madeleine Bettina Stern, *The Pantarch: A Biography of Stephen Pearl Andrews* (Austin, Tex., 1968).

55. O. S. Fowler, *Love and Parentage* (New York, 1843), p. 87.

56. "The New Theories of Marriage," *Christian Union*, 26 July 1871. On the issue of Free Love, no less a respected personage than Elizabeth Cady Stanton had this to say: "We are one and all free lovers at heart, although we may not have thought so. We all believe in a good time coming, either in this world or another, when man and woman will be good and wise, when they will be 'a law unto themselves,' and when therefore the external law of compulsion will be no longer needed" (Elizabeth Cady Stanton Speech, "On Marriage and Divorce," 1870, in *Signs* 1[Autumn 1975]: 265–68).

57. The *Chicago Tribune* reported that Beecher received many love letters from women. "He receives love letters by the ream and cord. . . . His wife reads them before he does" (*Chicago Tribune*, 24 June 1874, p. 1).

3 THEODORE TILTON

1. ET testimony, PCIC, Marshall, *True History,* pp. 191–92. On the character of Plymouth Church see Stephen Morrell Griswold, *Sixty Years with Plymouth Church* (Chicago, 1907), p. 28, and Thompson, *History of Plymouth Church.*
2. New York City Directories, 1830–1840.
3. "Solved—Is Insanity the Key to the Beecher Scandal?", *Brooklyn Eagle,* 1 August 1874, p. 1.
4. TT testimony, *Trial,* 1:456–57.
5. For an analysis of the Gospel of Love see McLoughlin, *The Meaning of Henry Ward Beecher.*
6. HWB, "Man's Accountability to God," 16 May 1847, in Thompson, *History of Plymouth Church,* pp. 29–57.
7. TT testimony, *Trial,* 1:456–57.
8. Clifford Clark, "The Changing Nature of Protestantism in Mid-Nineteenth Century America: Henry Ward Beecher's *Seven Lectures to Young Men,*" *Journal of American History* 57, no. 4 (March 1971): 832–46.
9. Plymouth Church, Brooklyn, Book 21, Minutes, Baptisms, Admissions, May 8, 1847, to December 8, 1865.
10. TT testimony, *Trial,* 1:458–59.
11. Marshall, *True History,* pp. 93–100.
12. For a history of the *Independent,* see Frank Luther Mott, *A History of American Magazines,* 3 vols. (New York, 1938), 2:367–79.
13. HWB testimony, *Trial,* 2:735.
14. Griswold, *Sixty Years,* p. 21.
15. William Hayes Ward, "Sixty Years of the *Independent,*" *Independent* 65, no. 3132 (1908): 1347.
16. ET testimony, PCIC, Marshall, *True History,* p. 190.
17. TT to Henry C. Bowen, 5 January 1860, Beecher Collection, Box 1, Library of Congress.
18. Ward, "Sixty Years of the *Independent,*" pp. 1347–48.
19. HWB testimony, *Trial,* 2:735.
20. TT to ET, 2 December 1866, ibid., 1:503.
21. HWB testimony, PCIC, Marshall, *True History,* p. 256.
22. For Theodore Tilton's public career, see Ward, "Sixty Years of the *Independent,*" pp. 1345–51; Eugene Benson, "New York Journalists: Theodore Tilton," *Galaxy,* September 1869, pp. 355–59; L. P. Brockett, *Men of Our Day* (New York, 1868), pp. 612–18; Edwin Terry, "Theodore Tilton as Social Reformer, Radical Republican, Newspaper Editor, 1863–1872" (Ph.D. diss., St. John's University, 1971); Sharon Ann Carroll, "Elitism and Reform: Some Anti-Slavery Opinion-Makers in the Era of Civil War and Reconstruction" (Ph.D. diss., Cornell, 1970).
23. Terry, "Theodore Tilton," p. 73.
24. Ward, "Sixty Years of the *Independent,*" p. 1347.
25. Robert D. Benedict to Stephen Hitchcock, 4 December 1850, William Page Papers, Archives of American Art, Smithsonian Institution.
26. HWB, "Moral Affinity the True Ground of Unity," 6 December 1868, ser. 1, pp. 285, 286.
27. Ibid., p. 289.
28. Eighth Census of the United States, Population Schedules, Brooklyn, New York, Ward 6.
29. ET testimony, PCIC, Marshall, *True History,* p. 191.
30. Ibid., p. 192.
31. HWB testimony, *Trial,* 2:740.
32. ET testimony, PCIC, Marshall, *True History,* p. 189.
33. TT to ET, 31 July 1865, cited in *Chicago Tribune* (hereafter CT), 13 August 1874.

34. Ibid.
35. Sarah Putnam testimony, *Trial*, 2:154.
36. Samuel Wilkeson testimony, ibid., p. 302.
37. Isabella Oakley testimony, ibid., p. 245. Also, Bessie Turner testimony, ibid., p. 467.
38. ET testimony, PCIC, Marshall, *True History*, p. 198.
39. Ibid., p. 191.
40. Ibid., p. 190.
41. Bessie Turner testimony, *Trial*, 2:466.
42. Sarah Putnam testimony, *Trial*, 2:161.
43. HWB, "The Strong to Bear with the Weak," 25 October 1868, *Plymouth Pulpit*, ser. 1, p. 122.
44. TT to ET, 1 March 1868, CT.
45. TT to ET, 17 December 1866, ibid.
46. Bessie Turner testimony, PCIC, Marshall, *True History*, p. 391; and *Trial*, 2:466, 533.
47. TT to ET, 1 March 1868, CT.
48. TT to ET, 15 January 1869, ibid.
49. HWB, "Love of Money," 22 November 1868, *Plymouth Pulpit*, ser. 1, pp. 251–52.
50. TT testimony, *Trial*, 1:629.
51. TT to ET, 23 March 1866, 27 January 1866, and 1 December 1866, CT.
52. TT to ET, 1 February 1867, ibid.
53. TT to ET, 6 December 1866, *Trial*, 1:503, 494.
54. TT to ET, 9 January 1865, CT.
55. TT to ET, 4 January 1867, ibid. Theodore's infidelity appears to have taken place between December 7, 1866 and December 31, 1866 in Dubuque or Clinton, Iowa. There are numerous fragments of evidence for this but one particular letter makes it clear. Over two years later, when Elizabeth knew of the affair, Theodore returned to Clinton, and on February 20, 1868, wrote: "the old fragrance has gone out of the 'prairie rose'! The flower is still comely, interesting, and agreeable, but I marvel at myself for once thinking it so fragrant above all the rest of the garden. It is gone forever! It can never be to me henceforth anything but a common flower. This figure of speech is a mystery which I think you will understand. . . . Faithfully yours—That word 'faithfully' means a great deal."
56. HWB, "The Strong to Bear with the Weak," 25 October 1868, *Plymouth Pulpit*, ser. 1, p. 122.
57. Ibid., p. 116.

4   ELIZABETH TILTON

1. This figure computed from Plymouth Church Records, Register of Members, Book 38, Plymouth Church, Brooklyn, New York.
2. HWB, "Moral Affinity the Ground of True Unity," 6 December 1868, *Plymouth Pulpit*, ser. 1, p. 285. Clifford Clark, in his biography of Beecher, argues that Beecher was not anti-institutional in the same way as Emerson and the Transcendentalists, and that he never preached quite the same radical individualism. Clark cites Beecher's strong support for the family as the basic social institution and quotes an 1849 sermon that states "the family is *the* most important *institution on earth*." I would agree that Beecher did not strive to *abolish* social institutions, but he did argue for a radical change in the basis of institutions—so radical, in fact, that their very nature was altered. Beecher's tendency to declare conventional ideas about family and sexuality followed by a series of qualifications had the effect of making him appear more conservative than he really was. It probably gave him the feeling that he was being honest with both his audience and himself. I do, however, believe Clark is right when he describes Beecher's increasingly institutional out-

look after the adultery trial. By 1884 Beecher has become much more conservative with regard to social institutions.

3. HWB, "Love of Money," 22 November 1868, *Plymouth Pulpit,* ser. 1, p. 235; and "Moral Affinity," pp. 304, 305.

4. For women's role in the family, see Barbara Welter, "The Cult of True Womanhood 1820–1860," *American Quarterly* 18 (Summer 1966): 151–74; Phillida Bunkle, "Sentimental Womanhood and Domestic Education, 1830–1879," *History of Education Quarterly* 14, no. 1 (Spring 1974): 13–30; Kirk Jeffrey, "The Family as Utopian Retreat from the City," *Soundings* 55 (1972): 21–41. For women's health problems in the nineteenth century, see Catherine E. Beecher, *Letters to the People on Health and Happiness* (New York, 1855); Ann D. Wood, "The Fashionable Diseases," *Journal of Interdisciplinary History* 4 (Summer 1973): 25–52; Carroll Smith-Rosenberg, "The Hysterical Woman: Sex Roles and Role Conflict in Nineteenth-Century America," *Social Research* 39, no. 4 (Winter 1972): 652–78.

5. For hints as to the nature of relationships in the boardinghouse, see ET to TT, 28 February 1868, *Trial,* 1:492–93; ET to TT, 31 January 1868, ibid., p. 503; ET testimony, PCIC, Marshall, *True History,* p. 195.

6. Marshall, *True History,* pp. 103–6.

7. ET testimony, PCIC, ibid., pp. 190, 197.

8. Ibid., pp. 190, 191.

9. ET to TT, 31 January 1868, *Trial,* 1:503.

10. TT to ET, 9 January 1865, 3 March 1866, CT.

11. TT to ET, 4 January 1867, 31 December 1866, ibid.

12. TT to ET, 6 December 1866, *Trial, 1:494.*

13. TT to ET, 7 December 1866, ibid. Tilton's ideas on this subject are more fully explained in an article he wrote: "Love, Marriage, and Divorce," *Independent,* 1 December 1870.

14. TT to ET, 7 December 1866, *Trial, 1:494.*

15. HWB, "The Primacy of Love," 29 March 1874, *Plymouth Pulpit,* ser. 6, p. 50.

16. McLoughlin, *Meaning of Henry Ward Beecher,* pp. 91–92.

17. ET to TT, 11 January 1867, CT.

18. ET to TT, 7 January 1867, *Trial,* 1:448.

19. ET to TT, 14 January 1867, CT.

20. TT to ET, 26 January 1868, *Trial,* 1:617.

21. ET to TT, 31 January 1868, ibid., p. 503.

22. ET to TT, 3 February 1868, ibid., p. 451.

23. TT to ET, 9 February 1868, ibid.

24. Ibid.

25. TT to ET, 20 February 1868, ibid.

26. ET to TT, 28 January 1868, ibid., p. 449.

27. ET to TT, 29 February 1868, CT.

28. ET to TT, 31 January 1868, *Trial,* 1:503.

29. ET to TT, 1 February 1868, ibid., p. 489.

30. ET to TT, 4 March 1868, ibid., p. 449.

31. ET to TT, 8 March 1868, ibid., p. 490.

32. ET to TT, 20 February 1868, ibid., p. 491.

33. ET to TT, 17 February 1868, CT.

34. The Tilton children were Florence (b. 1858), Alice (b. 1859), Mattie (died in infancy), Carroll (b. 1864), Paul (born and died, summer 1868), and Ralph (b. 1869).

35. TT to ET, 3 November 1868, *Trial,* 1:500.

36. ET to TT, 26 January 1869, ibid., p. 450.

37. Byron Strong, "Toward a History of the Experiential Family: Sex and Incest in the Nineteenth-Century Family," *Journal of Marriage and the Family* 35 (August 1973): 457–66.

5   PLYMOUTH

1. Harold Coffin Syrett, *The City of Brooklyn 1865–1898: A Political History* (New York, 1944), pp. 13–19.
2. Henry R. Stiles, ed., *The Civil, Political, Professional, and Ecclesiastical History and Commercial and Industrial Record of the County of Kings and the City of Brooklyn, New York, from 1683 to 1844,* 2 vols. (New York, 1884), 2:815–24.
3. Henry W. B. Howard, ed., *The Eagle and Brooklyn,* 2 vols. (Brooklyn, 1893), 2:294–96.
4. Noyes L. Thompson, *The History of Plymouth Church, (Henry Ward Beecher) 1847–1872* (New York, 1873), p. 65.
5. Henry C. Bowen to HWB, 6 August 1847, Beecher Papers, Box 9, Folder 345, Yale.
6. Bowen to HWB, 26 March 1847, ibid.
7. Howard, *Life,* p. 172.
8. Henry C. Bowen to HWB, 6 August 1847, 1 September 1847, Beecher Papers, Box 9, Folder 345, Yale.
9. Stephen M. Griswold, *Sixty Years with Plymouth Church* (Chicago, 1907), pp. 28, 61.
10. Bowen to HWB, 1 September 1847, Beecher Papers, Box 9, Folder 345, Yale.
11. Bowen to HWB, 20 May 1847, ibid.
12. Bowen to HWB, 21 July 1847, ibid.
13. Barrows, *Shakespeare of the Pulpit,* p. 490.
14. Thompson, *History of Plymouth Church,* pp. 64, 160.
15. *Christian Union,* 9 October 1872, p. 306.
16. Stephen Griswold, *Sixty Years* (Chicago, 1907).
17. Plymouth Church Membership List, in Thompson, *The History of Plymouth Church,* pp. 237–89; United States Census, Ninth Census (1870), Population Schedules, Brooklyn, New York, Wards 1–12, 20, 22.
18. Griswold, *Sixty Years,* p. 17. Biographies of other members also indicate that a rural New England background was common. George Burt Lincoln, for example, was born in Hardwick, Massachusetts, in 1817, and left the farm at fifteen. Another farmer's son was Abraham Daily, born in Sheffield, Massachusetts, who left the farm for New York in 1858. Stiles, ed., *History of Kings County,* 2:866, 1244.
19. For economic conditions in New England, see James Henretta, *The Evolution of American Society 1700–1815* (Lexington, Mass., 1973); Percy W. Bidwell and John I. Falconer, *History of Agriculture in the Northern United States 1620–1869* (1925; reprint ed., New York, 1941), pp. 89–98.
20. Griswold, *Sixty Years,* p. 17.
21. Ibid., p. 16.
22. One example of many books portraying this image is Matthew Hale Smith, *Sunshine and Shadow* (Hartford, 1869).
23. Griswold, *Sixty Years,* p. 19.
24. Ibid., pp. 19, 21.
25. William Beach summation, *Trial,* 3:319.
26. HWB to Charles Beecher [November 1852], Beecher Papers, Yale.
27. Plymouth Church Records, Book 21, Minutes, Baptisms, Admissions, 1847–1865, 30 August 1847, Plymouth Church.
28. Ibid., 25 February 1848, 30 July 1847, 17 April 1848.
29. Ibid., 17 April 1848.
30. Ibid.
31. Ibid.
32. Plymouth Church Records, Book 36, Minutes 1865–1874, 7 January 1870, Plymouth Church.
33. *Brooklyn Eagle,* 9 January 1871.

34. Plymouth Church Records, Book 21, Minutes, Baptisms, Admissions, 1847–1965, 17 April 1848.

35. Ibid., 23 February 1850.

36. Ibid., 3 December 1858.

37. Plymouth Church to the Brooklyn Congregational Council, March 1874, in *The Brooklyn Council of 1874* (New York, 1874), p. 120.

38. Plymouth Church Records, Book 21, 3 December 1852.

39. Ibid., 11 December 1856.

40. Ibid., 17 December 1856.

41. Ibid., 11 December 1856.

42. Ibid., 17 December 1856.

43. Thompson, *History of Plymouth Church,* p. 160.

44. *Christian Union,* 1 January 1870, p. 8.

45. Henry C. Bowen to HWB, 26 March 1847, Beecher Papers, Box 9, Folder 345, Yale.

46. Abbott, *Henry Ward Beecher: A Sketch of His Career,* p. 124. Bowen, like Beecher, was always committed to antislavery rather than abolitionism. The *Independent* was a moderate paper until Tilton became the editor; after he was fired it returned to the conservative side of moderate.

47. For these disagreements between Bowen and Beecher, see the series of letters Bowen wrote to Beecher, 27 November 1856; 3 May 1860; 11 May 1861; 1 January 1863; all in the Beecher Collection, Box 1, Library of Congress. This series of problems was finally settled by arbitrator Charles Gould who awarded Bowen $1,000 in damages.

48. Henry Bowen biography, *The Great Brooklyn Romance: All the Documents in the Famous Beecher-Tilton Case: Unabridged* (New York, 1874), pp. 95–99.

49. TT, "The True Story," December 1872, in the *New York Tribune,* 6 March 1875; and in *Trial,* 2:716–19.

50. Bowen to HWB, 1 May 1862, Box 1, Beecher Papers, Library of Congress.

51. Bowen to TT, 14 June 1863, Beecher Collection, Box 1, Library of Congress. This letter is both strong evidence that Beecher was, in fact, an adulterer *and* that, despite Bowen's later denials, it was with Lucy that Beecher had committed adultery. It seems significant that Lucy's death prompted Bowen to use such strong language in his letter to Tilton.

52. Bowen to HWB, 31 July 1863, Beecher Papers, Box 9, Folder 345, Yale. Beecher family tradition has long held that Beecher exerted a decisive influence on the diplomacy of the Civil War when he was in England. He is supposed to have "persuaded" the English people and government, for that matter, not to give aid to the South. More recent historians have pointed out, however, that the decision was made by military events and the Emancipation Proclamation, and had little to do with Beecher's oratorical ability.

53. Bowen Scrapbooks, 1, no. 45, American Antiquarian Society, Worcester, Massachusetts.

54. Henry C. Bowen to the Examining Committee of Plymouth Church, 4 February 1876, *Independent,* 10 February 1876, p. 3.

55. *Brooklyn Eagle,* 20 February 1871. Also Howard, *The Eagle and Brooklyn,* 2:105.

56. HWB sermon on Lincoln, *New York Times,* 14 November 1864, p. 8; Beecher sermon on "Charity," *Brooklyn Eagle,* 10 January 1870; "Beecher Backs Conkling," *New York Times,* 9 October 1879.

57. HWB to Charles Beecher, n.d., in *The Autobiography of Lyman Beecher,* 2:476–77. Quoted in Hibben, *Beecher: An American Portrait,* p. 89.

58. HWB testimony, *Trial,* 2:736.

59. Terry, "Theodore Tilton," p. 73.

60. HWB to the Cleveland Convention, 30 August 1866, *Trial,* 2:476–77.

61. HWB to Leonard Bacon, 21 September 1866, Beecher Papers, Box 7, Folder 291, Yale.

62. Beecher's Calendar of Events, n.d., Beecher Papers, Box 72, Folder 29, Yale.

63. HWB to Leonard Bacon, 21 September 1866, Beecher Papers, Box 7, Folder 291, Yale.

64. Ibid.

65. *Brooklyn Eagle,* 7 August 1874.

66. HWB testimony, *Trial,* 2:836.

67. Hibben, *Beecher: An American Portrait,* p. 197; Clark, *HWB: Spokesman,* pp. 203–4.

68. TT, Editorial in the *Independent,* quoted in Ellis, *Free Love,* pp. 456–57.

69. It is impossible to quantify and statistically analyze these factions—as useful as that would be—because church records do not indicate how individual members voted on the various issues. There was a consistent group of about twenty-five members who opposed Beecher and several of these are identifiable as friends and supporters of Henry Bowen. A scrutiny of the records of the Church of the Pilgrims and the newer Clinton Avenue Congregational Church indicates that a significant number (perhaps thirty-five or forty) left Beecher's church to join these two churches. People may have joined Clinton Avenue Church because they moved closer to it. It was located in one of the newer, wealthier sections of the city. Church of the Pilgrims, however, was located in Brooklyn Heights only a few blocks from Plymouth Church. The reason for these parishioners' switch, then, was probably dissatisfaction with Beecher.

70. Plymouth Church Records, Book 36, 8 July 1870.

71. B. Franklin Cooling, *Benjamin Franklin Tracy: Father of the Modern American Fighting Navy* (Hamden, Conn., 1973), pp. 36, 38.

72. HWB sermon, "Charity," *Brooklyn Eagle,* 10 January 1870.

73. Frank Moulton testimony, *Trial,* 1:116.

74. *Christian Union,* 1 January 1870.

6   THE SCANDAL AND LOCAL POLITICS

1. *Brooklyn Sunday Press,* 6 July 1873. Reprinted in *Woodhull and Claflin's Weekly,* 19 July 1873, p. 12.

2. Harold Coffin Syrett, *The City of Brooklyn 1865–1898: A Political History* (New York, 1944), pp. 13–19.

3. "The Brooklyn Ring," *New York Times,* 26 October 1870 and 3 September 1875. In a conversation with a wealthy citizen of Brooklyn, McLoughlin made the following statement: "When I first entered politics, a poor man in Brooklyn could not get a nomination for office. I determined to remedy that state of things. When you rich men made a nomination, the nominee always had to pay his election expenses, and of course the poor man had no chance. Now, all that has been changed. When we make a nomination and our man has no money, we give him a thousand dollars to treat the boys, and we raise the money by levying on men of your class."

   McLoughlin was elected registrar in 1861 and 1864, defeated in 1867, and re-elected for the last time in 1870. He never held any other office. When he retired in 1873 he was undisputed leader of Brooklyn's Democrats—and did not relinquish power until 1903. Syrett claims that McLoughlin was not ambitious: "His sole aim was to maintain his ascendancy over Kings County Democracy. Influence beyond Brooklyn was always secondary." Syrett also says McLoughlin was a "simple, moderate man" who stayed in the background. He drank infrequently and was a devoted Catholic who attended church regularly. Syrett, *The City of Brooklyn,* pp. 72–73, 77.

4. Raymond A. Schroth, *The Eagle and Brooklyn: A Community Newspaper 1841–1955* (Westport, Conn., 1974); see Chapter 4, "The Age of Kinsella." Also *Brooklyn Sunday Review,* 5 July 1874.

5. Beecher and Kinsella both belonged to the Faust Club. *Brooklyn Eagle,* 30 October 1872.

6. Syrett, *The City of Brooklyn,* p. 20.

7. Ibid., p. 12.

8. Ibid., p. 77.

9. For a history of the rivalry between the *Eagle* and the *Union,* see the *Brooklyn Sunday Review,* 27 April 1873.

10. TT testimony, *Trial,* 1:596. Marshall, *True History,* p. 260.

11. *Brooklyn Eagle,* 27 October 1870.

12. John G. Sproat, *"The Best Men": Liberal Reformers in the Gilded Age* (London, 1968). Matthew T. Downey, "The Rebirth of Reform: A Study of Liberal Reform Movements 1865–1872" (Ph.D. diss., Princeton, 1963).

13. "Liberals," *Brooklyn Eagle,* 27 August 1874.

14. "A Jubilee at the General Committee Rooms—Speech by Boss McLoughlin," *Brooklyn Eagle,* 6 November 1874.

15. "Meeting of Reform Republicans," *Brooklyn Eagle,* 1 November 1870.

16. TT testimony, *Trial,* 1:596.

17. *Brooklyn Eagle,* 22 December 1870. The term "carpetbagger," of course, reflected the feeling of the Irish Democrats that Bowen and Webster were outsiders by virtue of their connections with the national Republican machine.

18. Ibid., 15 November 1870. The successful candidate was none other than Thomas Kinsella!

19. B. Franklin Cooling, *Benjamin Franklin Tracy,* p. 36.

20. *Brooklyn Eagle,* 26 November 1870. *Brooklyn Union,* 11 November 1870.

21. *Brooklyn Eagle,* 7 December 1870.

22. TT testimony, PCIC, Marshall, *True History,* pp. 145–46.

23. TT to ET, 15 January 1869, CT.

24. TT testimony, PCIC, Marshall, *True History,* pp. 145–46.

25. *Brooklyn Union,* 22 December 1870.

26. *Brooklyn Eagle,* 22 December 1870.

27. TT testimony, PCIC, Marshall, *True History,* pp. 145–46. Also present at this meeting was Oliver Johnson, a friend of both Bowen and Tilton. He later confirmed Tilton's version of the meeting.

28. Ibid.

29. "Mr. Moulton's Last Statement," 11 September 1874, ibid., p. 479.

30. TT to Henry C. Bowen, 1 January 1871, ibid., pp. 313–14.

31. "Mr. Moulton's Last Statement," 11 September 1874, ibid.

32. Tri-Partite Covenant, 2 April 1872, *Trial,* 1:237.

33. TT testimony, *Trial,* 1:430.

34. For the history of the *Union,* see *Brooklyn Sunday Review,* 19 April 1874, July 1874; *Brooklyn Eagle,* 1 August 1874; Syrett, *The City of Brooklyn,* p. 21.

35. Richard Salter Storrs to Clarence W. Bowen, 17 March 1896, Brooklyn, New York, Bowen Scrapbook, 1, American Antiquarian Society, Worcester, Massachusetts.

   The Examining Committee of Plymouth Church wrestled with the question of what to do about the "Bowen scandal" from 27 June 1873 to 1 December 1873. William West, who first raised the issue was instructed to come back later with "further and more complete specifications" (27 June 1873). As the meetings went on it became clear that there was a real power struggle within the committee—with subcommittees being appointed to "confer" and the opposing group passing motions to limit what the subcommittee could confer *on* (14 July 1873)! It is obvious that the committee members did not want all their deliberations to appear in the minutes—when things heated up it was usual to recess for an "informal conference" (9 October 1873). The crux of the stalemate was whether Bowen *and* Tilton should be accused of causing all the trouble or just Tilton. Everyone seemed willing to dismiss Tilton from the church but Bowen still had powerful friends on the committee who blocked attempts to make any accusations against him. This group fi-

nally won on October 16 when it voted down a motion to present Bowen with "grievances" and carried a motion to lay Bowen's case "on the table." At the next meeting on
October 23, after some prodding from Beecher, Tilton was "dropped" rather than excommunicated. This ended Tilton's case, but by November 13, Bowen's enemies again
raised the question of "taking charges to Bowen" which somehow passed (possibly because not all Bowen's supporters were present) but by 1 December 1873 the complaint
against Bowen was "dismissed." This all seems to indicate that Bowen was still a very
powerful figure in the church; it was not quite as easy to get rid of him as it was Tilton.
Plymouth Church, Records of the Examining Committee 1871–1900, Book 40.

36. The struggle between the reformers and the machine politicians was focused throughout
the 1870s on the issue of control of local government. Tracy and the regulars sought to retain as many departments of the city within the state and federal jurisdictions, thus cir-
cumventing the power of McLoughlin. The Democrats, of course, fought to gain more
and more authority on the ward level which the immigrant politicians controlled. The
Liberals, however, claiming nonpartisanship, began to agitate for a new city charter that
would structure the city government so that Yankee Protestants could hold local offices.
They proposed to make more offices mayoral appointees rather than locally elected by
the wards—a Yankee had more chance to capture a citywide mayoral election than of
winning ward contests.

   However, one event points up just how much animosity existed between the two Yankee factions. In a city charter proposed to the legislature in 1872 that had been drawn up
by the Liberals, Tracy and one of his lieutenants appeared as Republican delegates in Al-
bany, ostensibly to support the charter, but, in fact, took turns "decrying" it, thus effectively "sabotaging" it. Syrett, *The City of Brooklyn,* pp. 51–69.

37. Alexander B. Callow, Jr., ed., *The City Boss in America* (London, 1976), p. 51.

38. In 1872, Victoria Woodhull decided to run for president herself. Not taken seriously by
anyone else, Woodhull apparently was convinced she had a chance. Because of her recent
friendship (she claimed love affair) with Tilton, she expected his support. Tilton, however, was still committed to the Liberal Republicans, attending the convention in Cincin-
nati in the summer of 1872 that nominated Horace Greeley. Although Woodhull had
mentioned her anger at Beecher's sisters for attacking her in the *Christian Union,* there
seems good reason to suspect as another reason for the "bombshell" article her resent-
ment of Tilton for not supporting her political campaign. Johnson, *Mrs. Satan,* p. 105.

39. *Brooklyn Eagle,* 19 August 1874, 8 October 1874, 2 December 1874.

40. Ibid., 26 October 1874.

41. The immediate objective of the Liberals was, indeed, accomplished when their candidate,
Simeon Chittenden, was elected. In the long run, too, the Liberals, or Mugwumps as they
were later called, with the help of reform Democrats (even Kinsella turned into a reformer
by the 1880s) managed to reform Brooklyn politics. In the 1880s a successful movement
known as the "Brooklyn Idea" became the model for other cities seeking to curb corruption of machine politics.

42. "S. B. Chittenden—Nominated by the Democrats for Congress," *Brooklyn Eagle,* 26
October 1874. The article quotes from the petition and lists the ninety leaders of the Liberals who signed it.

43. Records of Church of the Pilgrims, Book 1, Admissions, 1844–1894, Plymouth Church.
(Because Plymouth Church and Church of the Pilgrims merged in the 1920s, all the records of Church of the Pilgrims are housed in Plymouth Church.) Thirty-one of the petition signers were Church of the Pilgrims members.

   No other church seems so heavily represented on the petition. Four of the signers were
Plymouth Church members. Three belonged to the Clinton Avenue Congregational
Church. Its minister William Ives Budington had also been a long-time critic of Beecher
and Plymouth Church but he was not as fully supported by his membership as was Storrs.

44. Plymouth Church records, Book 40, Membership Committee, 30 October 1871–5 January 1900, p. 86.
45. "Dr. Bacon's Speech," 2 April 1874, Marshall, *True History,* pp. 40–42.

7   TWO CHURCHES

1. Stephen Pearl Andrews, testimony, *Trial,* 3:389–404.
2. William Maxwell Evarts summation, ibid., p. 654.
3. Ibid., p. 656.
4. C.T. Christianson to J. T. Howard, 25 June 1874, Beecher Papers, Box 45, Folder 1987, Yale.
5. William H. Beach, Closing Argument, *Trial,* 3:816.
6. Stiles, *History of Kings County,* 2:1016–17.
7. *The Church of the Pilgrims Manual* (New York, 1876), pp. 51–60. Thompson, *History of Plymouth Church,* p. 160.
8. HWB Sermon Outlines, Beecher Collection, Library of Congress.
9. Richard S. Storrs, *The Church of the Pilgrims, Brooklyn, New York: Its Character and Work, With the Changes around It, during Forty Years of Pastoral Service* (New York, 1886), p. 18.
10. Richard Salter Storrs, "Manliness in the Scholar," in *Orations and Addresses* (Boston, 1901), p. 346.
11. *The Brooklyn Council of 1874* (New York, 1874), pp. 138, 146, 139.
12. William H. Beach summation, *Trial,* 3:319.
13. *Brooklyn Council,* p. 144.
14. Ibid. The day after the council's conclusion Beecher wrote the following letter to Moulton: "I am indignant beyond expression. Storrs' course has been an unspeakable outrage. After his pretended sympathy and friendship for Theodore he has turned against him in the most venomous manner—and it is not sincere. His professions of faith and affection for me are hollow and faithless. They are merely tactical. His object is plain. He is determined to *force* a conflict, and to use one of us to destroy the other if possible. That is his game. By stinging Theodore he believes that he will be driven into a course which he hopes will ruin me. If ever a man betrayed another he has. I am in hopes that Theodore, who has born so much, will be unwilling to be a flail in Storrs' hand to strike at a friend. . . . At any rate, while the fury rages in Council, it is not wise to make any move that would be *one* among so many, as to lose effect in a degree, and after the battle is over one can more exactly see what ought to be done. Meantime I am *patient* as I know how to be, but pretty nearly used up with inward excitement, and must run away for a day or two and hide and sleep or there will be a funeral. . . . No one can tell, under first impressions, what the effect of such a speech [Storrs's] will be. *It ought to damn Storrs.*" HWB to Frank Moulton, 25 March 1874, Marshall, *True History,* pp. 367–68.
15. This information about seating in New England churches was gathered from a study of the colonial records of the towns of Northampton, Hadley, Amherst, Pelham, and Hatfield, Massachusetts. See David Hackett Fischer, *Growing Old in America* (New York, 1977), pp. 78–79; Patricia J. Tracy, *Jonathan Edwards, Pastor* (New York, 1980), pp. 125–28.
16. Descriptions of Plymouth Church pew rental auctions were published in the *Brooklyn Eagle* every January. These reports described the bidding, listed the pew purchasers, the pews they chose, and how much they paid. Beecher defended the practice, insisting it was "democratic" religion, allowing those who had worked their way to the top to reap the rewards they deserved.
17. Stiles, *History of Kings County,* p. 1–16.
18. Barrows, *Shakespeare of the Pulpit,* p. 78.

19. Most Beecher scholars, including Hibben and Shaplen, have assumed that his parishioners were upper and upper-middle class, as Storrs's church actually was. This error stems from the fact that Beecher's more *visible* parishioners *were* wealthy merchants and professionals who lived on Brooklyn Heights. No one has made any effort to collect data on *all* the members. An exception is Clifford Clark in his biography, *Henry Ward Beecher* (1978), who recognizes the marginal middle-class status of many Plymouth Church members.

20. *Lain's Brooklyn Street Directory and Buyer's Guide . . . 1870* (Brooklyn, 1870); United States Census, Ninth Census (1870), Population Schedules, Brooklyn, Wards 1–12, 20, 22. The initial ten-percent sample was selected by extracting from alphabetical membership lists every tenth name. For Plymouth Church, this resulted in a list of 400 names and for Church of the Pilgrims, 72 names. When the name was a woman's, we attempted to gather data for her husband, if known. Because these lists covered all members since the founding of both churches, many of our people had died or moved away by 1870—the year we searched in the Census or Directory. Thus our results: the location of 130 or thirty-three percent of the Beecher and 55 or seventy-five percent of the Storrs sample was quite high. But, the sample is biased toward more stable, well-to-do church members.

21. *Brooklyn Sunday Sun,* 14 June 1874.

22. Stiles, *History of Kings County,* pp. 1281, 1297.

23. "J. Carson Brevoort," ibid., p. 1320.

24. In examining Plymouth Church membership records, one is struck by the large numbers of young working-class men and women who join the church—especially during revival years—but who soon disappear and are dropped from the rolls. One can only speculate on what hundreds of people felt when the Gospel of Love failed to work for them.

25. The phrase was used by Frank Moulton to describe what drove Tilton to prosecute Beecher. Tilton, like Church of the Pilgrims members, felt threatened by loss of social as well as economic status.

26. *Brooklyn Eagle,* 23 July 1872; Howard, *The Eagle and Brooklyn,* 2:304.

8   THE HIGHER SPHERE

1. HWB, "The Strong to Bear with the Weak," 25 October 1868, *Plymouth Pulpit,* ser. 1, p. 118.

2. Theodore Tilton, "The True Story," December 1872, *Trial,* 1:592.

3. HWB testimony, *Trial,* 3:795.

4. ET testimony, PCIC, Marshall, *True History,* p. 193.

5. HWB testimony, *Trial,* 3:737.

6. TT to HWB, 30 November 1865, ibid., 2:738. This letter has been used by Hibben and Shaplen to demonstrate the closeness between the two men, ignoring the spirit in which Tilton wrote it—in disillusionment with his idol.

7. TT to ET, 6 December 1866, *Trial,* 1:494.

8. TT to ET, 27 December 1866, ibid., pp. 494–95.

9. TT, "Love, Marriage, and Divorce," *Independent,* 1 December 1870.

10. Bessie Turner testimony, *Trial,* 2:474. The testimony given by Elizabeth "Bessie" Turner was important in both the church and civil trials. Bessie was a teen-aged girl who lived in the Tilton household acting as a kind of "mother's helper." Her status was considerably above that of the other Irish servants—she was treated almost as an adopted child in the Tilton family. In her testimony, her gratitude to and affection for both the Tiltons are obvious. She was clearly torn between the two when the scandal became public—but, after some vacillation, demonstrated that her devotion to Elizabeth was stronger. She appeared genuinely mystified by Theodore's treatment of a woman Bessie regarded as almost a saint.

11. TT to ET, 31 December 1866, CT.

12. ET to TT, 28 December 1866, *Trial*, 1:493.

13. HWB testimony, ibid., 2:735.

14. HWB testimony, PCIC, Marshall, *True History*, p. 256; TT testimony, *Trial*, 1:619.

15. ET testimony, PCIC, Marshall, *True History*, p. 192.

16. ET to TT, 28 December 1866, *Trial*, 1:493.

17. Ibid.,

18. ET to TT, 25 December 1867, *Trial*, 1:499.

19. TT, "Love, Marriage, and Divorce," *Independent*, 1 December 1870.

20. TT testimony, *Trial*, 1:560; HWB testimony, ibid., 3:21.

21. TT statement, Marshall, *True History*, pp. 116–17.

22. HWB, "The True Value of Morality," 18 February 1872, *Plymouth Pulpit*, ser. 5, p. 47.

23. HWB, "Moral Honesty and Moral Earnestness," 20 October 1872, ibid., p. 111.

24. HWB, "Motives of Action," 20 November 1872, ibid., p. 206.

25. HWB, "As to the Lord," 6 October 1872, ibid., p. 83.

26. "Mr. Moulton's Last Statement," 11 September 1874, Marshall, *True History*, p. 479.

27. HWB, *Norwood* (New York, 1868), p. 74. One of Beecher's favorite images was that of a "nest" and he used it repeatedly in sermons and the novel. For example, in one of his sermons, he said: "The world is good for a nest, but it is bad for a flying place. It is a good place to be hatched in, but it is a bad place to practice one's wings in. If a man has power to fly, he does not want to be confined to a nest. The glory and power of the eagle is never known while he lives on his cliff—not till he has abandoned that and sought his new home" ("What is Salvation," 29 September 1872, *Plymouth Pulpit*, ser. 5, p. 70).

28. HWB, "On the Temporal Advantages of Religion," 6 July 1873, *Plymouth Pulpit*, ser. 5, p. 368.

29. TT testimony, *Trial*, 1:619.

30. TT, "Sworn Statement," 20 July 1874, Marshall, *True History*, p. 116.

31. TT testimony, *Trial*, 2:72.

32. Emma Moulton's testimony, *Trial*, 1:725 (italics added). Apparently Beecher blamed Elizabeth for both the actual adultery and the scandal. He told Emma Moulton, "Poor child, she is trying to repair the wrong she has done in confessing it—in confessing *her* sin. But it is too late."

33. HWB, "Love of Money," 22 November 1868, *Plymouth Pulpit*, ser. 1, pp. 239–43.

34. HWB, "The Value of Deep Feelings," 12 December 1868, ibid., p. 312.

35. ET to TT, 7 February 1869, *Trial*, 1:491. Elizabeth wrote only seven letters to Theodore between October 1868 and July 1870. In a letter written March 18, 1869, she apologized for not writing more often. For her activities in the Equal Rights Association, see her letters of March 13 and 20, in the *Chicago Tribune*.

36. *Revolution*, 24 February 1870, Elizabeth Tilton listed as editor of the Poetry Column.

37. ET to TT, 13 March 1869, CT.

38. Lydia Maria Child to TT, 27 May 1866, James Fraser Gluck Collection, Buffalo Public Library, Buffalo, New York.

39. TT to ET, 14 February 1867, *Trial*, 2:502.

40. TT to ET, 7 December 1866, *Trial*, 1:495.

41. TT to ET, 15 March 1868, CT.

42. TT to ET, 7 December 1866, *Trial*, 1:495.

43. TT to Anna Dickinson, [May or June] 1870, Dickinson Collection, Box 13, Library of Congress.

44. Laura Curtis Bullard to Anna Dickinson, 24 May 1870, Dickinson Collection, Box 6, Library of Congress.

45. TT to Anna Dickinson, [May or June] 1870, Dickinson Collection, Box 13, Library of Congress.

46. "Tilton Traduced," *Brooklyn Eagle,* 26 January 1871.

47. TT to Anna Dickinson, [May or June] 1870, Dickinson Collection, Box 13, Library of Congress.

48. ET to "My Dear Friend and Sister," 13 January 1871, Marshall, *True History,* pp. 349–50. This letter refers to problems the "friend" was having with other members of her family—which indicates the letter was to Bullard.

49. Bessie Turner testimony, PCIC, ibid., p. 392.

50. HWB testimony, *Trial,* 3:31.

51. TT statement, Marshall, *True History,* pp. 116–17; *Trial,* 1:396–97.

52. Aurora Phelps to William Maxwell Evarts, c. 1875, Beecher Papers, Box 45, Folder 2007, Yale.

53. HWB testimony, *Trial,* 3:743.

54. ET testimony, PCIC, Marshall, *True History,* p. 197.

55. ET to TT, November 1870, ibid., pp. 535–36.

56. Bessie Turner testimony, *Trial,* 2:477.

57. TT, *Tempest Tossed* (New York, 1874), pp. 553, 554.

58. Ibid., p. 554.

59. TT to ET, 7 December 1866, *Trial,* 1:495.

60. On the events surrounding the first time Elizabeth left Theodore, see HWB testimony, *Trial,* 3:12; Bessie Turner testimony, ibid., 2:494; TT testimony, ibid., 1:558, 618.

61. Eunice Beecher advised Elizabeth to divorce Theodore "on the ground of his impurity, his bringing improper persons to the house, his abuse of her and the children, and his vulgarity and profanity" (Eunice Beecher testimony, PCIC, 14 July 1874, Beecher Papers, Box 87, Folder 219, Yale).

   Beecher agreed with his wife in the following note: "I incline to think that your view is right, that a separation and settlement of support will be wisest—and that in his present desperate state her presence near him is far more likely to produce hatred than her absence" (HWB to Eunice Beecher, December 1870, *Trial,* 3:132).

62. ET testimony, PCIC, Marshall, *True History,* p. 212.

63. For the circumstances surrounding Tilton's blaming Beecher for his loss of "place, business, and repute," see TT, "The True Story," *Trial,* 2:716–19; HWB testimony, ibid., p. 868; Charles Storrs testimony, ibid., p. 671; Samuel Wilkeson testimony, ibid., p. 295.

64. ET to Dr. Storrs, 16 December 1872, *Trial,* 1:137; HWB testimony, ibid., 3:31. The original letter of confession has apparently been lost, but the following are the letters of retraction (dictated by Beecher) and recantation (dictated by Tilton): "December 30, 1870-Wearied with importunity and weakened by sickness I gave a letter inculpating my friend Henry Ward Beecher under assurances that that would remove all difficulties between me and my husband. That letter I now revoke. I was persuaded to it—almost forced—when I was in a weakened state of mind. I regret it, and recall all its statements—E. R. Tilton. P.S. I desire to say explicitly that Mr. Beecher has never offered any improper solicitations, but has always treated me in a manner becoming a Christian and a gentleman. Elizabeth R. Tilton" (Marshall, *True History,* p. 317).

   "December 30, 1870—Midnight; My Dear Husband—I desire to leave with you, before going to sleep, a statement that Mr. Henry Ward Beecher called upon me this evening, asked me if I would defend him against any accusation in a *Council of Ministers,* and I replied solemnly that I would in case the accuser was any other person than my husband. He (H.W.B.) dictated a letter, which I copied as my own, to be used by him as against any other accuser except my husband. This letter was designed to vindicate Mr. Beecher against all other persons save only yourself. I was ready to give him this letter because he said with pain that my letter in your hands addressed to him, dated December 29, 'had struck him dead, and ended his usefulness.'

"You and I both are pledged to do our best to avoid publicity. God grant a speedy end to all further anxieties. Affectionately, Elizabeth" (ibid., p. 318).

65. Charles Storrs testimony, *Trial*, 2:672; Emma Moulton testimony, ibid., 1:721; HWB testimony, ibid., 2:893; HWB to Frank Moulton, 1 June 1873, ibid., 2:867.

66. On Reade and *Griffith Gaunt:* "Perhaps the most successful of all sensational novelists was Charles Reade . . . he determined to attract popular attention while at the same time writing novels with a social purpose. *Griffith Gaunt,* a highly colored story of bigamy, murder, and mistaken identity among eighteenth century gentry, was less significant for its attack upon a worldly gentry than for its almost pathological sensationalism. . . . the work [was] a scandalous success" (James D. Hart, *The Popular Book* [New York, 1973], p. 123).

67. ET to TT, 29 July 1871, *Trial*, 1:540–41.

68. Charles Reade, *Griffith Gaunt or Jealousy* (London, 1866), p. 230.

69. ET to TT, 29 June 1871, *Trial*, 1:540–41.

70. Emma Moulton testimony, ibid., p. 722.

71. ET to TT, 29 June 1871, ibid., pp. 540–41.

9   THEODORE TILTON AS SCAPEGOAT

1. HWB testimony, *Trial*, 2:868, 792–93.

2. Oliver Johnson to Anna Dickinson, 17 August 1874, Dickinson Collection, Library of Congress.

3. *New York Daily Graphic*, 25 July 1874, quoted in Hibben, *Beecher: An American Portrait*, p. 265.

4. HWB testimony, *Trial*, 2:895.

5. HWB, "Abhorrence of Evil," 15 November 1868, *Plymouth Pulpit*, ser. 1, p. 199.

6. TT testimony, *Trial*, 1:413.

7. Francis Moulton testimony, ibid., p. 222; HWB testimony, ibid., 2:855; 1:237.

8. *New York World*, 22 May 1871. TT testimony, *Trial*, 1:413.

9. TT, *Tempest Tossed* (New York, 1874), p. 67.

10. HWB testimony, *Trial*, 2:836.

11. HWB testimony, PCIC, Marshall, *True History*, p. 297.

12. Theodore Tilton, "Victoria C. Woodhull, A Biographical Sketch."

13. Francis Moulton testimony, *Trial*, 1:227.

14. HWB testimony, PCIC, Marshall, *True History*, p. 274.

15. Charles Storrs testimony, *Trial*, 2:672.

16. TT to Henry Bowen, 4 April 1872, Marshall, *True History*, p. 326.

17. HWB testimony, PCIC, ibid., p. 274.

18. *Woodhull and Claflin's Weekly*, 2 November 1872, ibid., pp. 28–30.

19. TT testimony, *Trial*, 1:580.

20. Tilton was, in fact, campaigning in New Hampshire when Woodhull wrote her "bombshell" article.

21. In addition, Harriet Beecher Stowe's novel *My Wife and I* (New York, 1871) had been written specifically to ridicule Victoria Woodhull.

22. Francis Moulton testimony, *Trial*, 1:225.

23. HWB testimony, *Trial*, 2:855, 868.

24. TT testimony, *Trial*, 1:592; 2:716–19.

25. TT testimony, ibid., 1:537.

26. HWB statement, 13 August 1874, Marshall, *True History*, p. 279.

27. HWB to Frank Moulton, 1 June 1873, ibid., pp. 280–81.

28. TT testimony, *Trial*, 1:612.

29. "Dr. Bacon's Speech," 2 April 1874, and TT to Dr. Leonard Bacon, 21 June 1874, Marshall, *True History*, pp. 40–42, 42–63.

30. HWB to Frank Moulton, 1 January 1871, *Trial*, 1:65.

31. Frank Moulton's statement, Marshall, *True History*, p. 479.

32. CT, 4 August 1874, p. 1.

33. *Brooklyn Sunday Sun*, 26 August 1874.

34. Ibid., 2 August 1874.

35. E. C. Stedman to Whitelaw Reid, n.d., quoted in Hibben, *Beecher: An American Portrait*, p. 243.

36. "Report of the Investigating Committee, Plymouth Church," 27 August 1874, Marshall, *True History*, p. 432.

37. CT, 1 October 1874.

38. Oliver Johnson to Anna Dickinson, 17 August 1874, Dickinson Papers, Library of Congress.

39. Ibid.

40. William Maxwell Evarts summation, *Trial*, 3:663.

41. Ibid.

42. Benjamin Tracy's opening speech, *Trial*, 2:9.

43. Ibid., pp. 6, 8.

44. HWB, "Motives of Action," 20 November 1872, *Plymouth Pulpit*, ser. 5, p. 212.

45. Tracy's opening statement, *Trial*, 2:9.

46. HWB, "Love of Money," 22 November 1868, *Plymouth Pulpit*, ser. 1, p. 254.

47. Tracy's opening statement, *Trial*, 2:8. This fear of overstimulation and passion running rampant, particularly when one is alone, probably had a great deal to do with the Victorian horror of masturbation. After all, this activity combined two things that were threatening—overexcitement and solitude. See Nissenbaum, *Sex, Diet, and Debility*, pp. 25–30; Graham Barker-Benfield, *Horrors of the Half-Known Life* (New York, 1976).

48. William H. Beach's closing argument, *Trial*, 3:816.

49. *Independent*, 10 February 1876, p. 16.

50. *Independent*, 18 November 1875; *New York Sun*, 2 and 3 March 1876.

51. Shaplen, *Free Love*, p. 266.

52. *New York Times*, 16 April 1878, Examining Committee Records of Plymouth Church, Plymouth Church, Brooklyn, New York, 10 June 1878, p. 298.

53. Shaplen, *Free Love*, p. 272.

54. Clifford Clark argues that Beecher maintained his "central" position in the community. Clark, *HWB: Spokesman*, p. 228.

55. Gerald McFarland, *Mugwumps, Morals, and Politics* (Amherst, Mass., 1975), p. 16.

56. Clark, *HWB: Spokesman*, p. 252.

57. McFarland, *Mugwumps*, pp. 36–39.

58. Liberal newspapers across the country had condemned Beecher. Laura Stedman and George M. Gould, *Life and Letters of Edmund Clarence Stedman* (New York, 1910), quoted in Hibben, *Beecher: An American Portrait*, p. 243; Shaplen, *Free Love*, pp. 257–58.

59. Clark, *HWB: Spokesman*, p. 266–67.

60. "Report of Plymouth Church Investigating Committee," 8 August 1874, Marshall, *True History*, p. 432.

Bibliography

I. PRIMARY SOURCES

A. Manuscripts

Beecher Collection, American Antiquarian Society.
Beecher Collection, Schlesinger Library, Radcliffe.
Beecher Family Collection, Yale University Library.
Beecher, Henry Ward, Letters, Houghton Library, Harvard.
Beecher Papers, Amherst College.
Beecher Papers, Library of Congress.
Beecher-Tilton Scandal Scrapbooks, Brooklyn Public Library.
Beecher-Tilton Scandal Scrapbooks, Long Island Historical Society.
Bacon Family Papers, Yale University Library.
Bowen Family Collection, American Antiquarian Society.
Church of the Pilgrims Records, Plymouth Church of the Pilgrims, 75 Hicks Street, Brooklyn Heights.
Anna E. Dickinson Papers, Library of Congress.
William Maxwell Evarts Papers, Library of Congress.
James Fraser Gluck Collection, Buffalo Public Library.
Victoria (Claflin) Woodhull Martin Papers, Southern Illinois University Archives, Carbondale.
Plymouth Church Records, Plymouth Church of the Pilgrims, 75 Hicks Street, Brooklyn Heights.
William Page Papers, Archives of American Art, Smithsonian Institution.
Lewis Tappan Papers, Library of Congress.
Theodore Tilton Collection, Library of Congress.
Theodore Tilton Papers, New York Historical Society.
Theodore Tilton Letters, Houghton Library, Harvard.
United States Bureau of the Census, Ninth Census (1870), Population Schedules, Brooklyn, New York, Wards 1–12, 20, 22.

B. Newspapers

Brooklyn Eagle 1870–1880. Brooklyn Public Library.
Brooklyn Sunday Press. Long Island Historical Society.
Brooklyn Sunday Review. Long Island Historical Society.
Brooklyn Sunday Sun 1873–1876. Long Island Historical Society.
Brooklyn Union 1870–1875. New York Historical Society.
Chicago Tribune 1874–1876.
Christian Union 1870–1876.

Frank Leslie's Illustrated Newspaper 1872–1876. American Antiquarian Society.
The Golden Age 1871–1875.
Harper's Weekly 1872–1878. American Antiquarian Society.
Independent 1848–1878. Amherst College, American Antiquarian Society.
New York Times 1872–1878.
New York Tribune 1872–1878.
Puck's 1874–1879. Forbes Library, Northampton, Mass.
Revolution 1868–1872.
Woman's Home Companion 1873–1876. Smith College.
Woman's Journal 1870–1875. Smith College.
Woodhull and Claflin's Weekly 1870–1876.

C. Books

Abbott, Lyman, ed. *Henry Ward Beecher: A Sketch of His Career*. New York: Funk and
    Wagnalls, 1883.
Barrows, John Henry. *Henry Ward Beecher: The Shakespeare of the Pulpit*. New York: Funk
    and Wagnalls, 1893.
Beecher, Mrs. Henry Ward [Eunice Bullard]. *From Dawn to Daylight: The Simple Story of a
    Western Home*. New York: Derby and Jackson, 1869.
———. *Motherly Talks with Young Housekeepers, 87 Brief Articles*. New York: J. B. Ford
    and Co., 1873.
———. *All around the House; or How to Make Homes Happy*. New York: D. Appleton and
    Co., 1878.
———. *Letters from Florida*. New York: D. Appleton and Co., 1879.
Beecher, Henry Ward. *Seven Lectures to Young Men*. Indianapolis: Thomas B. Cutler, 1844.
———. *Star Papers: Experiences of Art and Nature*. New York: J. C. Derby, 1855.
———. *Life Thoughts*. New York: Sheldon, 1858.
———. *New Star Papers*. New York: Derby and Jackson, 1859.
———. *Eyes and Ears*. Boston: Ticknor and Fields, 1862.
———. *Norwood: Or Village Life in New England*. New York: J. B. Ford and Co., 1868.
———. *Lecture Room Talks*. New York: J. B. Ford and Co., 1870.
———. *The Life of Jesus the Christ*. 2 vols. New York: J. B. Ford and Co., 1871.
———. *Yale Lectures on Preaching*. New York: J. B. Ford and Co., 1872.
———. *Evolution and Religion*. New York: Ford, Howard, and Hulbert, 1885.
———. *The Plymouth Pulpit: Sermons Preached in Plymouth Church, Brooklyn, New York*.
    Series 1, 2, 5. London, 1894.
Beecher, Lyman. *The Autobiography of Lyman Beecher*. Edited by Barbara Cross. Cam-
    bridge: Harvard University Press, Belknap Press, 1961.
The Beecher-Tilton Investigation: The Scandal of the Age. Philadelphia: Barclay and Co.,
    1874.
*The Beecher-Tilton Scandal: Complete History of the Case from November 1872 to the Pres-
    ent Time*. Brooklyn, 1874.
Brockett, L. P. *Men of Our Day*. Philadelphia: Zeigler, McCurdy and Co., 1868.
The Brooklyn Council of 1874: Proceedings and Result. New York: Woolworth and Gra-
    ham, 1874.
The Brooklyn Council of 1876: Proceedings. New York: 1876.
*Brooklyn Female Academy: Circular and Catalogue, with the Fifth Annual Commencement
    Exercises*. Brooklyn, 1851.
Browning, Elizabeth B. *Last Poems by Elizabeth B. Browning—with a Memorial by Theo-
    dore Tilton*. New York: J. Miller, 1862.

Bungay, G. W. *Traits of Representative Men*. New York: Fowler and Wells, 1882.

A *Church in History: The Story of Plymouth's First Hundred Years under Beecher, Abbott, Hillis, Durkee, and Fifield*. Brooklyn, 1949.

Church of the Pilgrims Manual. Brooklyn, 1876.

Clinton Avenue Congregational Church Manuals. Brooklyn, 1857, 1862, 1866, 1872, 1880.

Dickinson, Anna. *A Ragged Register (of People, Places, and Opinions)*. New York: Harper and Bros., 1879.

Doyle, John E. P. *Plymouth Church and Its Pastor, or Henry Ward Beecher and His Accusers*. Hartford, Conn.: The Park Publishing Co., 1874.

Ellis, Dr. John B. *Free Love and Its Votaries*. New York, 1870.

Fairfield, Edmund. *Wickedness in High Places*. Mansfield, Ohio: L. D. Myers and Bros., Printers, 1874.

Fowler, Henry. *American Pulpit*. New York: J. M. Fairchild, 1856.

Fowler, Orson S. *Creative and Sexual Science*. New York: Fowler and Wells, 1875.

———. *Love and Parentage*. New York: Fowler and Wells, 1843.

———. *Phrenology Proved, Illustrated and Applied*. Philadelphia: Fowler and Brevoort, 1836.

The Great Brooklyn Romance: All the Documents in the Famous Beecher-Tilton Case. Unabridged. New York: J. H. Paxon, 1874.

Griswold, Stephen Morrell. *Sixty Years with Plymouth Church*. Chicago: F. H. Revell Co., 1907.

Howard, Henry W. B., ed. *The Eagle and Brooklyn*. 2 vols. Brooklyn: The Brooklyn Daily Eagle, 1893.

Howard, John R. *Henry Ward Beecher: A Study of His Personality, Career, and Influence in Public Affairs*. New York: Ford, Howard, and Hulbert, 1891.

———. *Remembrances of Things Past*. New York: Thomas Y. Crowell, 1925.

Howard, Joseph, Jr. *The Life of Henry Ward Beecher*. Philadelphia: Edgewood Publishing Co., 1887.

Knox, Thomas W. *The Life and Works of Henry Ward Beecher*. Hartford: The Hartford Publishing Co., 1887.

Lain's Brooklyn Street Directory and Buyers Guide . . . 1870. Brooklyn: G. T. Lain, 1870.

McFarland, Henry H. *Historical and Descriptive Sketch of the Church of the Pilgrims, Brooklyn, New York*. Brooklyn: H. M. Gardner, Jr., printer, 1871.

Marshall, Charles F. *The True History of the Brooklyn Scandal*. Philadelphia: National Publishing Co., 1874.

Napheys, George G. *The Physical Life of Woman: Advice to the Maiden, Wife and Mother*. New York: B. Maclean, 1870.

Oliver, Leon. *The Great Sensation*. Chicago: The Beverly Co., 1873.

Parton, James. *Famous Men of Our Times*. Boston, 1893.

Plymouth Church Manuals. 1850–1876.

Reade, Charles. *Griffith Gaunt or Jealousy*. London: Chapman and Hall, 1866.

Smith, Matthew Hale. *Sunshine and Shadow in New York*. Hartford: J. B. Burr, 1869.

Stiles, Henry R. *A History of the City of Brooklyn*. 3 vols. Brooklyn, 1867, 1869, 1870.

———, ed. *The Civil, Political, Professional and Ecclesiastical History and Commercial and Industrial Record of the County of Kings and the City of Brooklyn, New York, from 1683 to 1884*. 2 vols. New York: W. W. Munsell and Co., 1884.

Storrs, Richard S. *The Divine Origin of Christianity Indicated by Its Historical Effects*. New York: A. D. F. Randolph, 1884.

———. *The Church of the Pilgrims, Brooklyn, New York: Its Character and Work, with the Changes around It, during Forty Years of Pastoral Service*. New York: A. S. Barnes and Co., 1886.

———. *Orations and Addresses.* Boston: The Pilgrim Press, 1901.
Thompson, Noyes L. *The History of Plymouth Church (Henry Ward Beecher) 1847–1872.* New York: G. W. Carleton and Co., 1873.
Tilton, Theodore. *Sanctum Sanctorium.* New York: Sheldon and Co., 1874.
———. *Tempest Tossed.* New York: Sheldon and Co., 1874.
———. *Swabian Stories.* New York: R. Worthington, 1882.
———. *The Complete Poetical Works of Theodore Tilton.* London, 1897.
Tilton versus Beecher, Action for Crim. Con. 3 vols. New York: McDivitt, Campbell and Co., 1875.
Tracy, Benjamin F. *The Case of Henry Ward Beecher.* New York: G. W. Smith and Co., 1875.
[Treat, Joseph.] *Beecher, Tilton, Woodhull: The Creation of Society.* New York: The Author, 1874.
Williamson, Francis P. *Beecher and His Accusers.* Philadelphia: Flint and Co., 1874.

II. SELECTED SECONDARY SOURCES

Aries, Philippe. *Centuries of Childhood: A Social History of Family Life.* New York: Random House, 1962.
Bacon, Theodore D. *Leonard Bacon, A Statesman in the Church.* Benjamin W. Bacon, ed. New Haven: Yale University Press, 1931.
Barker-Benfield, G. J. *The Horrors of the Half-Known Life.* New York: Harper and Row, 1976.
Bidwell, Percy Wells and Falconer, John I. *History of Agriculture in the Northern United States 1620–1860.* 1925. Reprint. New York: P. Smith, 1941.
Boyer, Paul. *Urban Masses and Moral Order in America 1820–1920.* Cambridge: Harvard University Press, 1978.
Bunkle, Phillida. "Sentimental Womanhood and Domestic Education, 1830–1870." *History of Education Quarterly,* 14, no. 1 (Spring 1974): 13–20.
Burnham, John. "The Progressive Era Revolution in American Attitudes toward Sex." *Journal of American History* 59 (1973): 885–908.
Carter, Paul A. *The Spiritual Crisis of the Gilded Age.* DeKalb, Ill.: Northern Illinois University Press, 1971.
Calhoun, Daniel. *Professional Lives in America 1750–1850: Structure and Aspiration.* Cambridge: Harvard University Press, 1965.
Carroll, Sharon Ann. "Elitism and Reform: Some Anti-Slavery Opinionmakers in the Era of Civil War and Reconstruction." Ph.D. dissertation, Cornell, 1970.
Caskey, Marie. *Chariot of Fire: Religion and the Beecher Family.* New Haven: Yale University Press, 1978.
Clark, Clifford E. "The Changing Nature of Protestantism in Mid-Nineteenth Century America: Henry Ward Beecher's Seven Lectures to Young Men." *Journal of American History* 57, no. 4 (March 1971): 832–46.
———. *Henry Ward Beecher: Spokesman for Middle-Class America.* Urbana: University of Illinois Press, 1978.
Cooling, Benjamin Franklin. *Benjamin Franklin Tracy: Father of the Modern American Fighting Navy.* Hamden, Conn., 1973.
Cott, Nancy. *The Bonds of Womanhood: "Woman's Sphere" in New England, 1780–1835.* New Haven: Yale University Press, 1977.
———. "Passionless: An Interpretation of Victorian Sexual Ideology, 1970–1850." *Signs: A Journal of Women in Culture and Society* 4 (1978): 219–36.
Demos, John. *A Little Commonwealth: Family Life in Plymouth Colony.* New York: Oxford University Press, 1970.

Douglas, Ann. *The Feminization of American Culture.* New York: Alfred A. Knopf, 1977.

Downey, Matthew T. "The Rebirth of Reform: A Study of Liberal Reform Movements 1865–1872." Ph.D. dissertation, Princeton, 1963.

Dyer, Brainerd. *The Public Career of William Maxwell Evarts.* Berkeley: University of California Press, 1933.

Elsmere, Jane S. *Henry Ward Beecher: The Indiana Years, 1837–1847.* Indianapolis: Indiana Historical Society, 1973.

Filler, Louis. "Liberalism, Anti-Slavery, and the Founders of the *Independent." New England Quarterly* 27 (September 1954): 291–306.

Foster, Frank Hugh. *The Modern Movement in American Theology.* New York: Fleming H. Revell Co., 1939.

Gadlin, Howard. "Private Lives and Public Order: A Critical View of the History of Intimate Relations in the United States." *Massachusetts Review,* Summer 1976.

Gordon, Michael. *The American Family: Past, Present, and Future.* New York: Random House, 1978.

Greven, Philip J., Jr. *Four Generations: Population, Land, and Family in Colonial Andover, Massachusetts.* Ithaca: Cornell University Press, 1970.

Grisaffi, Philip E. "Beecher-Tilton Investigation of 1874." M.A. thesis, St. Francis College, Brooklyn, New York, 1968.

Goode, William J. *World Revolution and Family Patterns.* New York: The Free Press, 1963.

Henretta, James. *The Evolution of American Society 1700–1815.* Lexington, Mass., 1973.

Henry, Stuart Clark. *Unvanquished Puritan: A Portrait of Lyman Beecher.* Grand Rapids, Mich.: William B. Eerdmans Publishing Co., 1973.

Hibben, Paxton. *Henry Ward Beecher: An American Portrait.* New York: George H. Doran Co., 1927.

Horner, Charles F. *The Life of James Redpath and the Development of the Modern Lyceum.* New York, 1926.

Jeffrey, Kirk. "The Family as Utopian Retreat from the City." *Soundings* 55 (1972): 21–41.

Johnston, Johanna. *"Mrs. Satan": The Incredible Saga of Victoria C. Woodhull.* New York: G. P. Putnam's Sons, 1967.

Kett, Joseph F. "Adolescence and Youth in Nineteenth-Century America." *Journal of Interdisciplinary History* 2 (Autumn 1971): 283–98.

Lancaster, Clay. *Old Brooklyn Heights: New York's First Suburb.* Rutland, Vt.: Charles E. Tuttle Co., 1961.

Lasch, Christopher. *Haven in a Heartless World: The Family Besieged.* New York: Basic Books, 1977.

Lockridge, Kenneth A. "Social Change and the Meaning of the American Revolution." *Journal of Social History* 6 (Summer 1973): 403–39.

McFarland, Gerald. *Mugwumps, Morals, and Politics, 1884–1920.* Amherst: University of Massachusetts Press, 1975.

McLoughlin, William G. *The Meaning of Henry Ward Beecher: An Essay in the Shifting Values of Mid-Victorian America.* New York: Alfred A. Knopf, 1970.

McPherson, James M. "Grant or Greeley? The Abolitionist Dilemma in the Election of 1872." *American Historical Review* 71 (October 1965): 43–61.

Merideth, Robert. *The Politics of the Universe: Edward Beecher, Abolition, and Orthodoxy.* Nashville: Vanderbilt University Press, 1968.

Mott, Frank Luther. *A History of American Magazines.* 3 vols. Cambridge: Harvard University Press, 1938.

Nissenbaum, Stephen. *Sex, Diet and Debility in Jacksonian America: Sylvester Graham and Health Reform.* Westport, Conn.: Greenwood Press, 1980.

Rosenberg, Charles E. "Sexuality, Class, and Role in Nineteenth Century America." *American Quarterly* 25 (May 1973): 131–53.

Rugoff, Milton. *The Beechers: An American Family in the Nineteenth Century.* New York: Harper and Row, 1981.

Sachs, Emanie. *"The Terrible Siren": Victoria Woodhull (1838–1927).* New York: Harper and Bros., 1928.

Schroth, Raymond A. *The Eagle and Brooklyn: A Community Newspaper, 1841–1955.* Westport, Conn.: Greenwood Press, 1974.

Shaplen, Robert. *Free Love and Heavenly Sinners.* New York: Alfred A. Knopf, 1954.

Shorter, Edward. *The Making of the Modern Family.* New York: Basic Books, 1977.

Sklar, Kathryn Kish. *Catherine Beecher: A Study in American Domesticity.* New Haven: Yale University Press, 1973.

Smith-Rosenberg, Carroll. "The Female World of Love and Ritual: Relations between Women in Nineteenth Century America." *Signs* 1, no. 1 (Autumn 1975): 1–29.

———. "The Hysterical Women: Sex Roles and Role Conflict in Nineteenth Century America." *Social Research* 39, no. 4 (Winter 1972): 652–78.

Sproat, John G. *"The Best Men": Liberal Reformers in the Gilded Age.* London: Oxford University Press, 1968.

Stern, Madeleine B. *Heads and Headlines: The Phrenological Fowlers.* Norman: University of Oklahoma Press, 1971.

———. *The Pantarch: A Biography of Stephen Pearl Andrews.* Austin: University of Texas Press, 1968.

Strong, Byron. "Toward a History of the Experiential Family: Sex and Incest in the Nineteenth Century Family." *Journal of Marriage and the Family* 35 (August 1973): 457–66.

Syrett, Harold Coffin. *The City of Brooklyn 1865–1898: A Political History.* New York: Columbia University Press, 1944.

Terry, Edwin. "Theodore Tilton as Social Reformer, Radical Republican, Newspaper Editor, 1863–1872." Ph.D. dissertation, St. John's University, 1971.

Welter, Barbara. "The Cult of True Womanhood." *American Quarterly* 93 (Summer 1966): 151–74.

Wiebe, Robert H. *The Search for Order 1877–1920.* New York: Hill and Wang, 1967.

Wood, Ann D. "The Fashionable Diseases," *Journal of Interdisciplinary History* 4 (Summer 1973): 25–52.

Wyatt-Brown, Bertram. *Lewis Tappan and the Evangelical War against Slavery.* Cleveland: The Press of Case Western Reserve University, 1969.

Index

Affinity: in Brooklyn politics, 90; in family
and community, 54, 131–32; in Plymouth
Church, 44; to replace organized religion
and duty, 29, 116; in sex and marriage, 6,
19, 114, 115, 140, 149; in social class, 44,
109, 110, 144
Andrews, Stephen Pearl, 3, 36, 94
Anthony, Susan B., 3, 4, 119
Antislavery, Theodore Tilton's involvement
in, 41, 51, 77

Beecher, Eunice Bullard, 31–34, 124
Beecher, Henry Ward: adultery trial of, 11,
17, 96–97, 141–44; affair of, with Elizabeth Tilton, 8, 116–17; approach to ministry, 70–72; childhood of, 19–21; college
years of, 22–23; demands Elizabeth Tilton's retraction of confession, 9, 125; effects of scandal on, 11–12, 145–46; historians' treatment of, 12–14, 19, 146;
idealization of women by, 21–22, 29–31;
introduction to Plymouth Church of,
66–67; marriage of, to Eunice Bullard,
31–34; marital difficulties of, 8, 32–34; as
novelist, 13, 18, 114, 117, 146; and "policy of silence," 7, 131, 136; popularity of,
4–6, 29–30, 37; as reformer, 12; relationship of, to Free Love, 1, 93, 112, 116; religious development of, 23–29; as representative of American culture, 6, 13, 16,
27, 31; seduction of Lucy Bowen by, 9,
34, 75; sermons of, 19, 21, 27, 35, 37, 54,
112, 116, 117–18, 143, 146; and support
of "machine" politics, 90
Beecher, Lyman, 19–22
Beecher marriage, 8, 31–34

Beecher-Tilton scandal, 1, 7–12, 130–31;
historical treatment of, 12–13, 16; relationship to the changing role of women,
14, 146–48, 150; religious and political
origins, 16–17
Blood, Colonel James, 3
Bowen, Henry C.: antagonism toward
Henry Ward Beecher, 8, 76, 78, 79, 81;
background of, 65, 76; excommunication
from Plymouth Church, 11, 145; friendship with Henry Ward Beecher, 75; as
founder of Plymouth Church, 65–67, 73;
as publisher of *Brooklyn Union*, 8, 83–84;
as publisher of *Independent*, 42; pur-
chases *Brooklyn Union*, 82; quarrels with
Theodore Tilton, 8, 84, 87; role of, in
Brooklyn politics, 88–89; role of, in scandal, 87–88; Theodore Tilton's revelation
of scandal to, 8–9, 87; testimony at second church council, 11, 34; wife's seduction by Henry Ward Beecher, 9, 34, 75
Bowen, Lucy M., affair of, with Henry Ward
Beecher, 9, 34, 75
Brooklyn: growth and expansion of, 64; political conflict in, 82–86, 89–91; relationship of, to national politics, 90–91
Brooklyn Eagle: endorses Democratic
"machine," 83; rivalry of, with *Brooklyn
Union*, 82; role of, in scandal, 85, 87, 89,
121; support of Liberal Republicans by,
85
Brooklyn Union: dismissal of Theodore Tilton by, 88; editorial policies of, 84; rivalry
of, with *Brooklyn Eagle,* 82; role of, in
scandal, 8, 83; Theodore Tilton as editor
of, 83–84

Bullard, Laura Curtis, 119, 120–21
Butler, General Benjamin, 3, 131

Calvinism, 39–40, 53
Child, Lydia Maria, 43, 119
Christian Union, 11, 78, 81, 88
Congregational Councils: first council, 10,
   94; role of Richard Salter Storrs in first
   council, 99; second council, 11, 145
Congregationalism, 64–65; Henry Ward
   Beecher's approach to, 132, 148; traditional view of, 133
Church Investigating Committee, 10–11,
   138, 140, 148
Church of the Pilgrims: economic and occupational profile of, 104–10; founding of,
   64–65; membership of, 98, 101; and rivalry with Plymouth Church, 95–96, 97,
   100, 101; role of, in scandal, 91–92, 93,
   97

Democrats, 82–83, 89, 90, 91

Evarts, William Maxwell, 96, 141

Family: Beecher family, 19–22; historical
   changes in, 14–15; Richards' family,
   40–41, 45; Tilton family, 38–39
Fowler, Orson, 22–23, 36–37
Free Love, 2–3; Henry Ward Beecher's relationship to, 1–2, 6, 93, 112; similarity of,
   to the Gospel of Love, 6, 147; stigma of,
   116

The Gospel of Love, 6; dangers of, 145, 149;
   influence of, on family and community,
   109, 131, 148, 149, 150; influence of, on
   religious institutions, 111, 131, 133; influence of, on sex and marriage, 149; origins of, 18–19, 21–22, 24; similarity of,
   to Free Love, 6
Greeley, Horace, 91, 136
Griffith Gaunt (novel), 126–27
Griswold, Stephen, 67–69

Howard, John T., 65, 75–76, 77, 78, 90

Independent, 41, 42, 43, 75, 77, 78, 81, 87,
   88

Kinsella, Thomas, 83, 85, 86

Liberal Republicans, 85–86, 89, 90, 91, 109
Love, 28, 36–37, 56–58

MacFarland Scandal, 79, 93
McLoughlin, Hugh, 83, 85, 90–91
Marriage: Beecher marriage, 31–34; and the
   Gospel of Love, 149; the "new marriage,"
   15, 37, 113, 115, 128; radical view of, 1,
   36; and social class, 44–53, 109; Tilton
   marriage, 14–15, 40–41, 44, 46–48, 53,
   55–63, 113, 115, 122, 128
Ministry: changes in, 26–27; Henry Ward
   Beecher's approach to, 26, 29, 67, 70–73;
   Richard Salter Storrs's approach to, 65,
   99; traditional role of, 25–26
Moulton, Emma, 145
Moulton, Frank: excommunication of, from
   Plymouth Church, 145; protests at
   Church Investigating Committee, 138;
   and role in scandal cover-up, 9, 130–31,
   132, 137

Nest-hiding, 8, 18, 117
Newspapers: *Brooklyn Eagle*, 82, 83, 85,
   87, 89; *Brooklyn Sunday Press*, 82;
   Brooklyn Sunday Sun, 139; *Brooklyn
   Union*, 8, 82, 83, 84, 88; *Christian Union*,
   11, 78, 81, 88; *Chicago Tribune*, 139,
   140; *Golden Age*, 9, 132, 135, 136, 137,
   138; *Independent*, 7, 41, 42, 43, 77, 78;
   New York Observer, 41; *New York
   World*, 132; *Revolution*, 119, 120–21;
   roles of, in Brooklyn politics, 82–83, 84–
   86; roles of, in scandal, 17, 82, 137;
   Woodhull and Claflin's Weekly, 1, 89

Phrenology, 22–23
Plymouth Church: changes in, under ministry of Henry Ward Beecher, 70–73; and
   church discipline, 71–72; Church Investigating Committee of, 10–11, 138, 140,
   148; dismissal of Theodore Tilton by, 10;

economic and occupational profile of, 104–10; and excommunication of witnesses against Henry Ward Beecher, 11; factionalism in, 78–81, 87; founding of, 64–67; loyalty of, to Henry Ward Beecher, 144–45; membership in, 54, 101; and pew rental, 101; recruits Henry Ward Beecher, 67; "Silver Wedding Anniversary" at, 29–30; social and economic functions of, 41, 42

Political parties: Democrats, 82–83, 89, 90, 91; Liberal Republicans, 85–86, 89, 90, 91, 109; "machine" politics, 90, 95–96; Regulars, 89; role in scandal, 71, 82, 91–92

Radicalism, 2, 4
Republicans, 77, 86, 89–92
Revolution, 119, 120–21

Sexuality, attitudes toward, 35–37, 52, 57, 113–14, 116, 118–20, 122, 128–29, 147
Shearman, Thomas, 80, 107
Social class, 44, 46–48, 51, 107–10, 144
Stanton, Elizabeth Cady, 3, 4, 119, 140
Storrs, Richard Salter: antagonism toward Henry Ward Beecher and Plymouth Church, 17, 71, 93, 95, 99–100; background of, 97–98; manner of preaching of, 65, 98, 99; as pastor at Church of the Pilgrims, 65, 98; role of, in Beecher-Tilton scandal, 92, 137; speech by, to the first congregational council, 99
Stowe, Harriet Beecher, 12, 20

Tappan, Lewis, 34, 65
Tilton, Elizabeth Richards: affair of, with Henry Ward Beecher, 8, 116, 117, 118–19; confesses affair to Theodore Tilton, 40–41; death of, 11; and defense of Henry Ward Beecher, 10; effects of the Gospel of Love on, 130; effects of the "new marriage" on, 115; excommunication of, from Plymouth Church, 145; and *Griffith*

Gaunt, 126–27; letters by, of confession, retraction, and recantation, 9, 88, 125–26; marriage of, to Theodore Tilton, 40–41; and results of affair with Henry Ward Beecher, 118–19; sexuality of, 122, 128, 130; socio-economic background of, 38–39
Tilton, Theodore: career of, 41–46; criticizes local politics, 84–85; demands Elizabeth Tilton's written confession, 125; dismissal of, by Plymouth Church, 10; economic and professional insecurities of, 49–52, 113, 119, 122, 123; as editor of *Brooklyn Union,* 84; as editor of *Independent,* 7, 41, 43, 84; friendship of, with Henry Ward Beecher, 7, 77, 113; friendship of, with Victoria Woodhull, 135; and jealousy of Henry Ward Beecher, 113; writes Henry Ward Beecher to demand resignation, 88; marriage of, to Elizabeth Richards, 15, 38–39; marital difficulties of, 8, 46–48, 55, 113, 115; as novelist, 123, 133–34; placates Victoria Woodhull, 132; as reformer, 43, 45, 51, 53, 120–21; religious background of, 39, 112; sexual infidelity of, 52, 56–57, 112, 114, 119; socio-economic background of, 38–39
Tilton marriage, 14–15, 40–41, 46–48, 53, 55–63, 113, 115, 122, 128
Tracy, Benjamin, 80–81, 86, 89, 91, 107, 142–43, 144
Transcendentalists, 24
Tri-Partite Covenant, 89, 132
Trial of Henry Ward Beecher, 11, 17, 96–97, 141–44, 145–46, 149

Women, changing roles of, 30–31, 33–34, 36, 54–55, 147–48
Women's rights movement, 2, 3, 43, 120–21, 147
Woodhull, Victoria, 1–4, 10, 12, 89, 92, 116, 132, 136, 147, 150
Woodhull and Claflin's Weekly, 1, 89